Praise For

Trials, Tributes and Tribulations

"No one knows crime in Eastern Kentucky like Ken Taylor. Forty years fighting violence, corruption, stealing and scamming. Crack the cover of this one and enjoy the ride. I certainly did."

—David Grise, author of *Bogustan; An Adventure in Diplomatic Misunderstanding*

"*In Trials, Tributes, and Tribulations,* Kenneth Taylor has written a fascinating look at the American legal system from the inside. As a federal prosecutor, he presents a wide variety of cases, from political scandals to bank robberies to environmental crimes. Each case has its own chapter, which keeps the book moving along. He explains the background of complicated cases without getting bogged down with too much detail. It is a highly readable book that will keep you engaged. Most importantly, the book is authentic. Kenneth is willing to admit his mistakes and explain his choices. We have all finished legal books and thought, that author has never been near a courtroom. When you finish *Trials, Tributes, and Tribulations* you will know you have been reading about someone on the front lines."

—Richard Spees, author of *Capitol Gains* and *Capitol Losses*

"As someone who is not a legal expert, Taylor's true stories about the legal system read like a fast-paced novel. His experience as a prosecutor offers a fascinating glimpse into the complexities of federal courtroom drama. *Trials, Tributes, and Tribulations* is serious, funny, and educational—all at once. I loved this book."

—David Randal, author of *Kelsey's Crossing*

"*Trials, Tributes, and Tribulations* is a fascinating glimpse behind the scene of criminal trials. Ken Taylor's true stories make a reader wonder how many other crooks get away with their evil deeds! He explains the rationale and methods of bringing complicated cases to trial, while striving to remain objective and even find a bit of humor in it all. There's never a dearth of criminals in society, and it's refreshing to see that some of them—whether involved in laundering votes for public office, scamming investors in bogus oil-drilling deals, running drugs, or fencing stolen property—really do get put behind bars when lawyers such as Taylor are on the job."

—Carol Ann Tardiff, coauthor of *Blindsided: A Memoir of Love, Loss, and Legal Abuse*

"Ken Taylor gives a veteran prosecutor's perspective on many of the biggest federal cases in recent Kentucky history—a diverse collection of more than thirty stories that covers all the seven deadly sins except gluttony. (Taylor compensates for that by including an extra dose of greed.) The cast of defendants is rich: political scoundrels, brutal killers, pain-pill pushers, bank robbers, wife beaters, crooked promoters, a Kentucky basketball hero, a governor's mistress and more. More than a simple 'greatest hits' collection, Taylor acknowledges his mistakes and examines a couple of cases he lost."

—Tom Loftus, government and politics reporter (1976–2025) for *The Courier-Journal, The Kentucky Post,* the *Kentucky Lantern*

"Ken Taylor served as a federal prosecutor for more than 30 years in the Eastern District of Kentucky, which stretches from the state capital and elegant horse farms in the center of the state to the often hard-pressed coal counties of Appalachia, and where the number of public-corruption convictions per capita rivaled much more populous places such as Chicago many years.

Now, in Trial, Tributes, and Tribulations, Taylor has opened a window into some of the most high-profile corruption cases and others from his career, providing insight into the inner workings of the legal system, courtroom strategy and the lighter moments that can occur even when the stakes are high. It's a great read for anyone interested in the law, politics or history."

—Bill Estep, Southern and Eastern Kentucky reporter (1985–2025) for the *Lexington Herald Leader*

"Ken Taylor prosecuted public corruption, among other serious crimes, during his career as an assistant US attorney in Kentucky. The principle that government officials shouldn't use their positions to enrich themselves might sound naive to some these days, but Taylor took it seriously enough to send offenders to prison when the law allowed. In his engrossing new memoir, Taylor reveals the behind-the-scenes stories of the federal government's pursuit of crooked Kentucky politicians and their entrenched cronies and bagmen, all of whom believed they could game the system and get away with it, and most of whom were wrong."

—John Cheves, government accountability and investigative reporter (1997–present) for the *Lexington Herald-Leader*

"Having worked (and played) with Ken Taylor and his colleagues for decades and knowing some of the compelling stories he tells in the authentic voice of Eastern Kentucky firsthand, I urge any student of American justice to attend to his fun, important book, which reflects the ethos and soul of doing the right thing under law."

—Richard Pilger, former director, Election Crimes Branch, US Department of Justice

"Ken Taylor's highly readable first book, *Trials, Tributes and Tribulations*, is not only a fascinating ride through some of Kentucky's most notable criminal cases, but a tale of self-reflection by a prosecutor who devoted much of his career to pursuing justice and accountability for the United States government. The book has something for everyone. It is educational, interesting, and in places, funny. Just like a great trial lawyer, Ken grabs and keeps the reader's attention.

Using the famous, infamous, and run-of-the-mill criminal cases that make up Ken's remarkable career, Ken educates readers as he explains the law in practical and accessible terms before digging into each case's facts. From vote-buying scams and political kickback schemes to insurance fraud and organized shoplifting, Ken provides the reader with an understandable, behind-the-scenes look at a prosecutor's decision to seek an indictment and determination to put an accused on trial and convict them.

The book also confronts the trials and tribulations that Ken faced during his prosecutorial career: the ethical dilemmas, the conviction of an innocent man, an acquittal that still troubles him, and the mental strain of dealing with powerful people who escape indictment. Yet, after reading Ken's book, one is left with the knowledge that at least with this prosecutor, justice is blind—not political."

—Allison Connelly, former Kentucky public advocate and retired law professor, University of Kentucky, Rosenberg College of Law

TRIALS, TRIBUTES, AND TRIBULATIONS
by Kenneth R. Taylor

979-8-88824-962-8

Designed by Suzanne Bradshaw

Published by

köehlerbooks™

3705 Shore Drive
Virginia Beach, VA 23455
800-435-4811
www.koehlerbooks.com

TRIALS, TRIBUTES, AND TRIBULATIONS

A Career in Federal Criminal Court

KENNETH R. TAYLOR

VIRGINIA BEACH
CAPE CHARLES

Introduction

I HAVE HAD a rewarding and interesting career in criminal law from both sides of the aisle—defense attorney and prosecutor—though the latter was much more extensive than the former. Over the years, it was common for me to regale friends and relatives with stories of interesting cases or humorous events. Upon retirement, a number of those friends and relatives implored me to write it down. I composed this overview of memorable cases as an exercise in closure—a reliving of my career. The writing is its own reward. If any reader finds inspiration, insight, knowledge, or even entertainment here, so be it. Maybe my grandchildren and great-grandchildren will want to hear about "Poppy Taylor's" life in court.

Now, a little about my background.

I was born in Louisville, Kentucky, in 1955, where my father was studying at the Southern Baptist seminary. My parents divorced when I was four or five years old; my mother remarried, and I spent my formative years on a farm in Daviess County, near Owensboro in Western Kentucky.

I graduated from Daviess County High School in in 1973. I was a good student, but after graduation and with a hunger for adventure, I considered enlisting in the Marine Corps. I came close to signing the enlistment papers before changing my mind and enrolling at Bethel College (now Bethel University) in McKenzie, Tennessee.

In my single year at Bethel, I took a course in criminology and became intrigued with the criminal justice system. I transferred to Western Kentucky University for the rest of college and sought out similar courses there in the sociology department. I took a few courses in the government department, where it seemed all my fellow students planned on applying to law school, so I did the same. I did well on the law school admission test and was accepted at the University of Kentucky School of Law.

During my last semester at Western, in the spring of 1976, and a few weeks after my law school acceptance, I made another huge career decision. I was walking through the student center and was intrigued by the booth overseen by a Marine Corps officer selection officer (OSO)—essentially a recruiter of officers. I related to him my flirtation with enlistment right out of high school. He enticed me to sit down right there and take the officer qualification exam, which I passed with flying colors. We talked about my law school plan, and he outlined the law school program the Corps offered. I could attend Officer Candidate School (OCS) that summer (essentially boot camp for officer candidates) in Quantico, Virginia, receive a commission as a second lieutenant, and be released for three years for law school. After law school, I would be contracted for a three-year tour as a military lawyer, specifically a judge advocate general (JAG). This was a perfect plan for me—Marine Corps and law school. Because I exercised the option of spending my summers between law school years on active duty, working out of JAG offices in California the first summer and North Carolina the second, the summers of officer pay with free lodging enabled me to save money.

While in law school, I tried, where possible, to focus on criminal law. I took criminal law and procedure under esteemed professors Bob Lawson and Bill Fortune. I assisted Professor Lawson to update a Kentucky Criminal Law summary that he authored. As a member of the Kentucky Law Journal, I chose to write about the expungement of criminal convictions. My substantive criminal law course, however, was taught by the brilliant, but eccentric John Batt, who didn't seem interested in the nuts and bolts of the law. We spent a lot of time discussing the insanity defense.

In October 1979, following law school graduation, passing the bar exam, and being admitted to the Kentucky Bar Association, I began my commitment to the Marine Corps. I had to go through five months of platoon commander training at Quantico and then train for JAG service at the Naval Justice School in Newport, Rhode Island. I was assigned to Camp Lejeune where I served first as a defense counsel in courts-martial, then moved to prosecution, called "trial counsel."

In 1982, I was back in Lexington, Kentucky after the Corps, where I joined Eric Smith and Megan Lake as an associate in their partnership. I did primarily civil litigation but longed to get back into the criminal arena. Thus, I accepted employment as a public defender with the Kentucky Department of Public Advocacy (DPA). I represented indigent defendants, mostly in Garrard and Lincoln County, for three years.

In 1987, I accepted an offer to join David Thomas and Hunter Daugherty in a practice in Nicholasville. David held the public defender contract for that county, and I became his sidekick in that practice. I handled many criminal cases during that three-year stint in Jessamine County, and I was accepted as an approved attorney for appointment as a public defender in federal court in Lexington. In the latter capacity, I became acquainted with several of the federal prosecutors in the United States Attorney's Office and was encouraged by them to apply for a job opening there. So, in 1990, I accepted an offer to become an Assistant United States Attorney (federal prosecutor). I retired from that office thirty-two years later, in 2022. During my law career, I tried well over 200 criminal trials, 108 of them as a federal prosecutor.

Upon retirement I began writing this book. But the final product is not as extensive as I had originally intended. That first manuscript contained two distinct sections, one entitled "For the Defense" and another entitled "For the United States." In the former I discussed ten or twelve defense counsel cases from the 1980s, each from my public defender days through my private practice in Nicholasville. The majority were murder cases. Therein I discussed self-defense, battered woman's syndrome, the insanity defense, the "choice of evils" defense, and many other intriguing issues.

At a legal ethics seminar recently, I learned that I was laboring under a misapprehension about an attorney's ethical obligation to protect the confidences of his former clients. I thought that so long as I avoided revealing the confidential statements made to me by the client, I was on safe ground. I was free, I thought, to relate my observations, thought processes, opinions and discussions with others who were not my client. What I learned was that I should not reveal anything that I learned as a result of the attorney-client relationship that is not generally known or sourced to a third person—not myself. This gave me great pause, as I had related many things about the case and the client that were not sourced to anything but my memory. So, I had that portion of the manuscript reviewed by an expert in attorney-client ethics. My suspicions were validated. Ethical traps permeated those cases. Sanitizing them to pass ethics muster would render them plodding and uninteresting. So, I made the very difficult decision to delete that portion of the book and go just with my thirty-two-year prosecution career.

Why did I choose these particular cases to discuss? Primarily, these are the cases I found most interesting and memorable, some because of their notoriety and press coverage and others because of humorous and memorable events. A lot of what follows is from my memory. I realize that memories are faulty and that others may remember the events differently. I tried to avoid legalese or getting too deep in the weeds factually or legally. I tried to write in a way and tone that is inviting and fun

Special Tribute

THROUGHOUT THESE STORIES, I pay tribute to colleagues, agents, analysts, witnesses, defense counsel, judges, and others who have impacted these cases. While revising, I realized that the one person who impacted many of my cases, in more ways than anyone, is sparsely mentioned. Paralegal Rebecca Woolums has been in and around my work since 1998, working quietly, tirelessly, and efficiently, without fanfare. So, I give her a special acknowledgment here. Thank you, Rebecca, for keeping me in line, focused, and (usually) out of trouble.

Ralph Baze

Assault Rifle Murder

In January 1992, the airwaves and print media in Kentucky were filled with news of the brutal slaying of two law enforcement officers in rural Powell County, Kentucky. Powell County Sheriff Steve Bennett, and his deputy, Arthur Briscoe, were shot in the back with a powerful assault rifle while trying to serve a warrant from Ohio on Ralph Baze at his rural mountain cabin.

Baze, a thirty-something felon, had warrants pending against him from Ohio, where he had formerly lived. He had recently moved to Kentucky, where his wife of a few years had roots, in part to avoid arrest. The couple lived in that remote cabin only yards away from his wife's son by a prior marriage; the son and his wife occupied another small house. To say that Baze and his stepson did not get along well would be an understatement. I was never aware of the source of their dispute, but it had become intense. According to Baze, the stepson had shot at him one day, prompting Baze to travel to Ohio, where he had connections, enabling him to purchase an SKS assault rifle for his protection. The transaction was illegal because Baze, as a felon, was prohibited from possessing a firearm.

Back in Kentucky with the new rifle, Baze placed it strategically where he could access it quickly. But the stepson had another card to play. Apparently, the stepson knew of the warrants in Ohio and alerted the Powell County sheriff's office of them and of the fact that

Baze was in their jurisdiction. The Kentucky sheriff's office contacted Ohio authorities, who confirmed that the warrants were still valid and that they would proceed with the prosecution of Baze if he were arrested; they requested Powell County to pick him up.

DEPUTY BRISCOE FIRST went alone that morning to execute the arrest. He approached the cabin and Baze's wife answered the door. Briscoe explained that he had warrants for Baze and asked if he was home. Baze's wife lied and said Baze was not present. Baze, who had seen the police car drive up to the house, was secretly listening to the deputy and slipped out the back door. Briscoe, following police protocol, went next door to speak with a neighbor (in this case, the stepson) for any information about Baze's comings and goings. While there, Baze was spotted running into the woods behind the house carrying a large rifle.

Briscoe returned to Baze's cabin where he encountered him on the back porch armed. Baze held the rifle by his side and bluntly told Briscoe he wasn't going anywhere. Baze said he knew how the system worked—that he would be in jail for months waiting to clear his name on these trumped-up Ohio charges. Deputy Briscoe stared Baze down and moved his hand toward his 9mm pistol. Baze began to lift the rifle, but his wife grabbed his arm. Deputy Briscoe retreated to his car, knowing that he was severely outgunned. Baze, in turn, fled for the hills and trees.

Briscoe drove away and radioed the dispatcher for backup. Sheriff Bennett was in a cruiser in the area and immediately responded. Briscoe and Bennett arrived back at the cabin at the same time, with Briscoe in front. The two men stepped out of their cruisers with guns drawn; Briscoe had briefed Bennett over the radio about the previous confrontation with the rifle-bearing felon Baze.

What the officers didn't realize was that Baze had not left the immediate area; instead, he had circled around and hid behind a tree overlooking the location where the arriving cruisers would park. When Bennet and Briscoe alighted from their cars, their backs were to Baze.

Witness accounts differ on what happened next: Baze's wife said Baze stood as if to surrender, and a gunfight erupted. She couldn't tell who fired first, but circumstantial evidence indicated that Baze ambushed the two officers. Sheriff Bennett was shot three times in the back as he tried to jump into the back seat of his cruiser. His gun was never fired. Baze's rifle blew the lawman's organs apart, and he died instantly.

Briscoe ran from the scene but was struck in the back by Baze's bullets. Baze approached the prone officer, saw a twitch of his hand as if he was reaching for his gun, and shot him in the back of the head.

Baze collected Bennett's .357 revolver and Briscoe's 9mm automatic pistol and headed for the hills again. Somehow, Baze traveled on foot several miles to a remote house in Estill County. The resident at the house refused to let him enter; Baze told the resident that he had shot the two officers in self-defense. The resident agreed to call the police so Baze could surrender. In short order deputies arrived and took Baze into custody. Baze told the arresting officers that the sheriff and deputy had opened fire on him while he was in the process of surrendering.

Baze was charged with two counts of first-degree murder in Powell Circuit Court. The commonwealth attorney promptly filed a notice of intent to seek the death penalty, making this a capital case. The significance of this designation was that the defense of Baze would be monitored, if not taken over, by the death penalty section of the Kentucky DPA. A group of anti-death penalty advocates in that section would begin the process of delay and legal maneuverings designed to keep Baze alive. It started with pretrial motions challenging every imaginable aspect of the constitutionality of the prosecution and, if possible, appeals, writs of mandamus, or prohibition. (Mandamus asks an appellate court to command a lower court to take some action; prohibition requests an order prohibiting the lower court from taking a designated action.) This kind of case could take several years to move through the court system.

I HAD BEEN following press accounts of the case for several weeks. I saw clear federal crimes involving the firearms Baze possessed, but the state had a more pressing interest in this case than the federal government. However, I saw an opportunity to significantly expedite the overall system of justice while simultaneously obtaining a federal conviction of Baze that would backup to the state system, lest any of the defense's efforts proved successful. I spoke with the state prosecutor and proposed the following: The feds would obtain an indictment of Baze for three counts of possession of a firearm by a felon—one count for Briscoe's 9mm, one count for Bennett's.357, and one count for Baze's SKS. Then, we would enter into a written comity agreement with the state prosecutor, wherein he would waive his right to go first with the state prosecution, provided we agreed to return Baze to state custody for trial after the federal prosecution.

I explained that I expected to obtain a thirty-year sentence for Baze, an unusually long sentence for felon in possession. Normally, such convictions result in a few years in prison under the federal sentencing guidelines, and the charge carries a maximum of ten years. But I saw aggravating facts in this case that would open the door to a thirty-year term. Baze had committed the more serious crime of murder while illegally possessing weapons. Using complex sentencing guidelines, I proposed that Baze be sentenced to ten years in prison for *each* of his three weapon's convictions. That added up to thirty years.

With the state prosecutor on board with my proposal, we took the Baze case to the federal grand jury and obtained that three-count indictment. The comity agreement was executed, and Baze was transferred to federal custody.

THE FEDERAL TRIAL of Baze involved an unusual evidentiary ruling that required all parties to tiptoe through the evidence surrounding the murders. Judge Karl Forester granted the defense's motion to exclude from the trial any evidence of the shooting of officers Briscoe and Bennett, on the grounds that such evidence would be overwhelmingly prejudicial. The jury would not have any background evidence demonstrating how Baze came to be in possession of the pistols. We called to testify the person from Michigan who sold Baze the rifle. Additionally, the arresting deputy testified that he arrested Baze at a home where he was in possession of that rifle and two pistols. But the jury never heard that Baze shot the officers. The jury was instructed to not consider or speculate as to why Baze was being arrested that day.

Surprisingly, Baze himself took the witness stand to defend his possession of the rifle. He explained that he bought the weapon to protect himself from his stepson, who he said had shot at him repeatedly during the prolonged dispute with him. He was trying to establish that despite being a felon, he was justified in arming himself. The judge ultimately denied the request for that instruction, holding that the threat was not imminent when he obtained the gun.

The jury convicted Baze of all three counts. However, at sentencing, Judge Forester foiled my plan for a thirty-year sentence when he ruled that the two pistol counts merged for sentencing purposes because they were obtained at the same time. So, Baze received twenty years. Per the comity agreement, Baze returned to state custody where he was tried and sentenced to death for the murders of Briscoe and Bennett. He remains on death row at the time of this writing.

A CLOSE FRIEND of mine at the US attorney's office was fellow prosecutor, Mike Murphy. In 1998, Mike met and married Teresa, the ex-wife of Deputy Briscoe. Teresa thus became a close friend of mine.

I've had many great times with Mike and Teresa over the years. I've stayed at their house, and they mine. We've had many meals together. The most memorable times were the years of bicycling together. Several years in a row, we did the Horsey Hundred—a one-hundred-mile bike ride starting in Georgetown on Memorial Day weekend, and we went on many bike excursions around the back roads of Fayette County. Teresa and Briscoe's son, Dennis Briscoe, who was fourteen when his father was killed, became a police officer himself. Over the years of my association with Teresa, we had several conversations about the progress of Baze's death penalty case—the delays, the appeals, and the lawsuits. This process was and remains especially hard for Dennis.

Norrie Wake

Salary-Kickback Scheme

Attorney Norrie Wake was a rising star in the Lexington political world in the early 1990s. In fact, many observers believed he was on track to run for Kentucky attorney general or even governor. The fifty-year-old had a sterling reputation as a lawyer and family man who was active in his church and community. He had been elected county attorney in 1985 and was a tough prosecutor who worked hard and implemented new programs and procedures. He had a penchant and talent for the performing arts, having acted in local theater, and was known to have a beautiful singing voice.

When he beat longtime incumbent E. Lawson King for county attorney in '85, he had taken advantage of several scandals that had rocked the King family and his office for several years. But the tables turned on Wake in the spring of 1993. Allegations trickled out from some of his former employees that the county attorney's office was involved in financial improprieties.

Wake was seeking reelection to his third term that year. He faced a primary challenge in the Democrat party from a law school classmate of mine, Margaret Kannensohn who had been made aware of the ex-employees' allegations and jumped at the chance to make that a campaign issue. She went public with her accusations, asserting that it appeared Wake had misused public funds related to child support enforcement. (Kentucky county attorneys are statutorily tasked with enforcing child support orders and they receive large amounts of state funds for that program.) Wake vehemently denied any wrongdoing and attributed the allegations to disgruntled former employees he had fired, claiming they had encouraged Kannensohn to join in a witch hunt against him as retaliation.

FOR SEVERAL WEEKS during February and March of '93, the dispute and acrimony between Wake and Kannensohn percolated through the local press. Wake was frequently defended by admirers who disbelieved the accusations and were quoted in the newspaper extolling his honesty and integrity. What Kannensohn didn't know as she began making public accusations against Wake was that one of those former Wake employees had approached the US Attorney's Office many weeks prior, which was actively investigating the allegations.

We obtained bank and other financial records through subpoenas. We interviewed many former employees. A strong case against Wake emerged, and by April, we were ready to present the matter for indictment to the grand jury. While evidence pointed to Wake diverting federal funds earmarked for child support enforcement to other purposes, that case was not that solid. Instead, we focused on a specific salary raise kickback scheme. Wake was charged with theft from a state agency of federal funds, conspiracy, and mail fraud.

I was only a couple of years into my federal career and had not yet carved out the niche of prosecuting public corruption cases that I would later develop. The case was assigned to one of the senior prosecutors, Jim Zerhusen, or "Z" as we called him. But Z asked me to assist him on the case, and I jumped at the opportunity.

From the moment our indictment dropped, the war of words began as Wake publicly defended himself. Whenever the press asked about the charges, he alleged that our office was politically aligned with his opponents and that the prosecution was politically motivated.

He repeated the allegation that the former employees were lying. He proclaimed that he would be exonerated. He never made an overture to our office about a guilty plea. Many prominent Wake supporters added to his defense in the press. They expressed extreme incredulity about the indictment. This was going to be a brutal battle with intense public interest.

The indictment was returned in April and the primary was held in May. Kannensohn trounced Wake—over thirteen thousand votes to around eight thousand votes. The general election was not until that November, so Wake was still the county attorney for the next several months. But because of the indictment, Wake was required to relinquish some of the criminal law functions of his office. The Kentucky attorney general appointed a stand-in to act in that capacity. But Wake refused to resign and vowed to defend himself.

Around the time of the election, an assistant county attorney came forward to our office with evidence against Wake. She had worked for Wake as an assistant county attorney for several years. And for most of that time, she was very close to Wake and his former law partner David Vest. Vest also worked at the county attorney's office as Wake's first assistant. At some point in the affiliation with Wake, this assistant county attorney realized that she had unwisely allowed herself to become involved in a scheme that she believed was bound to be discovered someday. She cut her losses by cooperating with the authorities. She had toyed with the idea of taking the case to the commonwealth attorney's (state prosecutor) office but eventually received advice to shop her case to the feds.

The assistant explained the scheme this way. In 1985, Wake had financed his campaign for county attorney with a bank loan. Those proceeds were then loaned to the campaign committee, and Wake was paying the note at the bank. As of 1989, when Wake was beginning his next run for office, he still owed about $35,000, which was listed as an outstanding debt on the books of his former campaign committee. Several employees involved in his '89 campaign thought that debt was a political liability, and they put their heads together to find a way that the debt could be retired.

They came up with a salary-kickback scheme. First, Wake was going to file a notice with the registry of election finance that he was personally forgiving the debt so it could be removed from the public records. Wake would seek authority from the state to give key employees a raise under the pretense that they were overworked with child support duties and needed additional compensation. The employees agreed to pay to Wake the amount of the monthly increase in their salary—less their additional tax liability—in cash. This would continue for one year, whereupon the employees would be allowed to keep their raises.

AT TRIAL, AT least six employees admitted to participating in this salary-kickback scheme. Three testified to having conversations with Wake about the arrangement. A few denied knowing about a linkage between the raise and the contribution. They indicated they were simply asked to contribute to retiring Wake's debt and did so to demonstrate that they were a team player.

Most of these employees testified that, each month, they put cash in an envelope and gave the envelope to another county attorney employee, who then delivered it to Wake. One employee testified that she wanted to give the money to Wake in person so he would remember her and her loyalty. We introduced bank records to show that, sure enough, Wake deposited the cash in his bank account in amounts matching the testimony and promptly wrote checks to the bank to pay off the loan.

Our case was strong. Six witnesses said it happened. At least one cried as she testified. She was having difficulty testifying against her employer, friend, and mentor. Another item of our evidence cast grave doubt on the truthfulness of Wake's entire defense. In essence, we showed that Wake's story about the cash payments had changed over time. During his opening statement for the defense, Burl McCoy conceded that Wake received cash from employees, but he didn't know it was part of a salary kickback scheme. He thought the employees were simply being supportive of his campaign. Z and I immediately realized that Wake had previously provided a different story publicly. We decided to disprove McCoy's opening statement.

We played a video of a television interview of Wake during his campaign wherein he was asked to address some of the allegations, including one that employees had given him cash under the table. He flatly denied ever receiving cash from employees. He went on to say that, once, employees got together and bought him an appliance to put in his lake cabin.

When the prosecution rested, it was Wake's turn to put on evidence. Most importantly, it was time for Wake to testify, something which we had been promised by defense counsel in opening statement. But Wake was in that old dilemma I often saw over the years; without testifying he couldn't win, but if he testified he was sure to lose.

Wake began his testimony with a transparent attempt to ingratiate himself with the jury. When a defendant toots his own horn about his history, accomplishments, and reputation, it comes across as a subtle plea that he should be acquitted because of who he is rather than the weakness of the evidence. After around forty-five minutes of testimony about his early years, I leaned over to Z and said we needed to try to shut this down. I suggested that we approach the bench and ask the court to instruct the defense to get to the point. We wanted to do this at the bench rather than in front of the jury because we didn't want it to appear we were obstructing the defense.

I stood and asked to approach the bench, where Judge Joe Hood sat. "Judge, I know the defendant has the right to personalize himself in front of the jury, and we don't oppose him doing that. But there has to be some limit. We've been here forty-five minutes, and I think we are now in the fifth grade. (Sarcasm). At this rate, we won't get to the subject matter of this case and the indictment for several days. I ask that the defense be directed to speed this along."

Apparently, Judge Hood was having some of the same thoughts as he nodded in agreement. McCoy acknowledged that the testimony was dragging and agreed to get on with it. Hood's ruling was a simple. "All right."

Wake's defense was that he did not know anything about a kickback scheme. He believed that the envelopes of cash were just his loyal employees voluntarily helping him pay off the campaign debt. He did not know the amount of money he was getting from them was related to the recent salary increases. If there was a kickback scheme, he wasn't part of it.

On cross-examination, Z dismantled Wake's story. Why would employees bring cash in envelopes monthly? Why didn't he question them? Hadn't he sought approval to obtain their pay raises? What motive did all these former employees have to lie about their conversations with him?

His answers were not convincing. But the most damning moment came when Wake discussed his allegation that the prosecution was politically motivated. While listing all the people who were benefiting from his prosecution, he volunteered about Z, "And I've heard about you and what you do. You just want another notch on your gun."

Neither I nor Z could believe what we had just heard. Z's reputation was that of a by-the-book, soft-spoken straight shooter. Z could make strong arguments, but he was always measured. I had never heard anyone mention Z being politically motivated or unfair. If that had been said to me, it might have some credibility. I developed a reputation as a bulldog who was sometimes overzealous in my advocacy, but that wasn't Z. This was purely self-serving bullshit.

Z tossed his ink pen onto the prosecution table and moved slightly toward Wake. He crossed his arms and said, "Well, why don't you just tell us all what you've heard about me and who said it?" Of course, Wake had no specifics, no names, no examples, just amorphous rumors. It was wholly unconvincing.

When Z finished, I leaned over and said, "I think we need to call Karen Caldwell to the stand."

Z's eyes opened wide at the US attorney's name, and he asked incredulously, "For what?"

I said, "Wake just put into evidence an allegation that this case was politically motivated and that you are a political hack. The person who approved this case, appointed you as lead counsel, and signed the indictment needs to refute those allegations. Let me see if the judge will allow this."

It was somewhat unusual. Normally, the thought processes behind prosecution decision-making are irrelevant at trial, but I felt Wake had opened the door. It wasn't so much that I thought the jury was biting on the politics argument, but I knew Caldwell would have the jury eating out of her hand. Why not vouch for our case a bit?

Though Z was skeptical, he listened to me. We approached the bench, and I made my argument to Judge Hood that we should be allowed to refute Wake's unfounded accusation with rebuttal testimony from Caldwell. Surprisingly, Hood did not have any trouble with the proposition. "We need to hear from Ms. Caldwell," Hood said.

During a break, we called Caldwell. At first, she recoiled at the prospect. She didn't believe it was appropriate. But by now, Z was for the plan, and he convinced her that, at this point, the judge was expecting to hear from her. Reluctantly, she agreed and came to the courthouse.

What happened next is part of office lore and a story that Z told about me at my retirement party. When the judge asked if we had rebuttal witnesses, I said, "Yes, but let me step out to see if she has arrived at the courthouse." So, as the jury, spectators, counsel, and court personnel sat quietly, wondering what was coming, I stepped out of the courtroom. I was pumped. I knew this was going to be dramatic, and my penchant for drama kicked in.

Caldwell was waiting in the hallway. Shaking her head, she asked if I was sure this was a good idea.

I said, "Yes, it's going to be great." I went over with her quickly my line of questioning: How did this case come to the attention of our office? What did she do to vet the case? Were there any political considerations? Did she assign Z to the case? Why did she pick him? Was she aware of any issues in the past with Z's abuse of his position for political purposes? Did she have any affiliation or friendship with those employees who testified in the case?

Now we were ready to rock and roll. I told Caldwell to stand just outside the door and that when she heard me call her name to enter, be sworn in, and take the stand. I entered the courtroom, walked toward counsel table, and flung open the gate to the bar of the court like a gunslinger entering a saloon. In a loud, dramatic voice I announced, "Your Honor, the United States calls United States Attorney Karen Caldwell."

All eyes turned toward the door as Karen walked in with a pleasant smile. She took the stand, then nodded and smiled at the jury. Caldwell came across exactly as I knew she would—professional, composed, measured, fair, and articulate. The jury hung on every word as she told them that she knew this case would have some political overtones, and for that reason, she had taken extra precautions to ensure that the process was above reproach. She appointed Z because he was considered to be the most cautious and thoughtful attorney she employed.

It was a beautiful moment.

DURING A WEEKEND recess, Z and I met to discuss closing argument. Originally, we had agreed that I would do opening, and Z would do closing. But as we discussed ideas for closing, and I had a lot of them, Z said, "You really would like to do this, wouldn't you?" I affirmed, and so I spent the rest of the weekend collecting my thoughts.

My closing argument may have been my all-time favorite. The courtroom was full of spectators, and the local press was present. Many of my colleagues from the office came to watch. But I felt organized and had a lot of good things to say, so it seemed to flow off my tongue. A couple of the nuggets stuck with me:

I pointed out that Wake's story about ignorantly and naively receiving cash could not be believed. I played the clip of Wake stating that he never received cash from employees. I said by the time trial came around, Wake knew he couldn't stick with that story because we had records of him depositing cash in the amount testified to by employees. I mocked his trial testimony about how he had forgotten the cash. How could someone remember the appliance he was given but forget that cash he received monthly for a year?

I addressed the incredible story of Wake not knowing why these attorneys, who all had checking accounts, would give him cash. I got somewhat dramatic with a personal story. I said, "I have an eight-year-old daughter, Sara, who is going through that phase where she wants to be treated like an adult and is offended sometimes when I think I'm giving good adult advice. If I say, Sara, look both ways before crossing the road,' she'll give me *that* look and say, 'Duh, Dad.' If I say, 'Sara, you need to buckle your seatbelt,' she would respond, 'Duh, Dad.'" (She didn't follow all my advice. Seven years later, she was struck by a car. She survived.)

I continued, tying my story into the case, "Ladies and gentlemen, I'll tell you now that if I told Sara that these envelopes of cash, every month around payday, were for the purpose of concealing something illegal, she would say, 'Duh, Dad.' But Norrie Wake, an attorney who has handled many financial and business-related cases, wants you to believe that he saw absolutely nothing sinister or suspicious about repeatedly receiving cash, such that he wouldn't even inquire as to its purpose and source. To that, I say, 'Duh, Mr. Wake."

In just three hours of deliberation, the jury convicted Wake of all charges. He was sentenced to twenty-one months in prison.

Surprisingly, he filed no appeal. Wake's fall from grace was sad. In addition to his prison time, he was disbarred in 1993 by the Kentucky Bar Association. Eight years after the conviction, Wake sought to have the license reinstated, a request that is customarily granted to a contrite and apologetic lawyer. But during a bar association investigation into the propriety of his reinstatement, Wake was defiant and denied wrongdoing. His request was denied, and he never again practiced law. He moved to Wayne County, Kentucky, and established a team leadership and adventure facility for business entities and corporations. Later, he moved to Rhode Island to be near family and died in 2020 at the age of seventy-seven.

David Whitis

Backseat Carjacker

In the early to mid-1990s, I prosecuted several cases under the federal carjacking statute. Carjacking essentially involves taking a car from another person at gunpoint. David Whitis was one of those cases.

Whitis was a large, muscular man in his thirties, a convicted felon and divorcee whom I believe was a construction worker. He met a woman, Jane Johnson, (not her real name) in 1993, and the two became romantically involved. Jane was also divorced and had custody of four children.

Whitis would later testify that the relationship was "like having a new toy," so intense and fulfilling. But over time, Whitis's jealousy and controlling behavior soured the relationship from Jane's perspective. Eventually, she broke up with Whitis. That didn't go over well with Whitis, who became a classic stalker. Jane obtained an emergency protective order (EPO) against him, which required Whitis to stay away from her.

ONE SPRING EVENING in 1994, Jane left her home in Richmond, Kentucky, to patronize a nearby bar out in the country, the Circle H Saloon. As she drove to the bar, she noticed Whitis behind her in his car. She bypassed the bar and drove to the Richmond police station, where she showed the officers the EPO and requested their assistance and protection. Police officers patrolled the area for a while but saw no signs of Whitis, so Jane resumed her planned evening of fun and socializing at the Circle H.

Jane spent several hours at the bar, dancing, and conversing, mostly with an old friend, William Tony Fowler. As closing time approached, Jane and Fowler left together to go to a local restaurant for coffee. They traveled in their separate vehicles so they could go directly home after visiting the restaurant.

A few moments after Jane pulled onto the road from the bar parking lot, she felt a jolt from behind, as though something hit the back of her seat. In the rearview mirror, she saw Whitis rising from the floor of the back seat with a gun in his hand. He put the gun to her head and ordered her to pull over. She complied, and Whitis got in the front seat with her. The two struggled, and Whitis pistol whipped her, opening a gash in her scalp that ultimately required four stitches.

Jane decided that resistance was futile and let Whitis get behind the wheel of the car. However, Fowler had driven by, and seeing Jane's car on the side of the road, he pulled over and got out. As Fowler approached the car, Whitis emerged and assumed a shooting stance as if aiming at Fowler, although Fowler would later admit on cross-examination that he never actually saw a gun. Whitis told Fowler to mind his own business and leave. From the car, Jane begged Fowler to leave as she feared Whitis would shoot him.

Fowler left and drove down the road for a mile or so. Then he turned around and returned to the scene. His intent was to follow Whitis and Jane until he could find a way to notify the police. When Fowler got back to the scene, Jane's car was gone. Fowler returned to the Circle H, where he called the police, who immediately began searching for the car, Jane, and Whitis. Based on the EPO, the earlier sighting of Whitis, and Whitis' history, the police had great concern for Jane's safety.

During this time, Jane had not been able to escape Whitis. He had driven her to an open field, where he told her he was going to kill her and then himself. Jane decided that her only chance to live was to convince Whitis that she still had feelings for him. She said they could spend some time together. Whitis drove to a nearby Red Roof Inn and rented a room. There, Whitis and Jane had sex and spent the night. Whitis told her that if she ever went to the police about what had happened that night, he would hurt her four children.

The next morning, Jane kept up her acting job and agreed to go with Whitis to a flea market, but she said she needed to go home first, change her clothes, and clean up the dried blood from her head wound. He agreed. They retrieved Whitis's car from the Circle H, and Whitis followed Jane to her home. Luckily, Jane's children had spent the night with a relatives and weren't home. Jane had an escape plan. She entered her house quickly, shut the door, and locked it. She called the babysitting relative and told them to lock their doors. She then called the police.

Whitis fled. Jane was treated for her head wound and a broken finger at a local hospital. Whitis was arrested the next day.

Whitis was charged with rape, kidnapping, and other offenses in state court. But as is customary in these types of cases, the local or state police shopped the case to the feds because of potentially better sentencing options and often more resources.

We took the case and charged Whitis with federal carjacking, felon in possession, and use of a firearm during a crime of violence. The latter provided a mandatory five years on top of any sentence he could receive on the other charges.

THROUGH PRETRIAL PROCEEDINGS, conversations with defense attorney Derek Gordon, and witness interviews, we learned something unexpected. Whitis intended to present a different version of events than the one outlined above.

Whitis was going to say that Jane was involved in a conspiracy with Fowler to frame him. According to Whitis's story, Jane had called Whitis, despite the EPO, and asked him to meet her at the Circle H, stating that she wanted to spend time with him. When he showed up at Circle H, she willingly got in the car with him and asked if they could get a room for the night. Everything that happened between them that night was consensual. He did not have a gun, and he never beat her. The wound on her head came from something else—perhaps self-inflicted. Fowler had lied about the roadside incident, Whitis contended.

So, the trial came down to which person or persons were lying, Jane and Fowler, or Whitis. I felt strongly that the jury would believe Jane and Fowler over a felon, but it was not a sure thing. Jane did not project an aura of the church lady next door. She was out carousing and drinking that night while her children were watched by others. By her own admission, she left the bar with Fowler. Circle H Saloon was not hosting a Baptist prayer meeting that night. It would be nice if we could corroborate our storyline with additional evidence.

We did have one compelling piece of evidence. Jane had told the police she recognized the gun that Whitis had brandished. She said she had purchased that gun for Whitis as a gift some months before. She gave them the gun store's name, and the police retrieved paperwork related to the purchase. We could identify the gun by make, model, and serial number. Jane had signed the paperwork because, as a felon, Whitis could not possess a firearm. This proved that Whitis had access to a firearm, but it did not prove that he brandished it that night.

We needed corroboration of Jane's story. I'm not sure who or what brought it to my attention, but I learned of another incident that debunked Whitis's denial of a weapons possession.

MY BEST MEMORY is that when news accounts of Whitis's assault on Jane were published, a woman, Mary Smith (not her real name) contacted Jane. Mary was the ex-wife of Whitis. She told a story that was eerily similar to Jane's experience. Five years prior and shortly after she divorced Whitis she claimed that Whitis called her to say that he had a check that was made out to her that he had received at their former marital residence. If she wanted it, she would have to come to his sister's home in Somerset. Mary made the trip but found no one at home when she arrived. She got back in her car to leave when Whitis suddenly came up out of the back seat, brandishing a gun. He drove her to an open field in the country and threatened her. Feeling threatened, Mary had sex with Whitis to placate him, she said.

Judge Karl Forester ruled that the evidence was admissible as a signature crime, noting that the distinct *modus operandi* (method of operating) made Jane's story significantly more believable. Mary did not initially report the assault and rape to police because she had no proof. But a few days after the assault, Whitis brutally beat Mary. This time there was medical proof, and Whitis was convicted of a felony assault.

The admission of Mary's testimony was hotly contested by defense attorney Gordon. Usually, this type of evidence, called "signature-crime evidence" is admissible to prove the identity of a perpetrator. If a person on trial is shown to have committed crimes similar to the one on trial by using a specific method, that can help prove that the defendant is the perpetrator. Here, the identity of the perpetrator was known. The issue was the credibility of the victims versus that of the defendant.

The jury believed the testimony of Jane and the others. It convicted Whitis. Judge Forester sentenced Whitis to a total of 248 months. The conviction was upheld on appeal, where the primary issue was allowing Mary's testimony. Both the lower court and the appeals court agreed the testimony was permissible.

Despite the serious nature of the trial, I have to relate a funny story that came out of it. With the issue being which side was telling the truth, the defense counsel, Gordon, set about to vigorously impeach anyone who gave testimony unfavorable to his case. In trying to show that Fowler made up the story about the kidnapping and the gun, he engaged in a rapid-fire series of questions designed to make Fowler stumble and falter, which he would be likely to do if he were making up details on the fly. To that point in his testimony, Fowler had come across as a no-nonsense, serious, unemotional witness.

> Gordon: *So, you gave us all these details about that night. Let me ask you, how many beers did you drink that night?*
> Fowler: *Three, I believe.*
> Gordon: *And what brand of beer was it?*
> Fowler: *Coors Light. (Pause) I'm a Silver Bullet Man.*

Fowler smiled while the jury and courtroom roared with laughter.

Robert DeZarn

Perjury

The highest-ranking member of the Kentucky National Guard is a flag grade officer known as the adjutant general. Appointed by the governor, this general serves at the pleasure of the governor. Other than this political appointment, the Guard is supposed to be apolitical. Promotions and retention should be based on merit, not cronyism or politics. A retention board comprised of a small group of officers appointed by the adjutant general and the governor meets periodically to determine which officers will be retained and which will be let go.

In 1992, over twenty officers were let go by the retention board—historically, an exceptionally large number. Those who were not retained were surprised, disappointed, and confused. No rational basis for who was canned and who stayed seemed to exist. Then some of them saw a pattern. Rumors had circulated that Adjutant General Robert DeZarn had developed a circle of politically motivated officers who were seeking to purge the Kentucky Guard of those officers who did not adhere to their brand of politics. There were stories about contributions for the reelection campaign of Governor Brereton Jones from guards at a Preakness Stakes (horse race every May) Party and another function. The pattern appeared to be that if you contributed to that campaign, you were retained. If you did not, you were fired. This would be clear violations of federal and state regulations and statutes.

The fired guards complained to the Department of the Army of the United States in the fall of 1992. Two inspector generals (or IGs) were assigned to investigate the complaints. They conducted numerous interviews of guards, including General DeZarn. Of particular relevance to this case, they asked DeZarn if the 1991 Preakness Party everyone was talking about was a Jones fundraiser. He emphatically denied that it was a fundraiser and said that he didn't see any cash change hands. The IGs concluded that the allegations could not be substantiated, and they closed the case.

A subsequent development caused the FBI in Lexington to look at the matter. A Guard officer by the name of John Julian was developed as an informant. I don't recall the life circumstances that made him agree to cooperate, but he had had some kind of falling out with DeZarn and was irked that he had escaped any consequences for what Julian knew to be true. Julian had been on the inner circle of officers who helped DeZarn raise funds for Jones in 1990 and 1991. Julian told of a meeting among a group of officers in early 1990. They hatched a plan to ask a list of officers to contribute $500 apiece to the Jones campaign. The funds were to be brought to a Preakness Stakes Party to be held at the home of former Adjutant General Billy Wellman. The FBI asked Julian to wear a wire to record conversations with guards who were in on the fundraising. The result was several incriminating recordings, confirming what Julian had said. In various interviews with guards, the FBI further corroborated that there had been an organized fundraiser in conjunction with the Preakness Party.

I WAS ASSIGNED to the case along with a colleague, E.J. Walbourn. We reviewed the transcript of the interview the IGs had conducted of DeZarn and immediately realized he had lied to them when he had denied that the Preakness Party was a fundraiser and in several other statements. We brought an indictment in 1995, and the case went to trial in 1996 in Frankfort, Kentucky.

It was during the defense's opening statement that we first realized that the defense was going to be working two rules, or maxims, of the law of perjury—the " literal truth" and "sharp contrast" rules. No longer were they saying that no cash was raised, the defense now was saying that the Preakness Party was in 1990, not 1991. DeZarn, they said, was confused when asked about the 1991 Preakness Party. That's because DeZarn had attended a Belmont Stakes party in 1991, so the mistaken year made him think the question was about *that* party. (The Preakness and Belmont are the second and third legs in the Triple Crown of horse racing, the Kentucky Derby being the first.) That Belmont party was not a fundraiser like the Preakness Party, so his answer about 1991 was the literal truth. Therefore, his answer "no cash at the 1991 Preakness Party" was not in sharp contrast to the truth that the party was in 1990. And the answer about 1991 was the literal truth because he did not raise cash at the 1991 Belmont Party.

Here is an example of the sharp contrast rule in action. Let's say a man is guilty of shooting and killing a person. He is interviewed by the police. He is asked, "Did you kill the man?" He answers, "I don't believe in killing." The answer comes across as a denial of guilt. But is not in sharp contrast with the truth. The answer is not perjury.

Here is an example of the literal truth rule. Let's say a man bowls at the local bowling alley every Tuesday night. But on a particular week he bowled Wednesday night also. On that Wednesday he is seen stealing bowling balls. He is interviewed by the police a week later. He is asked whether he was at the bowling alley last Wednesday night and he answers, "I bowl on Tuesdays." That is a literally true statement, so no perjury results, even though it was an attempt to deceive.

Hearing the defense theory during the opening statement, E.J. and I changed our case just a bit. Our goal became showing the jury that DeZarn understood the question about the Preakness Party, even if there was an error in the question about the year it occurred. We introduced evidence regarding that 1991 Belmont party to show that DeZarn wasn't misled by the mistake. That party involved about four couples who had a sit-down dinner together indoors. The Preakness Party was an outdoor cookout with dozens of people present. Governor Jones had made an appearance at the Preakness Party but not the other.

During the IG interview, DeZarn had made statements that clearly showed he was referring to that singular event known as the Preakness Party. He mentioned the governor's appearance. He described the outdoor barbecuing. He mentioned people who were there that were not at the Belmont party.

E.J. and I recalled an article we had seen from the Louisville *Courier Journal* months earlier when the allegations about the Preakness Party had first become public. A reporter asked DeZarn to address the allegations. The question by the reporter correctly identified the year as 1990. DeZarn denied that cash changed hands to the reporter, just like he did to the IG. Thus, the difference in the year made no difference in the answer.

During a lunch break, E.J. and I drove over to the state library in Frankfort, pulled up the microfiche of the *Courier Journal* newspapers, and searched for articles about our case, and bingo, we found the article that we remembered. Later, we introduced the article to make our point that the date mistake was not the cause of his false answer. The jury convicted DeZarn after about three hours of deliberation. The conviction was appealed. The Sixth Circuit Court of Appeals affirmed and issued an excellent opinion addressing the literal truth and stark contrast doctrines.

Elisha Jacobs

One Mean Man

Elisha and Lauretta Jacobs, then in their late thirties or early forties, lived as husband and wife in rural Knott County, Kentucky. Lauretta had four children by a prior marriage and had two more children with Elisha.

Lauretta was a stay-at-home mom, and Elisha worked a blue-collar job—I believe in a coal-mining-related position, though I don't believe he was an actual coal miner. By all accounts, Elisha was the domineering ruler of his castle and controlled—and sometimes abused—Lauretta. But Lauretta persevered in the marriage until one of her daughters reported that Elisha had sexually abused her. Lauretta filed criminal charges against Elisha, obtained a stayaway order, which is a type of restraining order, packed up all her kids, filed for divorce, and moved back to central Indiana, where she had relatives.

Elisha was enraged that Lauretta filed criminal charges against him. He wasn't about to let it pass without retaliation, and thus, started a series of actions that would essentially destroy the rest of his life. Feigning concern for Lauretta and the kids' financial well-being, Elisha called Lauretta and invited her to meet him at his parents' home in Knott County so that he could give her cash to help defray living expenses. Though such a meeting would have been in violation of the restraining order, Lauretta agreed to the meeting because she needed the money. But the meeting was a ruse.

As soon as Lauretta stepped out of her car that day in Kentucky, Elisha grabbed her and punched her in the mouth, sending blood gushing, and loosening her teeth. Elisha then brandished a single shot shotgun, pushed Lauretta into his truck, and began driving for the next several hours, all the while berating her for ruining their lives. Eventually, the couple wound up in Tennessee, initiating federal jurisdiction by crossing the state line.

Elisha rented a motel room. Lauretta, fearing for her life, acquiesced to having sex with Elisha. The next morning, Elisha apparently believed that everything was good between him and Lauretta and that she would not report the kidnapping, so he took her back to her car. Lauretta promptly reported the events to the police, and a warrant was issued for Elisha's arrest. He was jailed, pending trial, and Lauretta returned to Indiana, vowing to never physically meet Elisha again. Lauretta had filed new charges against him.

Enraged, Elisha felt like he had nothing more to lose. Unfortunately for Lauretta, a state judge in Kentucky had lowered Elisha's bond, and he was freed. He wasted no time and drove directly to Indiana, where he approached the house Lauretta was staying in with relatives. It was dark when he approached, and he cut off the electricity to the house, hoping that the occupants would come out of the dark home. When they didn't, he turned the lights back on and knocked on the door. When no one opened the door, he crashed through the big front window into the living room in front of Lauretta and the kids.

Elisha brandished a shotgun, grabbed Lauretta by the hair, dragged her out into the cold night air, across cornfields and downed barbed wire, cutting her leg. Eventually, Lauretta was able to free herself from a slumbering Elisha and made her way to a nearby highway, where she flagged down a passing car. The good Samaritan driver took her to a hospital, where she was treated and the police summoned.

Elisha, charged in Indiana state court with kidnapping and assault, pleaded guilty. He was sentenced to fifteen years, but his legal consequences had just begun. Social workers in Kentucky brought me the case to evaluate for federal prosecution under the relatively new Violence Against Women Act (VAWA). It was not a hard decision, as this was precisely the kind of case that VAWA was meant to address.

WE OBTAINED AN indictment against Elisha for kidnapping (the Tennessee incident), interstate travel to violate a protection order, interstate travel to commit domestic violence (the Indiana incident), and two counts of possession of a firearm during a crime of violence (one count for Indiana and one count for Tennessee). Those last two counts, dealing with firearm possession, known as 924(c) counts, were especially significant. The law provided that for the first 924(c), the defendant shall be sentenced to five years *consecutive* to any other sentence imposed, and on the second 924(c), the defendant shall be sentenced to another consecutive term of twenty years.

For the trial, Elisha asked the court to sever the two separate incidents—Tennessee and Indiana—arguing that they were distinct and separate crimes. More importantly, he argued, he did not contest the Indiana charge but had a defense to the Tennessee counts. He claimed the Tennessee incident was simply a romantic encounter between him and his wife and that everything was consensual. The request to sever was denied as the court found the two incidents were part of a common scheme or plan.

Lauretta was remarkably composed during her riveting testimony. The jury was moved by the testimony of few of the children who witnessed their dad bust through the living room window and take their mother from the house. But Elisha was still angry. At one point, while the jury was being escorted from the courtroom for a break, Elisha faced me and began mouthing off about something, the details of which I have long forgotten.

Instinctively, I turned to him and said, "You'll be better off just keeping your mouth shut."

He responded, "Who's going to make me? You?"

The marshals quickly ushered him out of the courtroom, much to my relief. I don't think I could have taken him, as they say.

The verdict was quick—guilty on all counts. At sentencing, several months later, Elisha was sentenced to just more than thirty years in prison. If he had not possessed a gun during the two incidents, his sentence would have been seventy months, or just under six years. Twenty years later, following a change in the case law, the details of which are too academic to analyze here, Elisha filed a motion to have the gun convictions set aside. Initially, a magistrate judge agreed with Elisha's reasoning, and the judge filed a report and recommendation setting those convictions aside. If sustained, Elisha would then be a free man.

We objected to the magistrate's recommendation, and Judge Hood, in a lengthy opinion, sustained the objection. Elisha appealed to the federal court of appeals, where the convictions were upheld. But it was a close call.

I recently learned that, with "good time" awarded, Elisha served his entire sentence and was recently released.

Dan Hale

Doctor RICO

In the early 1990s, an extended family in Mount Vernon, Kentucky, created a plan to scam insurance companies by using a particular line of insurance known as *daily indemnity hospitalization.* This type of insurance was the subject of extensive sales promotions by insurance companies around that time and seemingly lucrative.

The Ramsey family found loopholes, and a friendly doctor who would allow them to perpetrate a fraud that brought them millions of dollars over several years. Ultimately, it led to the imprisonment of more than a dozen family members, a Tennessee doctor, and an insurance agent. This scam, like most such crime schemes, probably started small, then grew as the scammers developed better techniques.

To understand the scheme, you have to know something about how these daily indemnity policies work. Everyone has seen the AFLAC duck and various celebrities on television hawking just such a policy. It is designed to supplement the insured's medical and health insurance, covering costs incidental to hospitalization that are not covered by the primary health policy. The theory is that when a person is hospitalized, the family incurs costs for travel, hotel, food, and the like that exceed normal budgeted expenses. Under the daily indemnity policy, a flat daily rate is paid for every day in the hospital—no receipts required, no questions asked, no justification needed.

The Ramseys noticed that when someone applied for a policy with one company, the application never asked, "Do you own any other daily indemnity policies?" The practical effect of this is that a person could buy an unlimited number of these policies. Let's suppose someone obtained twenty such policies, each paying one hundred dollars a day for each day of hospitalization. That amount of coverage would earn $2,000 per day, far in excess of any out-of-pocket expenses caused by the hospitalization. To afford the premiums for twenty policies, the applicant would have to be confident that a sustained hospitalization was in the near future. This required both a friendly doctor and feigned or staged injuries.

DR. DAN HALE of Morristown, Tennessee, was known to frequently hospitalize a group of Tennessee residents, all of whom had lots of daily indemnity policies, for suspicious injuries. I believe a local insurance agent, Jimmy Collake, had educated these people on the ins and outs of this type of policy and helped develop the scam. Collake was making tons of money selling dozens of these policies. At some point, Collake became acquainted with the Ramseys from Kentucky and steered them to Dr. Hale, who was making a lot of money on physician fees while the scammers were in the hospital. It became one big symbiotic relationship.

Over time, the Ramsey clan put together an elaborate scheme. A member of the family would obtain dozens of policies from Collake; they would injure each other in staged accidents, fall off ladders or put something heavy in a sock and hit each other. Then they would go to Tennessee to see Dr. Hale. Though they were careful to show a bruise or abrasion for the benefit of nurses and staff, most of their complaints of pain were faked or exaggerated. They became notorious among the staff and nurses, who noted a "Ramsey wing" in the hospital where the family members would visit each other and essentially party.

And they noticed that the hospitalizations were unusually long—far in excess of what any legitimate health insurance company would approve for such an injury. But health insurance companies were not scrutinizing these hospitalizations because the Ramseys were self-pay, and no single insurance company was out much money. The Ramseys together made tens of thousands of dollars each day and paid Dr. Hale and the hospital in cash.

After months of the scam's operation, Tom Isbell, an insurance fraud investigator in Tennessee, discovered a pattern. He saw accident reports where Ramsey clan members would be the victim one day and a witness the next. He saw the long hospital stays and the use of the same doctor. He saw that Morristown was an unlikely place for a Mount Vernon, Kentucky, family to seek medical care, much less hospitalization. It was clear what was happening. The challenge was going to be to prove it in court.

While Isbell was making his observations in Tennessee, another investigation was being opened in Kentucky. The daughter-in-law of Russell Ramsey, who was having a marital dispute with Ramsey's son, decided to come forward to law enforcement and implicate the family. Her allegations ultimately were referred to the US Postal Inspection Service in Lexington, where Inspector Lanny Miller was in charge. Miller took on the case himself and, after some initial investigation, brought it to the US Attorney's Office for prosecution.

I met Miller for the first time in my office one morning in 1993. He had asked that I be assigned to the case. He was there to brief me on the facts. As usual, Miller was dressed in sartorial splendor, and he was smooth and loquacious. I thought, *Who is this slick dude?*

But right there, a lifelong friendship started. We had several investigations and trials together. We went on numerous golf trips to Western North Carolina. He and his future spouse went with my wife and me on a dinner cruise on the steamboat, *Belle of Louisville*, for my fortieth birthday party. I attended their wedding, and we tailgated together at University of Kentucky football games.

OVER THE NEXT three years, we put together a huge case with lots of guilty pleas and two trials. At some point in time, my good friend and colleague Bob Rawlins asked to join the case as cocounsel. Bob was older and experienced—he was looking for new adventures in his career. He seemed like a good fit, and I welcomed him aboard. He became an integral and vital part of the trial team.

Eventually, the investigation resulted in guilty pleas from all the Ramsey family members, a trial of the Dr. Hale on racketeering charges, and a trial of the insurance agent Collake on mail fraud charges. The insurance policies were obtained through the mail. Thus, the use of the mail helped facilitate the fraud scheme, which constituted mail fraud.

Miller began the investigation with extensive interviews of Ramsey family members. He had the uncanny ability to show up at the workplace of a Ramsey daughter or son, chat them up a while, and soon have them believing he was their long-lost friend. He eventually hooked up with Isbell, and they put together an elaborate timeline of accidents, witnesses, hospitalizations, insurance policies, and insurance payments.

The first phase of the investigation focused on Mount Vernon and the Ramseys. The first indictment was brought in November 1993. It charged about eight members of the Ramsey family and a family friend, Randy Fyffe, with mail fraud. The family hired one lawyer to represent all of them—legendary Harrodsburg attorney Earl Dean. Dean was getting up in years and was once thought of as the go-to attorney in the Harrodsburg area. I knew him from my public defender work in Danville and Harrodsburg a few years prior. He was sometimes called "Honey Dean" because of his sweet singsong voice and demeanor. When he saw me, he often said, "Good boy, Ken."

I still chuckle thinking about my conversation with Dean as he got off the elevator in the federal courthouse in London, where the Ramsey clan was set to be arraigned. He immediately began asking about a potential plea offer. He said in that lilting voice, "You can tell they're guilty by reading the indictment." That is my goal with every speaking indictment—convince the reader of guilt. But Dean did not remain the attorney for all the family members. I convinced Judge Jennifer Coffman that Dean had a conflict of interest, in that some of the defendants had reached out to the postal inspector about plea bargaining. We simply could not deal with them while they were represented by Dean. She appointed counsel for some defendants and ordered those who had funds to hire an attorney. Eventually, all the first round of defendants pleaded guilty.

After months dedicated to bringing down the Ramsey clan, our investigative team turned its attention to Dr. Hale, his partner Gene Lynch (who died before indictment), and insurance agent Jimmy Collake. But first we had to establish that we had venue over their crimes. We could accomplish that if we could establish that they were coconspirators with the Ramseys. By law, a conspiracy can be prosecuted in any federal district where any overt act furthering the conspiracy has occurred. Because much of the fraud was initiated in the Eastern District of Kentucky, Dr. Hale could be prosecuted as a coconspirator here.

But our theory of conspiracy ran into an obstacle when we took a proffer (interview) from Ramsey and the others. We fully expected that Ramsey would tell us about very candid phone calls he had with Hale, planning out the mechanics of the fraud scheme. Perhaps we would hear that Ramsey would call Hale, who would take the call alone in his office, and they would discuss what injury would be faked and when the next group of scammers would arrive. We thought we would hear them discuss kickbacks and extra fees for Hale's complicity.

But what we learned, to our chagrin, was that Ramsey's relationship with Hale did not involve overt discussions of fraud. It was a wink-and-nod, unspoken relationship. We figured that Hale had to know it was a scam. There were so many red flags. But there were no overt discussions about fake injuries and accidents. There were a few nuggets of conversation that were telling, such as the time that Hale suggested that one type of accident or injury was better for him than another. Hale didn't like car accidents because the police got involved. But we had nothing of what we liked to call real dirty talk. So, we had to adapt our theory to the circumstantial evidence. We had to find evidence that Hale turned a blind eye to this obvious scam, and by doing so, he joined the conspiracy.

This new investigative plan involved many trips to Morristown, and the nearby Tennessee town of Bean Station, where Hale had a satellite office. Many nurses and hospital personnel told us that the scam was obvious to them. It was a running joke for them.

In addition, Isbell had once approached Hale and explained the scam to him—lest he had not already seen it and suggested that it stop. Hale blew him off saying he was there for the patients, not for the insurance companies. The scam had been brought to the attention of hospital administrators, but they had no incentive to shut it down because it was so lucrative. These were the nights in the hospital being paid for in cash. They didn't have to bill insurance companies and deal with denials of payment.

We interviewed former and current employees of Hale, including physician assistants, nurse practitioners, and office personnel. We heard stories about another kind of fraud that was even bigger than the hospital insurance scam. We learned that Dr. Hale was defrauding Medicaid and Medicare by performing unnecessary procedures and tests. Instead of referring his patients to an outside lab or testing facility, Hale purchased numerous devices and testing equipment, such as an EKG machine, CAT scan, and most unusual, an MRI machine.

An MRI machine is extremely expensive. The only way a general practitioner like Hale could justify the expense is if he planned to use it on a large scale, like a private MRI facility might do. We learned that Hale would meet with his staff and establish a contest to see who could order the most EKGs or MRIs. He taught his underlings how to elicit symptomatology to back up the testing orders. If a patient came in for a stubbed toe, Hale's people would probe their medical history until they found something, like a recent headache, that would justify ordering an MRI. One physician's assistant told us that when he first came to work for Hale, Hale took him aside and explained that Medicaid payouts were pathetically low and the only way a doctor can be fairly compensated is to run as many tests as possible and own as many of the testing machines as possible so the fee would stay in office.

We learned from the government officials who administered Tennessee's Medicaid program that Hale was the top Medicaid biller in the state and had been targeted for a fraud audit. The audit ultimately determined that a significant percentage of Hale's ordered tests and procedures, paid for by Medicaid, were unnecessary. All this evidence of Medicaid fraud was interesting, but we had no venue whatsoever over this conduct. We were told that the state Medicaid office had had no luck in getting a local prosecutor, state or federal, interested in taking the case. We decided then that we would pull another legal arrow out of our quiver and incorporate this new fraud scheme into our case.

That new theory of prosecution was RICO—Racketeer Influenced and Corrupt Organization Act. This act basically made it illegal to promote the unlawful activities of an enterprise that repeatedly engaged in a series of specified crimes. The original intent of the RICO statute was to address organized crime, like La Cosa Nostra and the Mafia. But over the years, federal prosecutors have used it to cover a wide range of organizational crime.

Here, our theory was that Hale's medical practice had become a racketeering enterprise. The underlying specified crimes was the insurance fraud with the Ramseys and the Medicaid fraud in Tennessee. So long as some of the racketeering activity occurred in the Eastern District of Kentucky, we had venue to prosecute the case. To be clear, however, we could not actually convict Hale of the

Tennessee Medicaid fraud. It simply could be introduced as part of the racketeering activity supporting the indictment.

THE TRIAL OF Hale began in February 1995 in London, Kentucky. It lasted four weeks and was essentially two trials in one. The first couple of weeks were devoted to proving the insurance fraud, and the last two dealt with the Medicaid fraud. It was an intense trial that required constant work. We often prepared witnesses at night for their testimony the next day. Legal issues arose constantly that required research and argument. The trial also was the source for two of the most gut-wrenching events of my career.

The first event occurred at the beginning of the trial in the opening statement. Though I was an accomplished public speaker and had had numerous trials to that point, I also had a little secret that few people—even those close to me—knew about. I was susceptible to panic attacks in public speaking settings. Twice before, I had experienced attacks. In one, I made an excuse and exited the setting before speaking. In the other, I had a moment to go to the restroom and gather myself before returning to speak. Is this opening statement, I was totally exposed and without recourse, other than asking for a recess.

My attacks were not the classic attacks one reads or hears about, with heart pounding and sweating with a desire to flee. I would describe it as an overwhelming sense of *I cannot do this.* My thinking would become paralyzed, and I would lose the ability to form a sentence. The experience would be triggered by an intrusive thought, like, *You have nothing of interest to say to these people.*

When it happened in the Hale trial, I stammered, fell silent, then turned to Judge Coffman and said, "Judge, can I have a recess?"

She obviously sensed something was wrong and granted the request. "Just let us know when you are ready to proceed," she said.

As I was leaving the courtroom, the defendant Hale—who

professed to be a religious man—looked heavenward and uttered, "The Lord God will deliver me from mine enemies."

Miller and I walked around the courthouse. I tried to explain what was going on, but Miller just said, "It's nothing. It's just a brain fart. You're going to be fine."

That encouragement was what I needed to hear. I vowed to return to the courtroom, dispense with my notes, and just talk to the jury, person to person, and tell them in plain English what this case was about. I knew the case inside and out. I didn't need to rely on notes. And that is what I did, and the rest of the opening went fine.

Though the immediate crisis was averted, the panic attack had a profound effect on my mental state going forward. Deep inside, I had a persistent nagging fear that this was the beginning of the end of my ability to do the job I loved. *What if this becomes a regular occurrence?* I feared developing a phobia of public speaking. I knew that each time I was called on to speak, I would remember the prior attacks and fear the embarrassment that would ensue from another attack.

The panic attack and the deep fears it engendered spawned another problem. Each night during the trial, after a day of courtroom drama where I was focused and energized, waves of depression overcame me. I had experienced depression before, which was fortunate because I knew I could cope and get through it, but it made the trial so much more difficult. Once the trial started each day, I would rally and perform well. But the evenings were tough. In the aftermath of the trial, I sought professional help for the recurring depression. I have been on an antidepressant ever since, and I can report that the treatment has been successful in keeping the depression at bay.

The Hale trial came to a successful conclusion with the defendant convicted on all charges. The conviction was upheld on appeal. Hale served several years in prison. I later learned that, after prison, he became involved in a business involving hormone replacement therapy. There were many allegations from his clients that the business was a scam, and it ultimately led to a civil action by the Tennessee attorney general for consumer fraud, resulting in the termination of his business.

I MENTIONED THAT there were two major unfortunate incidents arising from the Hale trial. The first was the panic attack and subsequent depression. The other was an unfounded allegation of professional misconduct levied against me by a judge on the Sixth Circuit Court of Appeals, based on a series of events that were taken out of context. The allegation requires some background to understand.

A basic rule of constitutional law is that a prosecutor has an obligation to turn over to the defense any evidence uncovered that is exculpatory—in other words, tends to negate guilt or mitigate culpability—or any impeachment evidence that can be used to challenge the credibility of prosecution witnesses. A classic example of this type of evidence would be prior inconsistent statements of witnesses. Therefore, it is important for prosecutors to examine the various prior statements of its witnesses to determine whether such inconsistent statements exist. Another tenet of this area of the law is that if a prosecutor is unsure whether an item of evidence is exculpatory or impeachment material, the prosecutor should reveal it to the judge for a court determination.

Another area of the law of criminal discovery comes into play in this story. It's called the *Jencks rule*. It provides that a defendant is entitled to discover the prior recorded statements of witnesses for the government so that the defendant can assess whether the statements are probative of the witness's credibility. But to be discoverable under Jencks, the statement had to be a verbatim or substantially verbatim statement adopted by the witness to be his own. A summary of the witness's statement, prepared by a government agent, technically was not a Jencks statement. However, if that summary contained exculpatory or impeachment material, the substance of that statement had to be disclosed. Therein lay the rub in this story.

When Russel Ramsey decided to plead guilty and cooperate with the prosecution, we set up what we call *proffer sessions*, wherein Ramsey would tell us everything he knew about his crime and Dr. Hale's involvement therein. The primary interview with Ramsey occurred in the postal inspector's office in Lexington. Miller, Rawlins, and I would ask the questions, and our paralegal, Glenda Glass, would take notes and ultimately write up a summary of the interview.

As previously discussed, we entered that interview with a preconceived notion that Ramsey would tell us about explicit dirty talk discussion between him and Hale about the fraud being committed. But from the beginning of the interview, Ramsey insisted that no such explicit conversations occurred. So, in the course of the discussion, he made two statements, which were summarized in a way that seemed profoundly inconsistent on the surface, but only because the context of the questions and answers was not adequately captured in the summary.

In response to our question about whether he ever talked openly with Hale about the scam, Ramsey said, "No, because I was trying to protect Hale." In other words, he wanted to give Hale plausible deniability. There would be no recording or witness to the "dirty talk."

As we listened to this story, our team began to believe that Ramsey, for some unknown reason, was trying to shield Hale from criminal liability. It just didn't make sense that, while admitting his own guilt, he would cover for Hale by claiming that there was no overt conspiratorial agreement.

At this point in the interview, Miller pointedly asked Ramsey, "Why would you want to protect Hale?" Ramsey responded, "I wouldn't want to protect Hale."

The first "I wanted to protect Hale" statement was in the context of back when they were presenting to the hospital for treatment. The second "I wouldn't protect Hale" was a reference to "right now" in this interview—two different contexts and two wholly different meanings. But superficially, this seemed to be a blatant inconsistency: "I wanted to protect Hale" and "I wouldn't protect Hale."

During pretrial disclosure of discovery materials, I was persuaded by Rawlins that we should not disclose summaries of witness interviews as Jencks material. I had recently started doing just that—out of an abundance of caution—even though, technically, they are not verbatim statements covered by the Jencks rule. At trial, defense counsel requested disclosure of all such statements. Following a standard rule, we asked the court to review the summaries to determine whether any of the statements summarized therein constituted Jencks or impeachment material.

Judge Coffman found several statements that she believed were discoverable as arguably inconsistent statements and provided those to the defense. She denied the request to see the statements in their entirety. Ramsey was then cross-examined on what appeared to be some inconsistencies with his trial testimony. To rehabilitate him on redirect, I asked Ramsey if he had been basically consistent with his story each time he told it, and he agreed.

DR. HALE HAD retained new defense counsel to pursue his appeal. One of the first motions new counsel made was to obtain access to the sealed witness summaries, which was granted by the court of appeals.

That's when all hell broke loose.

Predictably, the defense argued that the summaries contained substantial inconsistencies with his trial testimony, and thus, it had been denied exculpatory material. Apparently, a couple of the court of appeals judges agreed with that proposition. They did not get the nuances of the context of the different statements. In the appellate opinion, the writing judge highlighted the instance I mentioned above as a classic case of inconsistency—in other words, "I was protecting Hale" and "I wouldn't protect Hale." But the court determined that, while a Brady violation had occurred, it was harmless based on the overwhelming evidence of guilt.

But the victory on appeal did not insulate me from a professional misconduct allegation. I believe the allegations against me arose from an unwise decision I made during oral argument at the court of appeals in Cincinnati. One jurist on the panel, Judge Suhrheinrich, was especially animated by what he saw as a Brady violation. The Brady ruling requires prosecutors to disclose any evidence favorable to the defense. He pounded me with pointed questions about the issue. When I pointed out that trial judge Coffman had examined the material and agreed that what was not disclosed was not Brady material, he fumed, "Whose job is it to determine whether material is Brady? You or the judge?"

Of course, the prosecutor is the ultimate arbiter of that issue, but the recommended procedure when there was doubt was to bring the judge into the discussion. This answer did not impress him, and he continued hounding me on the issue. Exasperated, I said, "Your Honor, this case has been proven with overwhelming evidence. It would be unfair to the public and the citizenry to overturn a case for some error I have made. If you think I've done something wrong, punish me, not the citizens."

I learned through back channels later that this comment sent Suhrheinrich into orbit. He immediately implored the chief judge of the court to issue a show cause order, directing me to prove I had not violated my ethical obligations. The first allegation was that I had intentionally withheld Brady material, and the second was that I had suborned perjury by having Ramsey agree that he had always told essentially the same story.

One Sunday afternoon that summer following the oral argument, I went into the office after a round of golf to catch up on some paperwork. On my desk was the show cause order. My case had been assigned to a magistrate judge in Louisville for investigation. The allegations were made known then to two other investigative bodies, the Office of Professional Responsibility (OPR) of the Department of Justice and the Kentucky Bar Association. Over the next few months, I underwent an extensive investigation by these two entities and ultimately was exonerated by both. But I made one immutable change to my procedures going forward. I would always turn over in discovery the witness summaries, definitional nuances be damned.

Joe Douglas Helton

The Lady in the Lake

In the 1990s, before I began to specialize in white collar fraud and public corruption cases, I handled my share of what we called *drugs and guns cases.* I developed strong working relationships with several Bureau of Alcohol, Tobacco, and Firearms (ATF) agents. Among those was hard charging crime fighter Doug Robinson.

One day in 1999, Robinson happened to be in our office in Lexington, and he mentioned that he had recently been contacted by a sheriff's deputy in Magoffin County regarding an interesting case. The deputy wanted the case to be prosecuted by the feds for fear that the defendants would be treated leniently, due to local politics if the case stayed in Magoffin County. The fear of "home cooking" in the local courts based on a family's connection to local power brokers was a frequent refrain in Eastern Kentucky. If the public officials were perceived by influential families to have gone too hard after their boys, they would be sure to support someone else in the next election. The two perpetrators, Joe Douglas Helton and Harold Dean McCarty, came from large extended families, which translated into dozens of votes in elections for sheriff, commonwealth attorney, or circuit judge. ATF Agent Robinson said that he would like to take the case against Helton and McCarty, but that he doubted that I would join in because of the insufficiency of the evidence on the aspects of the case that gave it federal jurisdiction. In cases where guns are used in connection with drug distribution crimes, the United States government has jurisdiction that overlaps with state jurisdiction. But in this case, Robinson said, they had not recovered any drugs or firearms, even though they had a victim who had testified to the existence of both. I asked Robinson to go over the facts for me so I could assess these jurisdictional issues.

According to Robinson, this case came to the attention of law enforcement in Magoffin County in the early morning hours of June 4, 1999, when a call came into the sheriff's office from an elderly couple who lived in a remote home in the countryside. The couple reported that a bleeding, disheveled woman was on their porch wanting into the house, but they were afraid to let her in. State police and the sheriff deputies responded and found a Magoffin County resident Mildred Slusher on the porch. She could barely talk, was bleeding from several wounds, and in a lot of pain. She said she had been shot by Joe Douglas Helton but did not have the strength to elaborate. Nor was there time for a lengthy interview. She needed immediate medical attention.

It would have been a long drive for an ambulance to transport Slusher to the nearest hospital, so Slusher was air lifted by helicopter to the University of Kentucky hospital, where she underwent surgery for the bullet wound and other blunt force injuries. The bullet had entered in a downward direction from the top of the shoulder, traversed her torso, and exited from her buttocks. One of her lungs had collapsed. But she was strong and tough, and survived to tell her story, eventually testifying in court against her attacker.

When Slusher was well enough to speak to the police, they conducted an interview in the hospital at Lexington. Slusher knew that what she was going to say would cast her in an unflattering light, but she laid it all out there in brutal detail, a story that was indeed one of terror and a death-defying will to live.

IT ALL BEGAN at a house trailer in rural Magoffin County where Helton lived alone. Four individuals—two men and two women—were having a party. McCarty and Helton were entertaining Slusher and Molly Minix. All four were severely addicted to cocaine. Reading between the lines, I readily assumed the arrangement Slusher described as a drugs-for-sex party. The women would provide ample sex to the men, and the men would provide everyone with the cocaine. These parties would last as long as the drug supply.

In the late afternoon of June 3, Helton's cocaine supply had dwindled to about a dozen small bags, and not desiring to end the party so soon, he decided to score a new supply of dope. He knew a cocaine dealer who often traded drugs for physical items like televisions. Helton had a nice sixty-inch television that was worth some money. He asked Slusher to accompany him to the dealer's residence, where he would negotiate a trade.

Helton had the small bags of cocaine in his pocket as he did not want to leave them at home with McCarty and Minix; he knew they would snort it all while he was gone. But for some reason, he also did not want to have the drugs on him when he got to the dealer's place. So, in full view of Slusher, Helton pulled over on the side of the road and hid the cocaine beside a signpost. Then he and Mildred continued to the dealer's residence and negotiated a deal. For the television and some cash, the dealer provided a nice quantity of cocaine.

Helton and Slusher returned to Helton's trailer. The men loaded the television in a vehicle, and Helton left alone to conclude the trade with the dealer. McCarty, Minix, and Slusher were all suffering from withdrawal, as it had been some time since their last hit. Slusher made the mistake of telling the others that she had seen Helton hide some cocaine by the road. McCarty convinced her to take him to the drugs. Slusher insisted that they take only a few of the small bags and leave the rest where they were, thinking that Helton might not miss a small amount and would not be too angry if he did notice. What Slusher did not realize was McCarty would later sneak out of the trailer and retrieve all the cocaine.

Helton stopped by the signpost on his way back to his trailer to retrieve his stash. When he found it missing, he was enraged. He knew of only one person who could have taken it, and he was hell bent on getting it back or making Slusher pay for stealing it.

Helton stormed into the trailer. He grabbed Slusher by her collar and threw her to the floor. He pulled out an automatic.45 caliber pistol, struck her on the head, and demanded that she give him the cocaine. Slusher pleaded and said she had only taken a small amount to relieve the withdrawal pains, but Helton wasn't having it. All the drugs by the signpost were missing. He dragged Slusher to the truck and drove her to the signpost. He again insisted that she tell him where the drugs were, and she again denied knowing. He fired his gun near her head.

Back at the trailer, Helton, still fuming, pushed Slusher to the floor and jabbed the gun into her shoulder, resulting in the weapon discharging. I don't believe Helton meant to shoot her at that point. That would have ended any chance of recovering the cocaine, and the shoulder is an unlikely target for someone bent on murder.

Slusher laid crumpled on the floor of the trailer. Now, Helton and McCarty were rattled. What were they going to do? They presumed that Slusher's wound was fatal, so the subject became what to do with her body. The two men picked Slusher off the floor and took her out to the truck, where they put her in the open bed. They then went into the trailer to discuss their next move.

But Slusher wasn't dead, just playing possum. Slusher used the cover of darkness for her retreat. She hid behind a propane tank some distance from the house. Within minutes, the men came out of the trailer to find Slusher gone. Helton jumped behind the wheel, turned on the headlights, and circled wildly around the yard looking for Slusher.

Eventually, Helton spotted Slusher behind the tank and captured her. He and McCarty found some old concrete blocks and rope and tied the blocks to Slusher's legs and hands while she lay in the truck. As the men pulled out from the yard, Slusher had no idea where they were going, but she noticed that they left the smooth blacktop and went down some bumpy gravel road. Then the truck stopped, and the men lowered the tailgate. They had backed up to a silt pond next to an abandoned strip mine operation.

The men jumped in the truck and threw Slusher and the concrete blocks into the water. Slusher thought she was as good as dead. But to her surprise, her feet touched the pond bottom well before her head submerged. Believing that it was best that the men thought she was drowning, Slusher alternated between ducking under the water and raising up just enough to breathe. She gurgled loudly to create the impression that she was, in fact, struggling in the water and trying to stay afloat.

Then she heard McCarty tell Helton, "Give me that gun."

Harold shot at Slusher three or four times, emptying the magazine. Each time he missed. McCarty and Helton pulled Slusher from the pond and over to a tree, removed the ropes and blocks, and sat and talked about what do with her. McCarty mentioned throwing her into an old oil tank where she may never be discovered. But the men were exhausted and strung out on drugs. Helton began to slumber. McCarty, frustrated, left on foot back toward the blacktop road they arrived on. Slusher saw her chance to escape.

It was now dawn, and Slusher could see her way through some woods. Despite her injuries, she was determined to escape. After walking through the woods for several miles, Slusher saw that she was on a ridge line looking down into a valley (or holler, in local jargon) where there was a farmhouse. She carefully climbed down the ridgeline and approached the home. She knocked on the door. She could see a face inside, but the person would not let her in.

She said, "I've been shot," but still no entry.

The person on the other side of the door said, "We're calling the sheriff."

That was Slusher's story as told to me by Robinson and later told to me in person by Slusher when I was preparing her testimony for trial.

ROBINSON BELIEVED SLUSHER'S story, but he questioned whether we could prosecute without the drugs in question and without a recovered gun. How could we prove that the substance Slusher claimed was at the center of these events—cocaine—was, in fact, cocaine with nothing to test? And without a gun to introduce into evidence, how could we prove Helton used a gun "during and in relation to" (the legal standard) a drug trafficking offense?

It occurred to me immediately that, though there were no actual drugs and guns to flash in front of the jury, we certainly would have great circumstantial case that both existed during these events. While drug testing is the conventional method of proving that a substance is a scheduled illegal drug, no law says that's the only way to prove it. Some legal research confirmed my intuition.

The nature of a substance is subject to the same rules of proof as any other fact or element of an offense. That is, any evidence, circumstantial or direct, that satisfies a jury beyond a reasonable doubt that a fact exists is sufficient to make a case.

In this case, we could prove that the substance being used by these four individuals was cocaine by the testimony of both Slusher and Minix. (We gave the latter immunity so she could not refuse to testify based on her Fifth Amendment right not to incriminate herself.) We could make them essentially expert witnesses on the nature of the substance they ingested. As cocaine addicts, they had a lengthy history of ingesting the white powder. In other words, they could testify that this stuff looked like a duck, quacked like a duck, and walked like a duck, and, thus, was a duck.

The use of the firearm would be proven by the testimony of Slusher and Minix, as corroborated by the medical evidence of a gunshot wound. Nothing in the law requires that the firearm be recovered and placed in physical evidence.

Helton and McCarty were indicted together, but their cases were severed for trial as it appeared that McCarty was going to use the defense that whatever he did in the case was a result of being coerced by Helton. Helton was also pointing the finger at McCarty as the main culprit.

The jury had no problem convicting Helton of conspiracy to distribute cocaine, using a firearm during a drug offense, and of being a felon in possession of a firearm. Ultimately, he was sentenced to sixteen years in prison. I believe he died in prison in 2015. McCarty pleaded guilty after the Helton trial.

A FEW SIDE notes are of interest. As I was preparing for trial, Robinson and I traveled to Salyersville to the home of Slusher. She lived in a modest ranch home with her father and her daughter. I expected to find a woman traumatized by the repeated brushes with death. I thought she may be emotionally fragile and require a lot of coaxing and reassurance. And to be sure, she was quite animated describing the events of that fateful evening. But it was as if she were describing a night where she slid off a road in a snowstorm. I'm not sure she realized just how close to dying she had come. I guess the life of a drug addict was so filled with daily drama that this was just more of it. But she did profess that she was leaving that life behind. I hope that she did.

After Helton's sentencing hearing, a court security officer reported to me that, as he was being led away to jail, Helton mumbled, "I should have tied the damn blocks around her neck." That would have been a nice little nugget of evidence if the case ever had to be retried.

When Helton's appeal was being argued before the Sixth Circuit Court of Appeals in Cincinnati, Judge Alice Batchelder interjected a question during a pause in my presentation. "Mr. Taylor, this really doesn't have any bearing on the legal issues before us today, but I'm just interested in your perspective on this. How do you explain Ms. Slusher being able to survive this ordeal?"

I responded, "Well, I guess you have never met a woman from Magoffin County. They make them tough out there."

That got a nice chuckle from the court.

Sonny Landham

Predator

Almost by accident, in the mid-1990s, I became the point of contact—and unofficial office expert—for VAWA (Violence Against Women Act) prosecutions. I say by *accident* because I just happened to be available to take a phone call from a woman's shelter in Lexington that was seeking possible federal investigation and prosecution of a domestic violence perpetrator. Like everyone else in the office, I had no formal training in the parameters of the relatively new legislation. It was background noise to me, and I did not foresee ever using the statutes.

Domestic violence was a state and local problem—until then-Senator Joe Biden sponsored the VAWA, which Congress passed in the mid-'90s. It established federal jurisdiction over certain cases of domestic violence, typically those that triggered the interstate commerce clause of the US Constitution.

So, I took on my best "fake it till you make it" persona and accepted the call. I took notes while frantically looking for literature attached to old emails. In those days, we did not have Google or other search engines to do quick research.

I told the caller I would investigate the matter and get back with the shelter as soon as possible. Thus began a blitz of phone calls to the Department of Justice in Washington (aka Main Justice), the FBI, and anyone else who might educate me. I learned how the new statutes worked and how the facts of this latest case fit into those parameters.

Over the next few months, I prosecuted the offender and obtained a guilty plea. As a result of my work on this initial case and a few similar ones brought to us by the same women's shelter, I was nominated for and received a Department of Justice Director's Award in Washington. But the most important result of this work was the relationships and networking between me and various domestic violence groups.

During the next five or six years, I was invited to join multidisciplinary working groups related to domestic violence, made up of state and local law enforcement, prosecutors, social workers, and the like. I spoke at a couple of conferences about VAWA's availability. And I prosecuted a number of VAWA cases, several of which went to trial. I thoroughly enjoyed my work in this area. However, it was short lived.

It turned out that VAWA was a wake-up call for state and local prosecutors and judges. For years, domestic violence was seen as all *domestic*, with little emphasis on *violence*. Prosecutors often soft-pedaled cases, and judges often probated or slapped offenders on the wrist. Thus, VAWA filled a void for domestic violence advocates for a period. The feds got the cases when we could find jurisdiction.

I had noticed that we weren't getting referrals any longer. Whether it was tougher state laws being passed or the state judicial system taking the subject more seriously, the pipeline dried up, and I went on to other areas of prosecution. All this background is to put the Sonny Landham case in a historical context.

I RECEIVED A call from a social worker in the Ashland, Kentucky area in the mid-to-late '90s about Belita Adams, who was being threatened and harassed by her ex-husband, Sonny Landham. I enlisted the help of our victim advocate at the time, Georgette Lilly, and we traveled to meet with Adams. We didn't realize at that moment that we were going to go on quite a ride with this case.

Landham was a force to be reckoned with, we learned. He was an acclaimed actor, having worked in action films with Arnold Schwarzenegger, Sylvester Stallone, Nick Nolte, and many others—including films like *Predator*, *48 Hours*, and *Lockup*. He was a hulking physical specimen (at least in his earlier years) and usually played a badass in the movies. (He started his film career making adult entertainment movies.) Most importantly, in my opinion, he was an egomaniacal narcissist.

Several years after I prosecuted him, Landham, who had no connection to Kentucky until this case but who subsequently made the state his home, ran for governor of Kentucky. He referred to the Democratic candidate, Ben Chandler as "Slappy Chandler," whatever that meant. (Probably a take on Ben's grandfather, Happy Chandler). He lost the primary, but it whetted his appetite for the limelight of politics. He tried a run for state senate, but the campaign stalled. He was a guest speaker at various right-wing organization meetings. Finally, in 2008 he challenged Mitch McConnell for his senate seat. To do this, he left the GOP to take up the banner of the Libertarian Party.

But the Libertarians dumped him within a month for his statements on the campaign trail. He called Arabs "camel-dung shovelers," and proposed that there be a total ban on Arabs in this country. He even advocated killing Arabs who would not leave. He said, "When you are in a war, you kill everything that moves." This was the mentality with which we were dealing.

Landham had married the much younger Adams a decade or more before the case. Their marriage was turbulent. Adams told of an incident where Landham shot a gun right past her head. He held her at knifepoint once and asked, "If you want to play Nicole, do you want me to play O.J.?" The marriage ended, and Adams moved to the Maysville, Kentucky, area where her grandmother had a farm.

Adams had come into some money when her father, a school superintendent in Florida, was murdered by a disgruntled employee.

Landham reappeared in the picture and convinced Adams to use her money to finance a movie and help him produce it. For a brief time, the relationship resumed. But eventually, things went off the rails again, and Adams tried to end all contact. Landham began a series of increasingly threatening letters. He began calling her and leaving threatening voicemail messages, calling her a "cunt who needed a bullet in the head." He also said things like, "I've done more to you with a Parker 51 than what happened to your father with a goddamn Taurus five-shot," and "I'm going to have all your children." He sent his daughter, Priscilla, a birthday package containing some item (I forget now what) that Adams interpreted as a threat.

Adams obtained domestic violence orders (DVOs) against Landham, but he repeatedly violated them by calling and threatening her. Landham also threatened Adams's mother, and she also obtained DVOs against him.

The domestic violence experts that Adams had consulted put together a written lethality assessment for her case. Experts in this area have developed a scale based on objective criteria and based on hundreds or thousands of real case studies that rate the likelihood of murder: Spoken words; actions of the people involved; life circumstances of the subject; history of violence; the physical abilities of the subject; perpetrator's access to weapons; perpetrator's social network (or lack thereof). Landham rated remarkably high on that scale. We believed we were working to save Adams's life—and possibly her two daughters.

We could prove that Landham had sent some letters across state lines and had traveled to Kentucky for no legitimate reason other than to stalk her, so we had federal jurisdiction under VAWA. We obtained an indictment at the Ashland grand jury and an arrest warrant for Landham.

But I had a charging problem, the extent of which I did not realize until it was too late. There was no question that Landham communicated real threats in the more than fifty phone calls. But the calls were of unknown time and date. Adams did not keep a log. The only threats we could date were mailed letters. The appeals court would later say that the threats we indicted were not true threats. We introduced the threats with a gun and a knife and the phone calls as prior bad acts, but they were not charged. While it was clear to the jury on the totality of the record that Landham was a dangerous man, the parsing of the language in separate counts of the indictment led to what I consider a defense victory by technicality.

At his arraignment a few days later, Landham appeared without a lawyer. I believe that he was asking to represent himself. I vividly recall that when Judge Henry R. Wilhoit asked him how he pleaded, Landham boomed, "Railroaded, Your Honor."

Judge Wilhoit, with a little smirk and a headshake said, "I'm afraid that's not a valid plea. I'll just go ahead and enter a not guilty plea on your behalf." He set the matter for trial and appointed Mike "Frenchy" Curtis to represent Landham.

The trial was not particularly noteworthy. It consisted largely of the testimony of Adams, the playing of the phone calls, and the introduction of the letters. Adams told of how these all scared her to death and how she truly feared for her life. Landham did not take the witness stand, but a juror later told me that Landham came across as arrogant and cocky during the trial with his facial expressions and body language.

Landham was convicted on several counts, acquitted on a couple, and the jury hung on a couple more. I moved to dismiss and not retry the hung counts, which would prove to be a mistake. Landham went off to prison, but not before his interesting speech at sentencing.

Landham went on about how badly he was treated by the justice system, in general, and then he got personal. He told Judge Wilhoit that the prosecutor (me) colluded with Adams to frame him. He said I had told her to make up false stories about shooting past her head and about threatening her with a knife. Then he turned and faced me directly and said, "What goes around, comes around. God gets revenge. Someday you will lose one of your children, someone close to you."

Judge Wilhoit told Landham, "In all my years on the bench I've never seen anyone waste their opportunity to speak before sentencing like you just did. You spewed venom the likes of which I have never seen." Landham's outburst confirmed just how threatening he was.

Unfortunately, as mentioned above, the Sixth Circuit Court of Appeals zeroed in on the conduct set out in each count of the indictment and said, in essence, these words do not describe a crime. I can't quibble with that sanitary analysis on a legal level—and, I guess, that's the level the court should be on. But it's just unfortunate that the true Landham, exposed by the prior bad act evidence and the phone calls, could not be considered by the court in determining whether a threat was made. Landham was free, though he had served two-and-a-half years, pending the appeal.

In hindsight, I should have spent more time with the charging decision to ensure what was reflected in the indictment was our best case. I shouldn't have dismissed the hung jury counts. I could have retried them. I just didn't see coming the reasoning of the appellate court.

After his vindication, Landham began his retribution. He held an informal press conference where he harshly criticized Judge Wilhoit, the court system in general, and me. His allegations were far-fetched and full of conspiracy theories about collusion and evidence fabrication. A reporter called me, and I responded, saying something to the effect that the trial was fair, that I disagreed with the appellate court opinion, that the judge was fair, and that Landham just could not let go of the case. That went to print, and Landham filed a lawsuit against me in state court for defamation, alleging that I had called him mentally ill and a liar. We removed the case to federal court, and ultimately, Judge Karl Forester dismissed me from the suit, citing my immunity from prosecution for performing my job.

Landham sued Adams and another attorney in state court. I think the court ultimately dismissed the lawsuit. He filed a multimillion-dollar lawsuit against the Department of Justice for wrongful prosecution. The court dismissed that lawsuit as well. Landham finally faded into the sunset and out of public view. I later learned that he suffered a serious injury in a car accident and died a few years later.

Greg Sargent

Bear Man

The Greg Sargent case that came across my desk in 1998 was unremarkable in terms of the nature of the charge—felon in possession of a firearm—but it had some unusual facts and procedural twists that make it noteworthy. The case started in the state court system with a complaint from Sargent's girlfriend to local authorities concerning Sargent harboring a black bear. Apparently, Sargent and his girlfriend had been arguing for an extended period, and in an act of vengeance, the girlfriend reported that Sargent was illegally keeping the bear in the woods in Eastern Kentucky. She and her sister also reported that Sargent was in possession of an AK-47 assault rifle; Sargent had a prior felony conviction, making such possession illegal. All this piqued the interest of state fish and wildlife officials.

Wildlife officers responded and quickly found the bear. They took it into state custody for eventual return to the wild. Sargent was charged with illegal possession of a wild animal. The officers found the rifle in a truck, but Sargent claimed in wasn't his and provided a story—one I've forgotten—about whose gun it was and how it got to the place and where it was found. His story was contradicted by the two women who described Sargent actively carrying and firing the weapon in the days leading up to their report to the police.

The case was taken on at the federal level by the ATF for

prosecution of a felon in possession charge. This looked like an easy case, and I expected a quick guilty plea. To my surprise, the defense attorney informed me that it was going to trial. My attempts to speak with the two sisters, who would be needed to testify about Sargent's handling of the firearm, were met with resistance. Both refused to be interviewed.

The sisters had regretted ratting out Sargent and would have to be compelled by subpoena to testify. I expected that they would be difficult witnesses for me, but I also expected that when pressed on the witness stand, the sisters would grudgingly tell the story of Sargent's handling of the gun. But they surprised me, and I surprised them back.

Of course, with testimony from the wildlife officers and state police officers who responded to the scene where the bear was located and the gun was found, I established that Sargent was near a loaded firearm and that he was a felon. However, I needed more than mere proximity to the gun to convict. I had to show that Sargent was exercising dominion and control of the weapon. I didn't have to prove he was the owner nor that he was the only person possessing the gun, but I did have to show he actively handled the gun. The sisters' testimony was going to provide that evidence.

Both siblings refused to meet with me prior to the trial. This confirmed that I was in for a wild ride, as I was going to have to treat them as hostile witnesses. As expected, at trial, the girlfriend recanted her prior statement to the police. She said that she was in an argument with Sargent and reported the bear out of spite. She said she added the part about him handling the gun as a little extra. She claimed he never touched the gun and corroborated his story about how that gun came to be in the truck. Of course, I cross-examined her about Sargent having influenced her to recant. She insisted that her previous story was a lie. Her sister took the stand and recanted and said she had joined the previous lie to help her sister.

All this put my case in some jeopardy. That's because of a rule in federal evidence law that a prior inconsistent statement of a witness is not substantive evidence. It can only be used for impeachment purposes. This may be a little nuanced for a person not familiar with the law, but it means that if a witness gives story *A* when first interviewed, then recants at trial and says *A* is made up, that story *B* is the truth, the prior statement is not considered to be valid evidence that *A* is true. The prosecutor can only point out that the witness is a liar.

I had to argue to my judge in this case that the story *A* involved here—that Sargent handled the gun—was supported by circumstantial evidence. I don't recall all my argument, and I don't recall whether we had tried to take fingerprints off the gun, but ultimately the judge agreed that Sargent and the sisters' story presented in trial—the story *B* in our analogy—was implausible and that the proximity of the gun to Sargent under these circumstances was sufficient to get the case to the jury. In my experience, jurors don't make the distinction between substantive and impeachment use of prior inconsistent statements, and they follow what is known in Kentucky state court as the Jett rule.

I've always loved the Jett rule announced by Judge Palmore many years ago, a common-sense rule that sets Kentucky apart from the model rules of evidence used in most states, and federal rules. The Jett rule (named after a case) simply says that if a witness says *A* one day and *B* another, the jury has free rein to decide, under all the circumstances, which is true—*A, B*, or neither. Is the witness' changed story a true heartfelt recantation, such that *B* is the truth, or has the witness been unduly influenced or coerced to recant, such that *A* is the truth?

AFTER THE TWO sisters' testimony, I was incensed. Their brazen disregard for the court system and the search for the truth was galling. I took an unusual action that started out controversial with my judge but ultimately got his blessing.

The siblings were kept at the courthouse for potential recall by the defense, so they were going to be around for my little procedure. I pointed out to the state police officer who had been present during their testimony that the sisters, under oath in front of the jury, had just confessed to filing a false police report. I suggested that he contact the county attorney in the appropriate county and swear out arrest warrants for them. This he did. Within a few hours and with the two sisters still present, the warrants were delivered to the Ashland federal courthouse.

When the case recessed at the end of the day and the sisters were released for the evening, they were met in front of the courthouse by state police officers, who placed them under arrest. Though I believed that their *A* version had been the truth, and the *B* version was perjury, I couldn't overlook the fact that they had confessed to lying about *A*. I discussed with the officers a plan of operation lest these witnesses again recanted in state court and said the police report was true. That would mean that their testimony in federal court was perjury, and I would indict them for that.

When the case resumed the next morning, the defense counsel asked to address the court out of the presence of the jury. He informed the court that something had occurred outside the courthouse the previous evening that he feared might have been witnessed by jurors and, thus, might prejudice his client. He said the state police arrested and hauled away the two witnesses who were obviously aligned with his client.

This seemed to push that particular button with Judge Wilhoit, one that is activated whenever he thinks official power has been abused. He was often quick to jump to that conclusion and go off on the perceived offender. He turned quickly to me and asked, "Mr. Taylor, did you know about this?"

I thought, *Well, here it comes–a blistering like only Wilhoit can administer.* I said "Yes, sir, I'm the one who suggested that it occur, that is, I asked the officers to get the warrant. I did not tell them where to execute it." Then I launched into a long explanation of how we can't let these witnesses toy with the legal system. They want the law to intercede in their affairs when it seems to be to their benefit, then they want to wreck the process they have put in motion. I believed the response to such conduct should be swift and certain.

My remarks seemed to mollify Wilhoit a bit, but he did conduct a group questioning of the jury before proceeding. Then, if anyone acknowledged having seen the arrests, we would go to individual questioning to determine whether there was prejudice to the defendant. The jury was assembled, and the judge questioned them in a manner that was designed to prevent prejudice if none had already occurred. He told them there had been an interaction between state police officers outside the courthouse after the trial. He did not say who was involved or precisely what had occurred. None of the jurors had seen anything out of the ordinary.

The trial proceeded, and Sargent was convicted.

Before releasing the jury after the verdict, Judge Wilhoit said, "You may be wondering what happened outside the courthouse last night." He explained. "Two witnesses, the girlfriend and her sister, as you heard, had told police some time ago that they saw the defendant handling the rifle. Then, here in court, they said that was false, that they had made that all up." He explained that in one proceeding or the other, the women had lied and that they were arrested on charges of filing a false police report based on their confession to that here in court.

I could only chuckle. The day before, it looked like Wilhoit was going to crucify me for having the witnesses arrested. Now, not only was he approving of the procedure, but he also seemed to imply that he put it all in motion.

James Taylor

No, Not That One

For several years during the late 1990s and early 2000s, I had an ongoing working relationship with Kentucky Employers' Mutual Insurance (KEMI). Their fraud investigators brought me several workers' compensation insurance (WCI) cases and worked with the postal inspectors or the FBI to investigate and prosecute them. The James Taylor case was clearly my most memorable one, primarily from a procedural and logistical perspective.

First, a little background on WCI and KEMI. WCI is a statutory insurance program that governs how workplace injuries are compensated for. WCI policies pay injured employees without regard to employer fault, but the amount an employee can recover is governed by law. WCI is mandatory for all Kentucky companies, with certain exceptions such as sole proprietorships or companies with no employees. If a company applies for WCI and is declined by all private companies, it can obtain insurance from KEMI, which is a quasi-private, quasi-public insurer of last resort for the state. It must take all applicants, but the premium it quotes could be so high that the applicant simply can't afford it, in which case, that company would have to cease operating. The underwriting of WCI involves an analysis of three factors—payroll, claims history, and the risk of injury inherent in the work.

Payroll is simply the number and level of compensation of

employees of each type—clerical, factory, farm, and so forth. Each employee is assigned a code that denotes the type and risk of the work that employee performs. The riskier the job, the higher the premium. For example, a tree-cutting service would incur a small premium for its receptionist who takes messages at a desk, and large premiums for the laborers who work in treetops with chainsaws.

The claims history analysis is expressed as an *experience modification factor* (EM). A company with a history of accidents that is consistent with national standards for a company of that type and size is said to have EM of one. If the company has a history of injury twice the size of the typical company, the EM is two. If a company had a history of injury half that of the typical company the EM would be 0.5.

So, in summary, the WCI underwriter uses a formula to calculate the premium, which multiplies a number that reflects the inherent risk for a particular job by the size of the payroll, then multiplies that by the EM. The premium is expressed as so many cents per dollar of payroll. The insured has a duty to keep KEMI updated with any changes to those factors—hiring of new employees, reporting of injuries (even if no claim will be made), and the change in an employee's duties. In injury-prone industries like coal mining, WCI premiums can be as much as the payroll itself. This creates an incentive to defraud the insurance company to lower operating costs and increase profits.

We had cases of fraud by companies involving manipulation and deception within the reporting of information in all three of these areas of analysis. Companies lied about the number of employees, the type of work they were doing, and the history of accidents. Sometimes a company would try to whitewash a horrible history of accidents by pretending to go out of business, when, in fact, they changed the name and pretended to be a new company, which meant they would start with an EM of one.

To prove it has WCI, each company is provided with a certificate of insurance by the insurance company, which the business must display at the worksite and provide to any other company upon whose premises its employees will work.

We sometimes found companies manipulating or even forging these certificates. That is what led KEMI to investigate James Taylor. The certificates of insurance didn't seem to match the coal company displaying them.

TAYLOR WAS A so-called insurance entrepreneur in Dallas, Texas. Taylor thought he had discovered a creative way to provide cheap WCI to the coal companies, but the plan was based on him deceiving both ends of the insurance transaction. The coal companies were paying him for bogus insurance; he was lying about the nature of the risk being insured against.

Taylor set up a shell company, Competitive Edge, Inc., and bought WCI from KEMI while representing on his application that all Competitive Edge employees were of the clerical, low-injury type. Then he advertised in Eastern Kentucky, offering cheap insurance for coal mining companies. He explained that the coal company would execute a joint venture agreement with his company, which he claimed automatically covered the coal company under his certificate of insurance. Unsuspecting and unsophisticated coal operators jumped at this offer and paid Taylor about two million dollars in premiums. Taylor never notified KEMI, the insurance company, about the addition of these employees, nor did he forward any portion of the premiums collected. In reality, the insurance that the mine operators paid for didn't exist.

The scheme was ended when KEMI auditors identified a problem with the arrangement. The certificates of insurance didn't match the name of the coal mine, and the joint venture agreement was pure hocus pocus. After a short investigation, we obtained a federal indictment in Pikeville for fraud-related offenses and money laundering.

Taylor and his wife drove to Pikeville from Dallas, Texas, for the arraignment. He told me later that he just wanted to see Eastern Kentucky and scope out its people. They would be the jurors on his case, he thought.

At the arraignment, we experienced for the first time Taylor's narcissistic personality. He was so full of himself. He was a handsome, dapper dude, well-tanned with a little bling, a nice car, and a beautiful young wife. He tried glad-handing and chatting with court personnel and our team in an obvious attempt to ingratiate himself with those in the system. He even volunteered information about the facts of the case, something defendants should never do. He claimed his business model was legal, and this was all a misunderstanding. No jury of laypeople would convict him of fraud.

Early in pretrial proceedings, the defense moved for a change of venue, citing the doctrine of *forum non conveniens*, which essentially holds that while the current venue is legally appropriate, it poses a severe inconvenience to litigants or witnesses. I was surprised when Judge Wilhoit granted the motion over our objection. He ordered that the case should be tried in Dallas. His logic was hard to contest as the majority of the overt acts in the case occurred in Texas. The defendant lived there as did most of the potential witnesses.

I had never experienced such a ruling, and it immediately raised logistical and procedural questions: Who would prosecute the case in Dallas, and who would preside? Would my office pay for us to travel to Texas and spend weeks trying the case? If we handed the case off to Dallas prosecutors, would they have enough interest in it to do a good job?

Fortunately, we were granted permission to travel and authorized funding for a prosecution team to go to Dallas. But we needed the concurrence of the US Attorney's Office there as well as their agreement to provide us with office space and other support. We spoke with the criminal chief there, who was very much amenable to us being visitors to their office. In fact, that office made us feel at home and welcome whenever we visited.

THE TRIAL TEAM consisted of me, my cocounsel, Bob Rawlins, FBI agent Joe Moutz, and a paralegal, Glenda Glass. Over the year or so we worked on the case, our team made three separate trips to Dallas. The first trip was for trial preparation, interviewing and preparing witness testimony primarily. That trip was notable for the now-humorous dynamic that played out among the team members.

Rawlins was a capable trial attorney. I had teamed up with him on several large cases, and we worked well together, offering complementary skills. One of Rawlins's strengths was his knack for planning. However, in some contexts this came across as control freakishness.

As soon as we got word we were going to Dallas, Rawlins jumped into action, planning our lodging. He wanted to insure we had a comfortable place to live and work. He focused on a Residence Inn in Dallas that was in a good location. As was his penchant, one of the reasons for selecting this Marriott-owned hotel, was that Rawlins owned stock in Marriott. But before committing, he visited a Residence Inn in Lexington and inspected its accommodations.

Then, there was the issue of travel. Rawlins had a van, so it was decided that he would drive to Dallas, transporting the boxes of records and equipment that we would need there. The other three of us flew there. Rawlins picked us up at the airport. What we experienced over the time we worked there caused the three of us to start calling Rawlins "Dad."

We were dependent on Rawlins for transportation. Rawlins decided our schedule to the minute. He determined where we would eat and what time we would depart. (We laugh now about Rawlins taking us to a Mexican restaurant that was part of a national chain because he owned stock in it, too, despite us being in the heartland of authentic local Tex-Mex cuisine.) Rawlins decided what time we left for the downtown office each morning and what time we would return. We had to borrow his van just to run to the store for provisions. On our second trip to Dallas, which was for the actual trial of the case, we all drove our own vehicle to have some independence.

The three-week trial was memorable for the obvious rapport we felt from the jury. It was palpable. We were somewhat a novelty to this Dallas jury, the hillbillies from Kentucky taking on a Dallas business executive. The defense dubbed us the Kentucky Headhunters, but it was obvious that the jurors loved us. They smiled, laughed mightily at my humorous comments, and were riveted by the evidence. It was also evident that they did not like or believe Taylor. On one occasion, as Taylor was trying to explain and justify some aspect of his business model, I witnessed one female juror turn to the man beside her and whisper, "That's bullshit." I easily read her lips.

The jury convicted Taylor of all counts after deliberating for a mere few hours. Judge Jorge Solis allowed Taylor to remain on bond pending sentencing—a bad idea. A few weeks later, US marshals in Dallas alerted us that they had received credible information that Taylor had fled the United States. The FBI in Dallas investigated and confirmed that Taylor had apparently fled to Cuba, with which this country does not have an extradition treaty. We asked the Dallas US Attorney's Office to present an indictment to their grand jury, charging Taylor with fleeing and related charges. That indictment was filed with NCIC (computerized crime records) so that Taylor could be immediately arrested if he was located.

We moved the court to go ahead with the sentencing of Taylor, in absentia. This required us to put on evidence that Taylor was aware of his sentencing date and had intentionally, not accidentally, failed to appear. Judge Solis sentenced him to just over ten years imprisonment.

A few months after sentencing, while I was at home one Friday night in Lexington, I received a call from an FBI agent in Houston. He had gotten my number from the US Marshals Office in Dallas. He wanted me to know that he had Taylor in custody. In fact, he was in a car with him at that very moment.

What I did next was not professional, and I attribute it to the bourbon I had consumed that evening. I asked the agent to put Taylor on the phone, and I had a little fun with him. We had developed that kind of conversational relationship during the trial. Taylor never missed an opportunity to strike up a conversation with any of us on the prosecution team. He was always taunting us about how he was going to be acquitted.

I said, "Hey James, good of you to show back up. How you been? Looking forward to your new home?"

He just mumbled something. It was not a good evening for him.

Apparently, Taylor had been living and working a small job under an assumed name in Houston, and someone had tipped off the authorities. We let the Dallas prosecutors proceed with the new charges against Taylor. Ultimately, he received a few more years tacked on to his original ten years.

After the trial, I received several communications from jurors. The foreperson wrote a very flattering letter to my boss, Joe Famularo, praising the excellent job done by the Kentucky Headhunters in Dallas. Another juror wrote to comment on the trial and told me some things about the deliberations. Later, the same juror wrote me to comment on Taylor's flight to Cuba. She had been following the case in the press. Disturbingly, a few weeks later, I received a letter from her husband explaining that she had a severe stroke. I wrote back wishing her a speedy recovery.

THE WASHABAUGHS

The Family Business

Tim Washabaugh and his wife, Nancy, of Lexington taught their two daughters, Misty and Solitaire, the family business during the 1980s and 1990s. That business was organized shoplifting. Misty would later testify that during the '90s, the family stole more than a million dollars.

The Washabaughs looked like any middle-class family living in the suburbs. They had a nice home, drove nice cars, were well spoken, educated, and in my limited interaction with them, they were amicable and respectable. But behind the facade was a dark side.

The family, along with a handful of unrelated enlistees, had developed a sophisticated shoplifting enterprise. They liked to travel several states removed from Kentucky so that they wouldn't run into people they knew. You see, Tim Washabaugh had already been convicted of theft and other charges in the past and was on the radar of the local police.

After checking into a hotel in a town with a Walmart, they would spend a day doing reconnaissance. They could tell which stores had which kind of theft prevention systems. They knew about cameras and could find dead or blind spots in a store. They knew about floor walkers who looked for shoplifting. Most importantly, they knew about door alarms that would sound if certain merchandise left the store without having been paid for.

They were masters of the division of labor. A team of four or five would perform separate roles. First, there was the loader, who would walk around with a shopping cart, loading it with the items they were interested in—razor blades, diabetic test strips, CDs and DVDs, and the like—small concealable items in high demand in convenience stores, the ultimate destination of this merchandise. One of them would walk around acting suspicious, attracting any floor walker's attention on the wrong person. The loader would push the cart and items into a camera blind spot and leave. Then other team members, one at a time, would conceal the items on their bodies. If there was no door alarm, they would walk right out with the merchandise. They had a different method for items that were tagged to trigger alarms at the exits. I found this to be ingenious.

First, one of them would buy one of the alarm-triggering items and pay for it, generating a receipt. Others would conceal in their clothing numerous other such items and stand by. Then the first one would take the item to the car in the parking lot and reenter the store, carrying the receipt. He would then take another identical item and leave the store without paying. When the alarm was triggered, he would stop and show the receipt to store security. While the alarm was going off, the standby players with all the loot would leave the store undetected because the alarm did not provide any further alert that additional tagged items were leaving the store. The stolen merchandise would be packaged back at the hotel and then mailed to prechosen fencers or grocery store owners who would sell it to the public.

IN EARLY 2001, something went wrong during a Washabaugh venture in Wagoner, Oklahoma. Misty and an accomplice were stopped by store security at Walmart and found to be in possession of large quantities of stolen merchandise. While in police custody, they confessed, and Misty began cooperating. The rest of the family fled town.

The Oklahoma authorities contacted the postal inspector's office in Lexington, as Misty had identified Lexington as the destination of much of their loot. Postal Inspector Al Chapa was assigned the case, and I was assigned as the prosecutor. Chapa and I flew to Oklahoma to view and retrieve the seized evidence and to interview Misty. We quickly built a case for interstate transportation of stolen property. We learned that Timothy Maxberry, a video store owner in Lexington, was the recipient of much of the stolen CDs and DVDs and was involved in an ongoing conspiracy. In April 2001, we indicted six individuals, including Maxberry.

The entire Washabaugh family ultimately agreed to plead guilty. But before they were sentenced, we had to try Tim Maxberry, who wouldn't cop a plea. He said that his address was being used as a drop for the merchandise, of which he knew nothing.

Misty Washabaugh provided credible, damning testimony against Maxberry. She laid out the inner workings of the conspiracy, as outlined above, and said that Maxberry was a knowing participant. The jury had no problem convicting.

Misty claimed to break clean from her former life. She started a new business cleaning homes and offices and vowed to refrain from shoplifting. I recall a conversation I had with her while preparing her to testify at the trial. She was talking about her new business and how it was growing.

I expressed incredulity at the prospect of clients allowing into their homes and businesses a convicted big-time shoplifter. She looked at me with disbelief. "You think I would steal from a regular person? We only do that to the Walmart's and big people." She had rationalized the shoplifting as being victimless. She saw it as a business—not as a crime.

Four family members were sentenced at the same proceeding. Judge Henry Wilhoit lectured the parents about their child-rearing. It was one thing to be a thief, but it was another to teach your children to be professional thieves, he said. His frustration with these defendants grew as the hearing progressed.

He first sentenced Nancy to about ten months and Tim to about eighteen. But he suddenly changed his mind and said, "No, I'm taking it back. You all have slid under the tag for too long." (Wilhoit often used sports metaphors.) Noting the probated sentences and short terms of incarceration in their past, he upped Nancy to sixteen months and Tim to twenty-seven.

When it was Misty's turn to be sentenced, Wilhoit took issue with her claim of being the ringleader. He felt she was just trying to mitigate her parent's sentencing. "I'm not buying it. You are no more the ringleader than the man in the moon. I may be from Grayson, but I've been around. I didn't ride in here on a turnip truck." It was classic Wilhoit.

BUT THE MOST poignant memory from the case came during the Maxberry trial, and it had nothing to do with the facts of the case. The trial started at 9 a.m. on September 11, 2001, with jury selection. Judge Wilhoit was doing some general questioning of the panel when the chambers door opened, and his law clerk moved briskly to interrupt the judge and whisper in his ear. The judge's eyes widened, and his mouth opened. He shook his head in disbelief and sat silently for a few moments, then spoke.

"Ladies and gentlemen, I need to ask you a few questions. Do any of you have any friends or relatives who are flying through New York today or who work in the Twin Towers on Wall Street? There has been a plane crash in New York City. Apparently, it crashed into one of the Twin Towers. There were no survivors, and it appears many in the building have perished. I need to ensure that all of you can continue with this trial and not be worried about something outside this case." None of the jurors expressed reservations about continuing, but of course, all in the courtroom were eager to get more details. We continued with jury selection.

It may have been twenty or thirty minutes later when the scene repeated. The clerk rushed in and conferred with the judge, who stopped my questioning of the jurors with the most serious look on his face. He addressed us: "Our country is under attack. A second plane has flown into the Twin Towers. This is not an accident. Let's all take a few minutes. We'll recess. I want you to think about whether you can be in a frame of mind to continue with this trial." The jurors were visibly shaken. But in the end, all indicated they would be able to serve without undue distraction.

During each break in the trial, we ran to the nearest television to get updates. It was a time of great unknown, and each minute brought new developments. The Pentagon was hit, a plane went down in Pennsylvania, the first tower fell, then the second. It was hard to concentrate on the case at hand. There was so much hunger for information.

The trial continued in the days following September 11. The events of that day caused a logistical problem in my presentation of the evidence. An essential witness, Postal Inspector Chapa, was expected to testify late on day two or early on day three. However, he had flown out West on some assignment with a plan to fly back in time to testify. But for days after 9/11, all commercial flights were canceled, and Chapa was stranded. I told Judge Wilhoit that I may need a recess until flights resumed, but the resourceful Chapa made that unnecessary. He went to the nearest postal service transit center, flashed his badge, and caught a ride on a cross-country mail truck. He arrived a day later than originally expected but in time to testify.

The Shalashes

Another Family Business

While working on the Washabaugh shoplifting case in 2000 and 2001, I became aware of a large fencing operation in Lexington. Misty Washabaugh told us that she sold a lot of stolen merchandise to Tareq "Derrick" Shalash and Ziyad "Tony" Shalash, who ran two warehouses.

Tareq handled mostly shoplifted baby formula on Horton Court, and Ziyad worked with drug store–type goods, like razor blades, diabetic test strips, and cosmetics on Pine Street. My colleague Dave Marye had recently prosecuted the head of the family, Mohammad "Big Man" Shalash, on charges of selling misbranded merchandise, like baby formula. It was widely believed that Big Man's repackaged baby formula was also stolen, but at that time, Marye didn't have sufficient proof to indict on that charge.

The Shalashes held their businesses out to the public as legitimate purchasers and repackages of surplus and discounted merchandise. But in the underground world of organized retail theft (ORT), thieves were aware that they could sell their stolen merchandise to the Shalashes with few questions asked. Shoplifters took their razors, diabetic test strips, and cosmetics to Pine Street, and truck hijackers would take their stolen loads to Horton Court. The Shalashes paid the thieves a fraction of the retail price, repackaged the goods, and then sold them to grocery stores and wholesalers. The stores paid less for

Shalash goods than they would have to pay a legitimate wholesaler or manufacturer, thereby increasing their profits.

As I turned my attention to the Shalash enterprise, I became aware of parallel investigations of their businesses out of Memphis and Ohio. The Memphis investigation focused on hijacked semitrailer loads of various commodities, including breakfast cereal and dish detergents. The Ohio investigation was putting together a large case against shoplifting rings, wherein much of the stolen merchandise was traced to the Shalashes in Lexington. Both investigations had already generated a lot of evidence against Ziyad, Tareq, and others. These investigations, taken together, convinced me that the Shalashes had a racketeering operation. Marye joined me, and we pooled resources and information with the Tennessee and Ohio investigators. Collectively, we put together an extensive indictment of the Shalashes, charging conspiracy, RICO, and interstate transportation and receipt of stolen property.

Paul Sherman was my primary contact with the Memphis investigation. Sherman was an interesting character. He was a college football lineman at Middle Tennessee State who had been drafted by the NFL's Philadelphia Eagles but only lasted a few years in the league. Now he was an undercover police officer. He was a burly man with a direct manner of speaking and disdain for boredom. For example, I asked him once if he had the expertise to explain to the jury exactly how his secret recording device worked. He shook his head and said, "Naw, all I know is how to turn it on, turn it off, and turn it in." Sherman did, however, clearly enjoy the drama, adventure, and even danger of his job. He was proud of his acting skills—the slick way he could convince the bad guys that he was one of them.

Sherman's latest gig was pretending to be a truck hijacker who was trying to unload his stolen loot. Memphis's investigation was aimed at battling a serious problem in Western Tennessee involving loads of goods being stolen from truck stops and loading docks, often as the result of inside jobs by truck drivers and dock workers. Sherman's role was to target the fencers like Tareq by offering them a great deal on the goods he was hawking. He would signal to known fencers, often in coded language, that his merchandise was stolen.

Under federal law governing the interstate transportation of stolen property there is a provision that the theft or receipt of property 'represented to be stolen' was the equivalent of property that was actually stolen. This made it possible for law enforcement to conduct sting operations. Sherman's unit worked with large corporations that provided truckloads of their products that the police could hold out as stolen. Kellogg's donated a load of Frosted Flakes. A baby formula manufacturer gave him a load of its product.

Over several months, Sherman delivered the feigned stolen goods to Horton Court. He was always wired for sound, and a police airplane would circle overhead to track his movements. Several successful sting operations were conducted, each with its own fake story. These became separate counts in the indictment.

Sherman had gradually developed a relationship with Tareq. In the beginning, Sherman was coy about the nature of his load. Basic undercover protocol says to avoid being too direct at first with a target. As the relationship developed, he became more open about the pretend source of his goods. He might tell Tareq that he had to switch trailers after taking the property so the police wouldn't be looking for it.

Tareq would say, "Man, don't tell me your business." That behavior played into a theory of prosecution called *deliberate ignorance* or *willful blindness*. It provides that a person cannot avoid prosecution by turning a blind eye to what is obvious—in this case that the goods were stolen.

Mark Barnhart worked with the Ohio task force targeting shoplifters. His team had developed inside informants that were outlining all the players in the business. One disgruntled insider was Brenda Craft (Not her real name). She became an important witness for us at trial. Craft was a member of the Arab community and educated us on cultural and familial relationships that helped us understand some of the behavioral dynamics inside the Shalash family. She interpreted some of the Arabic conversations captured on tape. She told us where the Shalash enterprise fit into the cottage industry of ORT.

OUR INDICTMENT IN the fall of 2001 charged Big Man, Tareq, Ziyad, and a distant relative from Ohio with the conspiracy. Soon thereafter, Big Man left the United States and traveled to his old country of Jordan. According to the family, Big Man died there on the West Bank and was promptly buried, as is Arabic custom. At the time, we did not believe the story of his passing.

The remaining defendants stood trial in August and September of 2002. The defense sought to have the two-week-old trial continued for a significant time because the trial dates would include the first anniversary of that horrible day, September 11, 2001. They said the defendants' Arab ethnicity would prejudice them in the eyes of the jury, and the anniversary of the attack by Arabs would be too much for jurors to ignore. Judge Forester denied the motion, holding that there would not be a day for years to come when the memory of that day would be erased.

Marye and I put on witness after witness who either did business with the Shalashes or had worked for them. The witnesses described the sellers of merchandise who arrived in panel trucks or station wagons with no signage. The Shalashes would write them checks for their goods, but then immediately cash their checks. The use of checks was part of their attempt to look like a legitimate business, should they be investigated. They employed another device, which I believe had the opposite of its intended effect. The Shalashes required sellers to sign a statement that the merchandise they sold was not stolen, as if that was an insurance policy against being accused of fencing stolen property. To me, it said, "I know there is a problem here."

The jury heard about loads of goods being stolen in Arkansas and Tennessee and landing in Lexington. They heard about all the goods coming in from Ohio. There was even some evidence of a load coming in from the East. In the closing argument, I took a large poster board and an easel and wrote *Lexington* in the middle, then put Pine Street and Horton Court under that. I placed *N*, *S*, *E*, and *W* on the four sides of the board to represent direction. I spoke of the Ohio evidence and wrote the names of those witnesses or events under the *N*. I spoke of the Arkansas thefts and placed those names under *W*. I spoke of the Tennessee thefts and put that beside the *S*, and the eastern event under *E*.

Then I summarized with a little flair and channeled my inner Ross Perot. I said while pointing to the poster, "If you go outside any late night in Lexington and cup your ear and listen, you can hear a giant sucking sound coming from Pine Street and Horton Court. That's the sound of the Shalash enterprise sucking stolen property from the north, south, east, and west." (Ross Perot, when running for president used this metaphor to describe jobs being sucked into Mexico).

The jury convicted the defendants on most counts. Judge Forester, over our objection, released the defendants on their recognizance pending appeal. He said they had shown for all court proceedings, had strong family ties to the area, and did not pose a danger to the public. A couple of months later, Judge Forester sentenced Tareq to seventy-eight months and Ziyad to eight. The brothers were allowed to remain out of prison pending their appeals.

DURING THE PENDENCY of the appeal, I received a phone call one day at my office from a Lexington police officer. He asked if I was the prosecutor from the Shalash trial. He said that officers had pulled over a car of so-called Hispanic actors (I don't recall the nationality) who had large sums of cash and some goods that had the appearance of having been shoplifted (multiple same items with the store tags still on them). They said they had just sold a bunch of this merchandise to one "Tony" on Pine Street.

I rushed to the scene with an agent, and we conducted an interview of several of these individuals. Sure enough, they described Ziyad and a typical Pine Street transaction. Ziyad had not skipped a beat, despite his conviction. We created an affidavit and obtained a search warrant for the Pine Street warehouse. Marye and I got some agents together and executed the search warrant. Unsurprisingly, we found the warehouse full of the same stuff that got Ziyad in trouble in the first place. We obtained a warrant for Ziyad's arrest, and the judge locked him up after a hearing in which agents testified, and we showed the pictures from the search.

The appeal was hard-fought, but the verdict was upheld. Back in Lexington, Judge Forester set a date for Tareq to report to prison in West Virginia. Of course, Ziyad was already in custody. The report date came and went, and Tareq was a no show.

An investigation determined that he had fled the country, presumably to Jordan, where his extended family lived. We indicted him again for fleeing and a warrant was placed in the law enforcement databases. Several years later, I received word that Tareq had been interviewed in Jordan by law enforcement officers on an unrelated matter. The United States does not have an extradition treaty with Jordan, so essentially, Tareq is living there as a free man but forever banished from the United States.

Patrick Donald

Bank Robber Extraordinaire

Bank robbery cases generally are not remarkable, especially the routine *note job* where the robber passes a note to a teller stating, *I have a gun. Fill up this bag with cash.* She complies, and he leaves. That was the case with Patrick Donald in Lexington in 2002. What makes the Donald case noteworthy is that I prosecuted him twice for bank robbery almost a decade apart. He sticks in my mind for his quiet, nonchalant demeanor in the face of serious accusations.

In 2002, Donald was a thirty-something year old residing in the St. James Apartments, a downtown Lexington government-subsidized temporary housing facility for disadvantaged people who were trying to transition back into society after some form of treatment or perhaps incarceration. I don't recall Donald's reason for being there.

One day in April that year, the National City Bank (now known as PNC), located just three blocks from the Saint James Apartments, was robbed by a man who used the stereotypical note and fled as soon as he received several thousand dollars of cash. Unfortunately for Donald, an employee of the St. James Apartments was at the drive-through teller window in her car and caught a glimpse of the man running from the bank. She wasn't certain but believed it to be Donald. She had seen him in the lobby of the apartment building that morning and the clothes of the fleeing felon were consistent with what she had observed him wearing earlier.

She waited for the police to arrive and told them what she had observed. The police pulled the video of the robber, and though somewhat grainy (why are these photos always poor quality?), the witness confirmed that the man on the film was consistent with Donald's appearance that morning at the apartments.

The police went immediately to Saint James and asked an employee at the front desk to see if Donald was home. He was. They asked her to summon him to the lobby. There they pulled Donald aside and asked him to account for his whereabouts all morning. Donald said he had gone outside momentarily for some now forgotten reason, but that was it. Otherwise, he had been in his little efficiency apartment all morning.

The police asked Donald for permission to search his apartment. He refused. The officers decided they had probable cause for a search warrant based on the eyewitness, the video recording, and Donald's proximity to the robbery. Though Donald was obviously not in the clothes seen in the photos, he had had time to change. Officers remained on the premises to keep tabs on Donald while others sought a search warrant. Donald was told he was temporarily detained in the lobby pending the warrant approval to ensure that any evidence was not destroyed.

With warrant in hand, officers had the apartment manager let them into Donald's apartment, and the officers began a thorough search. They found cash consistent with the amount and denominations taken from the bank and clothes consistent with those in the photos. Donald protested that the cash was savings from his work that he would be using to buy a car. Donald was arrested and taken into custody. Shortly, thereafter, the case was turned over to our office for federal prosecution, and I was assigned the case.

Donald and his attorney, Bill Swinford, put up a spirited defense despite the strong evidence for the prosecution. They tried to discredit the eyewitness, focused on the poor quality of the video photos, and also tried to establish that the cash was indeed from Donald's personal savings. But in the end, the evidence was too strong, and Donald was convicted. I don't recall the sentence he received, but it must have been only a few years because in 2012, Donald and I squared off again on another bank robbery.

In May 2012, two men robbed the Security Bank & Trust Co. in Maysville, Kentucky. Three tellers gave similar accounts of the incident. Two men entered the bank in winter clothing with masks over their faces. This was not a simple note job.

One robber clanked something metallic that was hidden in his pocket and loudly and angrily demanded that they fill his bag with money. The women believed that the one man had a gun, and they were frightened by his demeanor. The men were wearing latex gloves. There would be no fingerprints, and the bank surveillance photos would not be helpful.

The men fled on foot to a nearby tire store, where they jumped in a car and sped away. A tire store employee gave the police a good description of the getaway car, a silver Cadillac, vintage around '93 to '95, but he could not read the license number. A full account of the robbery, a description of the men, and the car description were published in the press around Central Kentucky.

The police received an anonymous tip that the robber was one Donald Patrick from Lexington. With Donald having a prior bank robbery conviction, the tip was plausible. Donald was located and interviewed. Of course, he denied involvement, but he could not provide a strong alibi. Telephone records were obtained using a grand jury subpoena and were analyzed. Sure enough, they revealed that Donald's phone was pinging off cell towers in the Maysville area sixty miles or more from Lexington and near the time of the robbery.

Donald was on supervised release in Lexington as a result of his prior conviction. His probation officer called him in to confront him about violation of his conditions of release. His interview contradicted some things he had told the police. I received a call from the probation officer for an evaluation of the strength of the case for prosecution.

I felt the case was just barely prosecutable based on the evidence we had at that time. It consisted of the fact that his phone records put him in the vicinity of the robbery, that he had lied about his movements, that his car matched the description, and that his race and build were similar to the robber in the photos. But it was Donald's previous conviction that cemented our belief he was the culprit. Typically, a prior bank robbery would be admissible in court only where it was of such a similar modus operandi that it would be considered a signature, substantiating the identity of the perpetrator.

But the two robberies were dissimilar. One was a note job, the other an armed robbery. One was a loner, the other a two-man job. One was on foot, the other in a car. I doubted that it would be ruled admissible, and if it were, I would be anxious about it standing up on appeal. We obtained an indictment, but I vowed to keep investigating, trying to shore up the evidence.

This is where I put on my detective hat and got down in the weeds with the evidence. While on a trip to Maysville with the FBI agents and cocounsel, Andy Boone, where we were going to interview the bank tellers, I had a thought that turned into a major development in the case. I asked the agents whether the Cadillac that was impounded by the Maysville police and was in storage in Maysville had been thoroughly searched. I thought that maybe we could swing by and look inside for additional evidence. I didn't know what we were looking for, but I had a strong hunch that we might find something interesting, like maybe a latex glove or a piece of matching clothing.

Within seconds of opening the back door of the Cadillac, I noticed a Walmart receipt on the floor. It was dated the same day as the robbery, but the Walmart in question was not in Maysville. It was on the north side of Lexington. I recalled that the phone records had placed Donald near that location several hours before the robbery. What was the receipt for?

Well, that would be latex gloves.

Agents went to Walmart in Lexington and authenticated the receipt. It was exactly what it purported to be. Someone in Lexington on the day in question had purchased two or more pairs of latex gloves and would have enough time afterward to drive to Maysville. Surveillance video of the purchase was downloaded. It clearly showed Donald as the purchaser. Outside, the video showed him entering the store from his Cadillac and then returning to it before driving away. Importantly, he had on some of the clothing items later appearing in the bank robbery photos. We purchased latex gloves identical to the ones reflected on the receipt and had the tellers acknowledge that they appeared to be like those worn by both robbers. Now our case was beyond solid.

We conferred with the defense counsel and disclosed our newly discovered evidence. As expected, after he conferred with Donald, we received a call. "What can you offer in the way of a plea deal?"

I said he could plead to the charge, but in order to get any leniency, he had to name his accomplice. If he agreed to testify against him, he could receive a *downward departure* from the sentencing guidelines for *substantial assistance.*

We reached an agreement in principle. Donald played us along, pretending to cooperate, but never really did. His accomplice was only known to him by a nickname. He gave a vague, vanilla description. He could not provide anything that would lead us to a real person.

We called him to the grand jury, and he played the same game. We ran down all the leads he gave us, but nothing proved fruitful. I tried for months to learn the identity of his accomplice and prove that Donald had committed perjury at the grand jury. But to this day, the other guy has not been identified.

At sentencing, we refused to ask the court to lower Donald's sentence. He had not been truthful or helpful. Judge Danny Reeves sentenced Donald to thirteen years in prison.

Phillip Cline

A Jealous Rage

In the late summer of 2001, I was contacted by a law enforcement agent, the identity of whom I have forgotten, alerting me to a case that was percolating through the local circuit court in Inez, Martin County, Kentucky, that needed federal attention if justice was to be done. It was related to domestic violence, and, at the time, I was our office's contact for Violence Against Women (VAWA) cases. The defendant, Phillip Cline, had political connections with county power brokers, and the commonwealth attorney was well known there for settling cases for next to no punishment. This was a serious case that deserved a serious prosecution.

The case involved a domestic abuser. He killed another man who had tried to intervene in a domestic violence incident. So, I presented the case to the criminal chief and requested that we open a criminal prosecution.

But I received some push back from our new US Attorney at the time, Greg Van Tatenhove. He had a logical question or two for me. Why is this a case the federal government should be involved with, and why does the federal interest outweigh the state interest? His position was that, while we may have federal jurisdiction with the charge of possession of a firearm by a man under a domestic violence protection order, the true gravamen of the case was assault and murder. "Shouldn't we defer to the state on this?" he asked.

What Van Tatenhove hadn't yet learned—coming from a congressional staff position in Washington—was that our office had historically stepped in to fill a gap in law enforcement in Eastern Kentucky. We often pursued federal charges that, while seemingly less serious, allowed us to deliver more fair and consistent justice for victims than they might have received through the state system, which was often entangled in local politics. I explained that there were real concerns about Cline being treated too lightly by local authorities. Van Tatenhove agreed with my reasoning, and I moved forward with the prosecution.

Cline had already been charged with murder in state court, but that did not preclude me from pursuing parallel federal charges. If, however, the state prosecution reached an adjudication—guilty or not guilty—before my case could come to trial, I would have to justify to supervisors at the Department of Justice in Washington why there remained a federal interest in the case. If I could get to the courthouse first, there would be no such issue. So, the race was on. As it developed, the state prosecutor seemed to be happy with our prosecution going first.

Phillip Cline and Jeanna Cline had had a tumultuous marriage for several years. Phillip was a husky, strong individual who treated Jeanna like chattel. That's not to say that Jeanna was always an agreeable and loving wife, but Phillip Cline had a grave anger issue. He could be explosive and violent. Jeanna had obtained at least four DVOs in the past, but as is common in domestic cases, she usually had them withdrawn to revive and heal the relationship. On the August night in question, Cline was subject to a DVO, but that fact was not without some confusion.

Some months prior in 2020, Jeanna had obtained an order that contained the most extensive type of condition available, that being a stay away order that essentially separates the spouses and often leads directly to divorce. But after weeks under that order, Jeanna, probably at Cline's insistence, moved the court to remove the stay away provision, again claiming that the couple wanted to reconcile. That request was granted, but the court only removed that one condition. The underlying protection order, with its no violence provisions, remained in full force. Immediately after rejoining Jeanna in the home, Cline beat her again. She responded by filing a new petition for a DVO, restoring the stay away position. Complicating matters, she failed to show up for court on the day her new motion was to be heard, and the court, consistent with its policy regarding such no-shows, dismissed the petition. But contrary to what the defense attorney later argued, the 2001 DVO had remained in effect, despite the new petition having been dismissed.

The effect of being under a DVO on the day in question was that Cline was prohibited under federal law from possessing a firearm. At the end of the fateful evening, several guns were taken off Cline by the police. In addition, subsequent investigation revealed other chargeable instances where Cline had purchased guns while under a DVO.

This was a good start, but I wanted something more serious than those possession offenses. So, I found another serious charge in the federal carjacking statute. That statute, passed during the spate of carjackings by professional criminals in the 1990s, made it a federal crime to take from the person of another, by force or violence, a car which had ever traveled in interstate commerce, which is the vast majority of all cars. But I used the plain language of that statute to prosecute a case that was not envisioned by Congress. You see, what the statute addressed was the increasing incidence of criminals hanging around the car rental offices near airports and watching as renters left. Then they would cause some accident or simply follow the renter to a stop sign, where they would jump the victims at gunpoint, commandeer the car, and steal their cash and possessions. My facts, though, still fit the statute, as you will see.

ON A WARM summer night, Cline and Jeanna were part of a group of people partying at a friend's home in rural Martin County. Everyone was drinking, laughing, and telling stories. As the night progressed and the beer supply diminished, two men said they were going to make a beer run. Shortly thereafter, family friend Luther Smith arrived. He and Cline engaged in a spirited conversation about war and the military. For some reason, however, Cline became angry at Jeanna. Perhaps Cline perceived she was giving their friend too much attention. But Jeanna saw one of his violent outbursts on the horizon. He was losing all rationality.

Cline left the room to use the restroom. Jeanna looked at Smith and said, "Don't leave me alone with him. He's going to hurt me. Get me out of here." The two ran from the house, got in Smith's car, and headed down the country road. Cline came storming out of the house after them. As bad luck would have it, the two beer runners returned, and Cline jumped in their car and instructed the driver to catch Luther's car.

A few miles away, the pursuing car caught up with Smith and Jeanna. Probably sensing a dangerous road-rage incident, Smith pulled over on the side of the road. Cline alighted quickly from the car and moved toward Smith. In a selfless and final act, Smith said to Jeanna, "He's not going to hurt you anymore." Smith got out of the car and confronted Cline.

Smith was slightly built compared to Cline. As such, he was no physical match. Predictably, the ensuing fight was over in seconds. Cline picked Smith up, raised him above his head and threw him violently to the blacktop. Smith lay writhing and groaning.

Cline jumped in the car with Jeanna. He pulled up the road, turned the car around and said to Jeanna, "So, you like that Luther, do you? Well, let's see how he likes this." With that, Cline sped toward the body in the road. Jeanna later said she couldn't tell whether the car struck Smith, but circumstantial evidence suggested that it had. The beer runners had left the scene momentarily for some reason, and when they returned, Smith was convulsing with his eyes rolling back in his head. The beer runners left to summon help for Smith. For some inexplicable reason, they did not remove his body from the roadway.

In the meantime, a man who was returning home suddenly hit something in the road—the same road where Smith lay. He would later say he thought it was an animal but had called the police after he got home because he began to suspect it was a person. In my estimation, the man knew he hit a human being but was afraid to stop and investigate. It was never firmly established which car struck the fatal blow. However, this was not a murder case, so we didn't have to prove causation.

Cline took Jeanna back to the trailer. He dragged her from the car and up a hill to an abandoned strip mine. There, he beat her and repeatedly threatened to kill her. The police were alerted by others at the trailer that Cline had dragged Jeanna up the hill. The officers drove up an old mining road and found the couple. After some confrontational moments, Cline let Jeanna go and surrendered.

THERE WERE A lot of pretrial motions filed by the defense, challenging numerous aspects of this indictment. They argued that the DVO had been rescinded, and thus, Cline could possess a firearm. They argued that what occurred here was not legally a carjacking. We prevailed on all their motions, and we went to trial.

Cline's trial defense was profoundly implausible, but I guess that was all he had. He testified that on the night in question, and without any provocation from him, Jeanna had run off with Smith while he was in the restroom. He followed them only to try to reconcile. He claimed that Smith attacked him, and he defended himself. He jumped into the car with Jeanna, who drove off with him voluntarily. When they got back to the trailer, he convinced Jeanna that they should go and spend some romantic time at a strip pit. He did not want another confrontation with Smith. He did not know then that Smith had been killed. He said Jeanna's conduct with him was consensual at all times.

The jury convicted Cline of five of the six counts charged. He was sentenced to 220 months of imprisonment.

Garland Woosley

Dingo Boots

In the early 1990s, Congress passed a federal carjacking statute to address a growing problem of violent thefts of automobiles from drivers on the highway. Armed criminals would jump unsuspecting drivers at intersections or stoplights and, at gunpoint, remove the victim from the car and drive away. The cars were either sold or chopped up for parts. In the years that followed, I used the carjacking statute to prosecute cases where the facts did not match this prototype but, nonetheless, met all the elements of the offense. The Garland Woosley prosecution was such a case. The Winchester, Kentucky police department had shopped the case to our office as a felon in possession firearm case, but after reviewing the facts, I determined it met the requirements of federal carjacking, giving us a much more serious charge to prosecute.

Winchester citizen Martha Crawford, (not her real name) left the Winchester Walmart after shopping one day in early 1994 and approached her car in the parking lot. As she began to put her key in the door lock, a man grabbed her from behind and put a hard object to her back. He commanded her to keep quiet and get in the car. The man took her keys, started the car, and drove away with Crawford in the passenger seat. He again poked her with some hard object and told her keep quiet. He told her to give him all the cash in her purse, and she complied. It wasn't much, maybe twenty dollars.

The man groused about the paltry sum of money. He turned onto Colby Road, heading out of town. He looked at Crawford and asked, "Is your pussy any good?"

Crawford whimpered, "I don't know."

He responded, "Well, we're going to find out. And if it's not any good, I'm going to kill you." Crawford, believing she was going to be raped and murdered and had nothing to lose, opened the door, and threw herself out onto the pavement, where she bounced and rolled onto the grassy shoulder.

The car thief hit the brakes. However, he saw that a woman in a following car had stopped to help Crawford. The carjacker sped away. The good Samaritan helped Crawford into her car and drove her to a police station where she was transported to a local hospital.

Investigators visiting the scene later were amazed by the fortuitous location of her exit from the car. If she had jumped sooner or later, she would have struck one of the many trees lining the road. As it was, she suffered severe road burn, a laceration of her forehead that required fourteen stitches, and several contusions and bruises.

The police began a search for the criminal and Crawford's stolen car. Over the next several days, an excellent police investigation identified the perpetrator as felon Garland Junior Woosley Jr. The Junior in the middle of the name was an actual middle name, not a reference to a father before him. But his father was also named Garland Junior Woosley, so the son was Junior Jr.

Several hours after the abduction, a patrolman spotted a car fitting the description of Crawford's missing car in the parking lot of an auto parts store that was almost directly across the road from the Walmart. It was now dark, and the patrolman noticed that the car lights were still on. A quick license check confirmed that this was the missing vehicle. The perpetrator apparently had ditched the car shortly after Crawford jumped. The police impounded the car and would later find two head hairs that were determined to be consistent with Woosley's hair.

The next day, news of the abduction was broadcast to the public, including information about the discovery of the stolen car at the auto parts store. A Winchester citizen, hearing that information, turned to his wife. "Honey, remember last night we stopped at that very auto parts store? There was a man standing in front of a car, and he had the car hood raised, and he looked like he was tinkering with the engine. And remember the lights of the car were on, but the motor wasn't running. Remember? I commented on the boots he was wearing. They were the old flat-toed Dingo boots that were popular twenty years ago." The man also recalled that the Dingo-boots-wearing man was gone when he exited the store minutes later, but the car was still there with the lights on.

The man called the police to report the possibility of having seen the perpetrator the night before. His rough description of the man generally fit the description provided by Crawford. He was able to produce a receipt for a car accessory he had purchased at that store immediately after seeing the man in the parking lot. The time and date of purchase was printed on the receipt. The police now had a precise time when the car was abandoned, and that time corresponded perfectly with other known times in the sequence of events. The police now had leads that looked promising. They had a rough description of the perpetrator. They figured that he lived close by the Walmart and the auto parts store, that he had no car of his own, and that he was probably unemployed and looking for money. One officer had a hunch that proved fruitful. He surmised that the criminal was probably penniless until he took the money from Crawford. He probably would have been eager to spend the money on tobacco, soda, snacks, or whatever craving he had going. The cop predicted that in a nearby convenience store at about the time the carjacker abandoned the car would be video footage of the perpetrator buying merchandise. The hunch was spot on.

The police pulled surveillance film from the store's camera, and sure enough, a man fitting the description could be seen entering, briefly shopping, and then paying for merchandise. The time of recording put it consistent with the man having walked from the abandoned car to the mini mart. As is common with such film, the image was somewhat grainy, but it provided information about size, race, and clothing.

The next day, the police published in the local paper still photos of the perpetrator taken from the store film. Immediately, the phone began to ring. Several individuals, most anonymously, identified the man in the picture as Garland Junior Woosley Jr. Some even provided his address.

The police went to Woosley's home and conducted an interview. Woosley denied being involved in the abduction. He admitted being the man in the video but that he had been there to buy lottery tickets and cigarettes. He said, other than that, he had been home with his mother all night. His mother corroborated his alibi.

The police asked Woosley if he would consent to a search of his bedroom. He grudgingly agreed. As soon as they opened the door to a closet, the police saw the Dingo boots. This style had become extremely rare. The chance that Woosley and another man by the abandoned car both had Dingo boots was unlikely. The police learned that Garland Woosley had a felony conviction. From arrest records, they were able to put Woosley's photo in a lineup for Crawford to view. She immediately picked out the picture of Woosley. Photos were also shown to the man and his wife who spotted the individual at the auto parts store parking lot. Both said Woosley appeared to be the man.

The police went back to the convenience store to check Woosley's description about what he purchased. The cashier who waited on him reviewed the footage again, and he was insistent that the man on film had not purchased lottery tickets. This he knew because retrieving lottery tickets would have necessitated him leaving the camera frame, which did not occur.

MARTHA CRAWFORD AND her husband were wonderful people—salt of the earth. I was amazed at Crawford's composure. Not only had she bailed out of a moving car, but she also did not seem to be overly traumatized by her close call with rape and murder.

As we worked on her expected testimony for trial, she wanted to know what kind of cross-examination she would get from the defense. I explained that they probably would treat her with kid gloves. The defense was not going to assert that she made up this story; it would be that she was confused and that the police used a suggestive photo array to get her to identify their client, Woosley, as the perpetrator.

But then I asked, "Just to be sure, is there anything in your past—any conviction, judgment, or adverse information—that I need to know about? Anything that could be brought out to question your credibility?"

Crawford thought and thought, then turned to her husband. "Do you know of anything?"

"Yeah, you missed Sunday school two weeks ago," he said, then laughed. This was the kind of person who Martha Crawford was. One factual issue required me to prepare Crawford's testimony regarding the use of a firearm by Woosley. At that time, an element of the carjacking statute was that a firearm was used, one that had traveled in interstate commerce. That element has since been removed. Now, the sole federal jurisdictional hook was that the car traveled at some time in interstate commerce. Because no gun was recovered here, the proof of that element was going to be solely Crawford's testimony. That was going to be a close question.

Crawford had never seen the gun. She had felt it when he poked her with it, and she had grabbed the barrel right before she jumped from the car. Woosley had made a statement or two from which one could infer he had a gun. But the truth was that if a jury had a reasonable doubt about whether a real gun—as opposed to a toy gun or other object—was used to simulate a gun, then we would lose that important count. Crawford had to understand the importance of her description of what she felt and what Woosley said. There could be no equivocation in her testimony on these points. Ultimately, her testimony was persuasive and Woosley was convicted on all counts, and the conviction was upheld on appeal.

Tina Conner

The Governor's Mistress

In September 2002, the Kentucky political world exploded with sensational and salacious news coming out of a press conference in Louisville on television station WHAS. Tina Conner, a little-known nursing home operator from far west Hickman County, Kentucky, came forward with a major allegation. She claimed she had a two-year sexual affair with Governor Paul Patton. During that time, she said the governor used his position and political influence to grant business favors to her and her husband. She said the affair began in 1997 and, when she broke it off in 1999, Patton retaliated by having nursing home inspectors cite her nursing home numerous occasions on safety and health charges. That led to her filing bankruptcy on the business. She said that Patton had ruined her livelihood and that she was not going to go down alone.

Conner outlined two significant ways Governor Patton had helped her during their affair. First, she had been having problems with getting Medicaid reimbursement for some of her nursing home residents. She said that in her presence, Patton called his chief of staff and told him to help her get the money. Within a couple of weeks, she had a large check. Secondly, and this is the most serious allegation, she said that her husband had a small construction company that didn't have much business. She decided to apply for a disadvantaged business enterprise (DBE) designation with the state. This program required state contracting construction companies to subcontract with a certain minimum percentage of minority and women owned and operated companies.

The problem that Tina's husband had was that, as a Caucasian man, he did not qualify for the DBE program. So, Tina produced a plan to circumvent the law. She would pretend to be the owner and operator of her husband's business. The paperwork would all be in her name. Then she would use her political influence with the governor to get the Transportation Cabinet, which administers the DBE program, to certify the business as DBE. Predictably, a cursory vetting of the company by the cabinet reflected that Tina had no construction experience and that she was clearly not the operator of the company. The application was denied. But Conner alleged that she called Patton, and he later told her that he told the cabinet secretary, "If Tina says she is the operator, then she is the operator. Get her certified." And that is what happened.

Conner provided significant details of the affair. She said it started in 1997 when she attended a political reception and fundraiser in Louisville and was introduced to Patton. As he spoke with her, Patton casually rubbed his arm on her breasts. Within a day of the encounter, Patton called her and asked that they get together. On nine or ten occasions over the next two years they hooked up at a hotel off Hurstborne Lane in Louisville and had sex while Patton's security detail, a state trooper, sat outside in a cruiser. The liaisons always began at 7 am and lasted four or five hours. Conner provided a TV station with phone records showing numerous calls between her and the governor, and presciently, she had saved hotel receipts.

Patton initially vehemently denied both the affair and any impropriety regarding business favors for Conner. He admitted he knew Conner and her husband, which of course he had to because he had appointed Tina to the state lottery board in 2000. But the governor claimed that their relationship was strictly professional. He attributed her allegations to financial desperation arising from her failing nursing home.

Within a couple of days of the press conference, Conner filed a sexual harassment lawsuit against Patton. This changed the landscape around the allegations drastically. Patton knew that the civil discovery process involved in a case like this would inevitably provide ironclad proof that Conner was telling the truth and that he was lying. For example, Patton's daily calendar would show that he was out of the office with his trooper by his side on the same days reflected on the hotel receipts. His state trooper would be deposed and, most likely, would decide that committing perjury for the governor was a step too far. Waiting outside while the governor had his tryst was just following orders. He could honestly say he didn't know who or why the governor was meeting someone there. But denying the hotel visits would end his career and perhaps land him in jail. It's a safe bet the trooper told the governor that he would not lie for him. Thus, Patton had no choice but to admit the affair. This he did in a blubbering, slobbering, Jimmy Swaggart-like, televised press conference a few days after the suit was filed.

SO, YOU ASK, what did all this have to do with the US Attorney's Office generally, and me particularly? The answer is that we always took special interest in allegations of wrongdoing by Kentucky Governors. So, what federal laws were being violated? A couple were on the table.

First, federal law makes it unlawful for an officer or agent of a state which receives more than $10,000 of federal funds in a year, to take something of value in exchange for official action worth more than $5,000. Thus, Patton being an agent of Kentucky state government, that government receiving millions of dollars of federal funding each year, and the favors alleged to have been conferred on her by the Gov being far in excess of $5,000, satisfied most of the elements of the offense. The only one left was that sex with Tina Conner must be *something of value*. As you can imagine, that led to jokes about how we were going to assess the value of this service. But legal research convinced me that we could meet that element, as the law indicates that anything can have a value if the receiver values it. There does not have to be a commercial market for the service.

But the real obstacle to proving this crime was establishing that when Patton received the sexual favors, he *intended* to be influenced in his official actions. It is just as plausible that he received the sexual favors thinking he was just getting lucky, and only later decided to help Tina with her business problems. This was all a very gray legal area, unless you had evidence, such as tape recordings, wherein the linkage between the sex and the favors was discussed.

The other federal statute in play was mail or wire fraud. If Tina Conner had received a DBE designation under false pretenses, that would constitute fraud on the government. And, if she used the mails or interstate wire communications in furtherance of that—and almost assuredly she did—it would constitute federal mail or wire fraud. And if Governor Patton was involved or if he knowingly facilitated the scheme—as Tina had alleged—he would be both an aider and abettor and a coconspirator. So, that is where we derived an interest in the case.

Now, why did I get the case? First, I was then establishing a niche in the office for public corruption cases, and this seemed to be up my alley. But the primary reason was my working relationship with the FBI agent assigned to the case, Joe Moutz. We worked together on several large cases in those days, and, as is customary, agents ask to work with someone they know, trust and like when they bring the case to our office. I gladly agreed to work with Joe. It just looked damn interesting.

Joe and I tried mightily to see if there was criminal liability on the part of the governor and his staff. We obtained business and state records pertaining to the DBE situation. We wanted to interview state officials who made the DBE decisions. We wanted to interview Patton. Unfortunately, Patton, through counsel, would only agree to answer written questions. The transportation secretary sent us word, though, that if called to the grand jury, he would take the fifth and not answer questions, so as departmental policy requires, we couldn't call him. So, when the investigation concluded, we could not make fire out of the smoke. We would not indict Patton.

All we had as evidence was Tina Conner saying essentially, "I committed fraud and Patton and the transportation secretary helped me." But we could not establish beyond a reasonable doubt that either man knew, at the time of their actions, that they were knowingly aiding and abetting a fraud scheme.

When the dust settled on the investigation, we were left with one stark realization. Tina Conner had repeatedly admitted the crime of mail fraud. In addition to the September 2002 press conference, she accepted almost every invitation to discuss her case. She even appeared on Dr. Phil's national program to discuss problems she was having within the family because of the public affair. She was on another national morning news program. In each case she said she obtained a DBE certification through fraud. Should we ignore that, give her a break because of the appearance of unfairness? It was a difficult decision and close call, but in the end, we decided to proceed.

We indicted Tina in the fall of 2003. She was shocked, having labored under the misimpression that because she had voluntarily revealed her crime—one that also implicated the governor—she would get a pass from the justice system. She changed attorneys, hiring prominent Louisville attorney Tom Clay.

Clay immediately made some public criticisms of Conner's former attorney, saying that he should never have let Conner go public with an admission of a crime. He should have kept her off TV and radio. He said the attorney did all this in the most public way to draw attention to himself, to the detriment of his client.

I always had a good working relationship with Tom Clay, and I did feel sorry for Conner's predicament. I believed her allegations. So, we offered Tina the opportunity to reveal other misconduct she may have uncovered in her various ventures and connections in state government, to obtain leniency in sentencing. Tina's proffer was unfruitful in that it provided no further leads to investigate. She told us of what she considered misconduct involving other people, but the conduct was not criminal. Nonetheless, attorney Clay made a strong argument for leniency for Connor. He pointed out that but for the horrible advice of her prior attorney, Tina would never have been indicted. So, we worked a deal where Tina would plead to a single count of mail fraud, and we would recommend to Judge Joe Hood that she be probated. And that is what happened. Conner was a convicted felon, but she never served a day in prison.

In a sentencing memo in Tina Conner's case, I criticized Governor Patton and the transportation secretary for stonewalling the investigation. I wrote that we could not satisfactorily get to the truth because of the lack of cooperation of these officials. I said Tina Conner was the only person being held responsible for the crime she uncovered and revealed, despite ostensibly having had the help of others. I wanted the court to know why we were recommending a probated sentence.

I also wanted to quash a false inference that some people were drawing from the fact that only Connor was being prosecuted. That inference was the Patton and others had exerted political influence to kill the investigation of them and simultaneously punish the citizen—albeit a criminally responsible one—who voluntarily spilled the beans. It looked like we were colluding with the public officials against the whistleblower.

AS PREDICTED, THE press reported on my comments about Patton and the transportation secretary. They sought out defense attorneys for comment on my comments. Some prominent members of the defense bar believed it was unfair for me to castigate someone not charged during the sentencing proceeding of another person. The transportation secretary's attorney said his client had the same right to exercise the Fifth Amendment as any citizen. Patton's attorney claimed he had cooperated fully, which was bullshit. Another attorney said my comments were unusual and disturbing.

Here's what I say about that. Admittedly, it would be improper for me to reveal the identities of people whose names had come up in the investigation but were not indicted because of insufficiency of the evidence, where the existence of their involvement was not already in the public domain. But here, Conner's allegations against Patton and the transportation secretary were widely reported from the beginning of the case. Secondly, as stated above, we needed to manage public perception of the fairness and thoroughness of the investigation and charging decisions. We needed to dispel what would be a false conclusion that Patton was exonerated of any wrongdoing, or that our office had been complicit in protecting the governor.

In response to the statement that these officials have the same constitutional rights as any citizen, let me say this. While it is a true statement, and while the legal advice to take the Fifth Amendment or answer only written questions may be professionally correct and superb advice, it does not mean that there should be no negative repercussions for public officials who take that route. In a jury trial, no mention can be made by anyone that the defendant, at some time, took the Fifth Amendment. Jurors are instructed not to consider the defendant's failure to testify. But the citizens who vote public officials into office are not bound by those instructions. They are free to draw an adverse inference against the public official who refuses to cooperate in an investigation.

Ross Harris

Vote Hauling

Jerry Garner was an FBI special agent in the Pikeville, Kentucky field office in the early to mid-2000s. He and I worked together on several cases during that time and became friends. One day, Jerry called to tell me that he had a lead on a new case and wanted me to review evidence and get my thoughts. I happily agreed, and on his next trip to Lexington, Jerry dropped off recordings of several phone calls.

Jerry explained that he had developed an informant who had made him aware of secret phone recordings of her talking to her ex-husband, Tom Varney. Tom was trying desperately to rekindle their romance and frequently called his estranged wife. But she wanted no more of the relationship, and, in fact, was angling to have him arrested. Varney often spoke of his access to drugs that he could get for her, so she decided to start taping their conversations to generate evidence she could turn over to law enforcement.

After listening to the various conversations, I reported to Jerry that the drug talk was interesting, but not nearly as significant to me as a discussion of what was obviously a vote-buying conspiracy. Thus began my first foray into the Eastern Kentucky world of vote buying. Over the next fifteen or so years I would become a specialist in those kinds of cases.

At the time, a political campaign was underway in Pike County, and one of the offices on the ballot was for district court judge. The two candidates vying for that office were the incumbent, Darrell Mullins, and the then-county attorney, John Doug Hays. Varney kept mentioning his involvement in that campaign to his wife. He said that wealthy local coal magnate and political influencer, Ross Harris, had developed a grudge against Judge Mullins. Harris had decided to use his vast financial resources to back the challenger Hays. Varney said they were spreading around money in the form of *vote-hauling* payments. He wanted to give one to the wife. He said vote hauling was just a figure of speech, that it's really vote buying. He explained that Harris had funneled money to spend on vote-hauling checks by using straw contributors. Kentucky has a $1,000 limit per donor per election on campaign contributions, but wealthy donors sometimes circumvent this law by funneling a single large contribution through individual donors.

Jerry and I did a quick review of campaign contribution records at the Kentucky Registry of Election Finance (KREF) and discovered that precisely at the time that Ross Harris came out in support of Hays, the Hays campaign reported $1,000 contributions from the friends, employees, and employees family members. This tended to corroborate what we heard on the tapes.

At the time, the district election officer in our office was Tom Self, who had handled vote fraud cases for many years. I went to Tom with what I heard on the recordings and what I was seeing in the KREF records. To my surprise, he was not overly alarmed. He said the vote hauling was a common practice in Eastern Kentucky and that there was an existing vote-hauling statute specifically authorizing it. The statute puts no limit on the number of vote haulers.

To me, however, this was a clear abuse of the vote-hauling statute. That statute was designed to authorize true transportation services—a form of a get out the vote effort. But this was a ruse, a disguised form of vote buying. Tom Varney admitted as much on tape. Whether something is legal or illegal is not governed by nomenclature. If what is really happening on the ground is vote buying, then it does not matter that you call it vote hauling. I decided to determine what these people did in exchange for their fifty-dollar check from the Hays campaign

Fortunately, state law required that the name and other identifiers of any person paid to haul voters had to be reported in the campaign's reports to KREF. Thus, we had access to a list of potential witnesses. We assembled a team of interviewers from many FBI offices and some Kentucky state troopers and planned a day or two of simultaneous interviews. Agents and troopers fanned out over the back side of Pike County, where most of these individuals were concentrated, and conducted dozens of interviews.

Each vote hauler was asked what the check he received was for. Most of them said for vote hauling. When asked who and how many people they hauled to the polls, not one of them had acted as a true provider of transportation services. Some said they hauled themselves. Some said they hauled their wife. "But weren't you going to transport her anyway, even if you never got a check?" We asked. "Well, yeah," one fellow said. "I looked around for someone to haul but everyone had a check." A few reluctantly admitted this was money to influence their vote.

We also interviewed Tom Varney and used the taped recordings of his criminal admissions to convince him to cooperate. From him and others he referred us to, we learned the logistics of this vote-hauling plan. Soon after Ross Harris funneled over $35,000 into the campaign, a planning meeting was set up in Harris's business office.

The group called themselves the committee to elect John Doug Hays. One of those present at the meeting asked, "Are we going to do vote hauling?" John Doug's wife, Brenda, who was serving as the treasurer to the campaign, then wrote out and signed 687 fifty-dollar checks, except that she did not put a name on the payee line. The checks were then divided up between several individuals, including Tom Varney, to take and distribute to voters. These check distributors were under orders to fill in the check once the voter agreed to take it and obtain the other information required for campaign reports. There was no discussion whatsoever as to the logistics of transportation services, such as how someone wanting a ride was supposed to contact the hauler. In short, our belief that this whole process was a form of vote buying was confirmed.

IN EARLY 2003, Ross Harris, John Doug Hays, Brenda Hays, Glenn Turner, and a handful of campaign workers who handed out the vote-hauling checks were indicted for conspiracy and vote buying. Harris, Turner, and Hays were also indicted for mail fraud based upon the mailing of a false campaign expenditure report, arising from a straw contribution scheme. Ross Harris had funneled tens of thousands of dollars into Hays's campaign by using the names of friends and relatives of Glenn Turner. This money was reported to KREF as individual $1,000 donations when, in fact, it was all one large illegal contribution from Ross Harris.

The motion practice in this case was extensive, contentious, and controversial. I moved the court to conduct an inquiry into whether some of the defense counsel had a conflict of interest. It was apparent to me that Ross Harris had hired attorneys to represent most of the defendants. The fear was that this was a method by which Harris could control the behavior of all defendants and prevent them from cooperating with the prosecution. This motion was met with strong disapproval from the defense attorneys in the case and the defense bar generally. They argued that it was an intrusion into the attorney-client relationship. They said that a lawyer is presumed to have the backbone to resist pressure from third parties that might influence their representation of their client.

I encountered this issue several times during my career. Here's how it typically played out. When multiple people were indicted for conspiracy or other jointly committed crime, the kingpin would hire lawyers for everyone involved. All the defense attorneys would enter into a *joint defense agreement,* meaning they worked together as a team. As a result, no one was willing to speak with the prosecution about cutting a deal—like offering testimony against the kingpin in exchange for a lighter sentence. This is an obvious conflict of interest in that the attorney has split loyalties—one to the person paying his fee and the other to his client.

For some unknown reason, the courts don't treat this conflict like other conflicts. Conflicts of interest, or the appearance of a conflict, for lawyers arise in many contexts. For example, a lawyer representing two clients in the same case has a potential conflict. A lawyer who will have to cross-examine a former client who is testifying against his current client has a potential conflict. A lawyer who is the spouse of the prosecutor has a potential conflict, as does the lawyer who has a business arrangement with an attorney on the other side of the case. In each of these cases, the law does not presume that the lawyer can set that aside. Hearings by the court or queries to the affected clients are typically conducted to determine whether there is an actual conflict and whether, if so, it can be waived. And that is what I sought here.

The court should inquire about the fee and see if the client truly wants to be represented by this attorney he didn't choose. Are they comfortable with the possibility of divided loyalty? The defense attorney may even subconsciously stay loyal to the kingpin (Harris here) to keep the money coming. Predictably, the court went with the conventional wisdom (or lack thereof) behind this presumption of independence and summarily denied my motion.

I filed a motion for a change of venue from the Pikeville docket to London or Lexington. I did so based on our observations that the defendants and witnesses were well known in Pike County. Many people had strong opinions about them—some favorable and some unfavorable. The court granted the motion and moved the trial to London.

After Harris hired new counsel, the defense filed a motion to reconsider and move the case back to Pikeville. The original attorney had not strongly opposed the venue change. But new counsel filed a lengthy memorandum reflecting surveys and containing other evidence and arguments. They wanted the case back in Pikeville.

The memorandum I filed in response to theirs is by far the most notorious pleading I ever filed, before or since. A quote from there made the national news and created a public relations nightmare for me. I made the argument that it would be impossible to seat a disinterested and competent jury considering the extensive local press coverage of the proceedings. I said, after we strike for cause all the potential jurors who have knowledge of and opinions about the case, "all that would be left to try the case would be illiterate cave dwellers." That was a metaphor for the type of person who does not read or listen to the news, is politically apathetic, and totally insulated from mainstream society. There aren't many such people, and they would not make good jurors. In Eastern Kentucky, the term *illiterate cave dweller* struck a sensitive nerve. Many people there resent the stereotype of the barefoot, uneducated hillbilly, and my reference seemed to be a play on that image. The cave dweller reference was mistaken to be a reference to underground coal mining. In short, many thought I was saying that once we got rid of the few good people, we would be left with the typical Eastern Kentuckian.

The press picked up the statement and obtained quotes of disapproval from many prominent citizens of the area. Letters to the editor condemned me. While I was on a golf trip with some buddies the day the story broke, I was mentioned on the radio as the chosen "idiot of the day." Relatives and friends of mine all over the country heard about it and thought I was in big trouble. Congressman Hal Rogers called my boss, Greg Van Tatenhove, and said I should be fired. Greg defended my use of the metaphor but did implore me to write a letter of apology to the *Appalachian News Express,* the Pikeville paper. I wrote the letter, but many say it wasn't a real apology. In fact, it has been included in anthologies of non-apology apologies.

My tap dance apology was intentional. I explained my intention to make the simple point that someone would have to have been living under a rock not to have an opinion on the case. What I was sorry about was my failure to see in advance just how people of that area might misinterpret the reference to be a regional slur. In due time, the storm blew over, I survived, and the case proceeded toward trial.

Fellow prosecutor Pat Molloy volunteered to join me on the case. He was a welcome addition to the team, as Molloy was a very experienced prosecutor in several different federal districts over the years. He also had a playful and fun-loving demeanor that helped with the stress of trial. We had a great time together during the preparation and trial, and we still tell funny war stories about it when we're together, like the time I had to borrow pants from Pat to get another hotel room key after I locked myself out without any pants on.

EARLY IN THE pretrial motion phase of this prosecution I made a motion to sever some of the defendants from others, and the motion was granted. Ross Harris and Glenn Turner would be tried separately from Hays and the money handlers. Things were going smoothly toward trial, but trouble was just around the corner. The case took on a different vibe when Ross Harris replaced his attorneys, Scott Cox and Mike Mazzoli out of Louisville, with a group from Barnes and Thornburg in Indianapolis, headed up by Larry Mackey. Mackey was a former assistant US attorney who led the prosecution of Oklahoma City bomber, Timothy McVeigh. At first, there was some collegiality and cordiality in our encounters, but that didn't last long.

Scorched earth is the only way to describe Mackey's defense style. I had to admire Mackey's thoroughness and work ethic, but I came to resent his accusatory approach. He was always accusing the prosecution of improper conduct, taking things out of context, or making up legal duties of a prosecutor, then arguing that we had violated them.

As an example, his team scoured the public records and court cases for any historical reference to any kind of questionable conduct by a prosecutor from our office. He pieced together unrelated bits of information, collected over many years and across different administrations, to support a motion to dismiss the indictment. He argued that there was a long-standing pattern of misconduct and unprofessionalism in the Eastern District of Kentucky, serious enough, in his view, to justify throwing out the case. The motion was pure horse shit—both procedurally and substantively. Of course, it got no traction with the court.

Harris's trial began in the fall of 2004 and lasted four weeks. We called dozens of poor people from Paw Paw and other small towns in Eastern Pike County to discuss their vote-hauling checks. Every morning a van met witnesses before dawn at a school in Phelps, Kentucky, to transport that day's witnesses to London. They were transported home together at the end of the day. None accepted our offer to be put up in a hotel in London. These were clannish homebodies. A few told us they had never been outside of Pike County or the westernmost portion of Virginia, just across the state line.

THE JURY GOT the case late in the afternoon, deliberated for two hours, and asked the court permission to go home and resume the next morning. Molloy and I still laugh about how that next morning one of the male jurors wore a shirt that looked like an American flag. That was a good sign that he was there to do his duty to God and country. The jury convicted the defendants on all charges.

The Hays trial followed within weeks. It was almost a carbon copy proof-wise. Tom Varney pleaded guilty to vote buying before trial and testified against Hays. We dismissed some charges against the check distributors just to simplify the proof and because they weren't seen as involved in the decision-making as we once believed. The Hays's jury deliberated for a whopping three to four days. They rejected the vote-buying allegations but convicted Hays of the mail fraud charge. However, on appeal, the court held that our theory of mail fraud—the *intangible right to honest services* theory—was improperly applied to an election finance situation, so Hays's conviction was overturned.

An outgrowth of the case bears mentioning. At both trials, we had called the straw contributors—friends and family of Glenn Turner—to grill them about their contributions to the Hays campaign. We knew they were going to deny that the money they gave was from Ross Harris, but their explanations of the source was so laughable we believed the jury would conclude they were lying. We had introduced bank records to show that these donors to the campaign deposited cash into their bank accounts either right before or right after writing a check to the campaign. When asked where the cash came from, all of them told of their secret cash stash—a Pringles can, a sock, a drawer.

After the trial, and with the confidence provided by the guilty verdicts, I drafted a letter to each of these witnesses. In so many words, it said, "You have a choice. I intend to indict you for perjury at the trial, or if you prefer, you can submit an affidavit admitting your perjury, and I would forgo prosecution." My goal was to put to rest Harris's and Turner's claim of innocence. That would have beneficial consequences in sentencing and in another related investigation involving a straw contribution scheme in another election, executed by many of the same straw contributors.

The effort proved successful. The contributors signed the affidavits, and I put them in the grand jury. We indicted Glenn Turner for perjury he committed during the investigation more than a year prior. He had testified at the grand jury, denying the existence of a straw contribution scheme, for which I now had unassailable proof. He entered a guilty plea in early 2005 and was sentenced to another term of imprisonment.

Fittingly, this vote buying scheme was unsuccessful. Judge Mullins defeated John Doug Hays to remain circuit judge.

A gratifying result of this case was that a short time after the trials, a state grand jury in Pike County issued an opinion and recommendation that the practice of vote hauling should be limited to one person per precinct and that each hauler should keep records of the miles driven and each person transported should be listed and an explanation provided as to why they needed a ride to the polls. I do not believe that the Kentucky General Assembly ever adopted that recommendation, but that report validated our belief that the citizenry was appreciative of our efforts. I am confident that, thereafter, the flagrant abuse of the vote-hauling statute was curtailed, because candidates knew we would be watching to see if the charade continued.

Bath County/Champ Maze

Voter Assistance Scam

In May of 2006 I received a call from Beth Maze, a circuit court judge in Owingsville, Kentucky. She had been referred to me because of my history of prosecuting vote fraud cases in Eastern Kentucky. As we spoke, she informed me that open vote buying was occurring in Bath County's primary election. Beth was concerned about this because her husband, Champ Maze, was on the ballot as a candidate for county attorney, and she believed that his opponent was involved in the vote buying. Well, we did take action, but what Beth Maze didn't know at the time was that her husband, Champ, was smack dab in the middle of a vote-buying scheme. Eventually, he would serve prison time for that and other crimes. It was a classic case of be careful what you ask for.

I had to explain to Beth that the federal government had a policy of not getting involved in overt voter fraud investigations while an election or campaign was underway. We could conduct covert investigations and observations but would not overtly investigate until the election was over. This policy of noninterference was designed to prevent us from being played or used by candidates to create a false narrative of fraud by a candidate's opponent. However, I had assured her we would look into the matter. I reached out to the FBI, and Special Agent Darrin Turpin was assigned to the case.

Thus began a series of investigations and prosecutions that would lead to the indictment and convictions of around fifteen individuals. It was a case with lots of surprises, twists, and turns.

DARRIN CONDUCTED A round of interviews to determine what the alleged vote buying looked like and what investigative methods could be used. What we learned was that a clear abuse of the voter assistance law was central to the scheme. One of the chief concerns of any vote-buying operation is the double-crossing vote seller who takes the money but doesn't vote as intended. Thus, different schemes have historically used different methods to verify compliance. Sometimes crooked precinct workers watch the seller vote and provide him with a ticket or other proof of compliance to take back to the buyer for payment. The voter assistance law provided an opportunity for these Bath County vote buyers to get what they paid for. They would send a co-conspirator into the voting booth with the vote seller under the guise of assisting them in casting their ballot. There was a major drawback for the buyers with this procedure; it created a paper trail for investigators to follow to identify the vote sellers.

OVER THE COURSE of my vote fraud prosecution experience, I followed the same general pattern of investigation. This technique was developed in response to my knowledge of what I called the anatomy of a vote-buying conspiracy. There are three layers or tiers of people with different roles, though often a person could be involved at more than one of these levels. At the top were the political movers and shakers and financiers. I dubbed them the *Boss Hogs*. Then there were the middlemen and handlers who paid the sellers, drove them to the polls, or provided other logistical support. These were the political wannabes looking to ingratiate themselves with the big guys. Then there were the actual vote sellers.

We always began our investigation with identifying likely vote sellers who we could interview. We learned that if you told a vote seller that he wouldn't be prosecuted if he admitted his crime, he would be surprisingly candid. These individuals are typically poor, addicted, and politically apathetic. They don't see anything immoral in their conduct and have no problem admitting it. Our goal was not to punish these folks, but to use them to go up the ladder to the middleman/handler and then to the Boss Hog who was financing the vote-buying conspiracy. The vote sellers would tell us who gave them the money and told them where to go. We would then go to these middlemen and hopefully flip them against the individuals at the top.

Identifying likely vote sellers typically involved interviewing poll workers, local law enforcement, and eyewitnesses to suspicious behavior. But in Bath County's case, we had a set of documents that identified them for us. That's because we were looking for persons who signed affidavits that they needed assistance in the voting booth to cast their vote.

Kentucky law governing voter assistance sets out a list of infirmities that justify allowing another person to provide assistance—an inability to read and write, blindness, and physical inability to complete the voting process, such as having no hands to flip a lever or hold a pencil. Voters are allowed to choose any person they desire to be their assister, but that assister must submit an affidavit that he will vote only as the voter instructs. Poll workers told us that there were a lot of red flags in the voter assistance process that year that they had never seen before. First, the number of people who requested assistance was over 550 voters, more than double the usual amount. Secondly, a handful of chosen assisters assisted numerous individuals, whereas typically a family member assisted one or two relatives.

One assister, Tammy Manley, hung out at the courthouse all day and was chosen by dozens of people to assist them. A review of the voter affidavits revealed a hairdresser, and a hazardous material truck driver swore they were blind. Poll workers pointed to several more individuals who swore they couldn't read the ballot when it was well known in town they could read well or had jobs that required literacy. In short, none of this passed the laugh test. We knew there was vote buying here; we just had to prove it.

DARRIN AND I developed a list of those voters who were assisted by Tammy Manley and several other individuals whom we suspected of being involved because of the number of nonrelatives they assisted. We assembled a team of agents and officers from the Kentucky State Police (KSP) and the FBI. One morning, this task force gathered at the KSP post in Morehead for a briefing. An FBI agent was paired with a KSP trooper as interview teams. We wanted a federal agent on each team so that the voters would be subject to the lying to the FBI statute if they didn't tell the truth. We gave the teams instructions to verbally immunize the witnesses in exchange for truthful information. The names and addresses of the voters were divided among the teams, and off they went for interviews.

Over the next two days, hundreds of interviews were conducted, and written summaries were generated and provided to us. From those, we built a list of the middlemen and assisters and got a clear picture of the mechanics of the conspiracy. The suspected illegal assisters had indeed gone into the voting booth and had voted a slate of candidates without any input from the voters[1]. The assister would then call a money person to confirm that the voting had occurred, and the seller would meet the money person at a designated location for payment.

We learned that there were vote buyers on both sides of most races on the ballot. Often, the middlemen competed for vote sellers, essentially bidding against each other. The standard fee for a vote was $50 but sometimes a voter could haggle for $60 or more. The voter

1 *A slate is a list of several candidates who are voted by the one assistor.*

would be instructed to go to the poll and hook up with a designated assister who would help them through the process.

Using our list of assisters and middlemen, we then set up interviews. Tammy Manley provided a lot of crucial information. Stunningly, she said Champ Maze, whose wife called to complain about the vote buying, had paid Manley and another woman to add his name to the slate of candidates they were voting for in the booth. It seems that Maze believed that he was going to lose the election if he didn't get involved. That's just how pernicious the culture of vote buying had become in Bath County.

We placed a number of these vote sellers in the grand jury. In July of 2006, we brought ten indictments against the assisters and money handlers. Most of them plead guilty once they saw the strength of the evidence against them. But the investigation was not over. We were going to try to obtain testimony and other evidence against the power brokers behind the scheme, such as business executive Sonny Swartz, county judge executive Walter Shrout, and Champ Maze. (Maze won his election by sixteen votes, which means that his vote buying paid off for him.) Essentially, our entire case against Champ Maze during this initial phase of the investigation was the testimony of Tammy Manley. We believed what she was telling us about Maze's involvement but did not trust that a jury would believe her over Maze in a trial. We allowed Manley to prove her story by getting Maze to admit his guilt in a recording. Maze had been reaching out to Manley for some time, but Manley had not spoken with him. She believed he wanted to influence her to not provide information against him. We had her call Maze and told him she would be by his office to speak with him.

Darrin wired Tammy with recording equipment and off she went to the meeting with Champ. She was instructed to tell Champ that she was being pressured by the FBI to tell everything and needed his advice. Ironically, she was to say that the FBI even wanted to wire her up and have a conversation with Champ. She would say she wanted to obtain leniency by wearing the wire, but she didn't want to make a case against Champ.

Maze told her things like, " . . . if you say you didn't get any money from me, no one can prove otherwise." He told her that they could arrange a silent signaling code that would allow her to alert him whenever she was wearing a wire around him. In essence, Maze was attempting to corruptly influence her—a clear violation of the obstruction of justice statute. Manley's testimony was thus corroborated.

WE INDICTED MAZE for vote buying and obstruction of justice in the fall of 2006. There was no discussion of a plea deal, and the case went to trial in February 2007 in Lexington. Maze had a very capable representation by Ned Pillersdorf and John Roach. His defense was that Manley was lying about Maze giving her the money for vote fraud. He had given her money only to help her out, something they said was common for Maze. As for the recordings, he was simply providing legal advice in the role of her lawyer. He was not obstructing justice.

On about the second or third morning of trial, we awoke to a blanket of snow over Central Kentucky. A clerk's recording that jurors and parties could call informed us that the trial was in recess for the day. We later learned that Champ and some friends used the time off to attempt to tamper with the jury.

Prior to jury selection, the parties in the case are provided with juror information sheets. There is revealed basic biographical information about the juror, such as occupation, age, marital status, place of birth, number of children, and so on. The parties use this to help in determining who should serve on a jury—or, more appropriately, who should not. In court, the jurors are only identified by an assigned number, but on these information sheets, we had their names.

When I arrived at the courthouse the morning following our

snow day, one of the other people we had indicted in the Bath County investigation, Sonny Swartz, was already there. He presented me with the juror information sheet on one of our jurors, and he told me a story about its significance. I don't recall the details, but it generally involved attempts by one of Maze's friends, Chuck Hart, to contact one of the jurors. The juror's fact sheet was left by Hart at the juror's place of work, and someone there had given the sheet to Swartz. Swartz correctly surmised that he needed to report the incident lest he be caught up in suspected jury tampering.

Before we called in the jury, I reported the incident to Judge Hood. He exploded. I had seen him mad before, but never to this extreme. He ordered the FBI to begin an immediate investigation and queried defense counsel as to how that jury sheet had gotten out on the street. John Roach confessed that he had given a copy of the forms to his client so that he could help in jury selection. Hood gave him one heck of an ass-chewing. He made it clear there were going to be repercussions for Roach. (Ultimately, Hood cooled off, and I don't believe Roach received any further repercussions.)

We went into recess for a while for the FBI to make phone calls and interview Swartz. The trial resumed while, simultaneously, FBI agents were out beating the bushes to flush out the facts of the snow day jury tampering. They learned that another friend of Maze was observing the trial on the day the jury was being selected. At the end of that day's proceedings, he overheard a conversation wherein Maze, Chuck Hart, and another person discussed trying to contact and influence jurors. The man warned them about such conduct and left. The man told the FBI that he was present in court the day when the jury tampering came to light. Champ asked this man to call his office and relay the instruction to his secretaries to get rid of the jury fact sheets.

The FBI learned that on that snow day, Maze, Hart, and Paul Goodpastor, the county PVA, met in the PVA office to determine the identities of the jurors and how to reach out to them. Goodpastor had been interviewed by the FBI and died of a heart attack later that day. Champ's secretaries confirmed that they had destroyed the jury forms when the tampering allegations arose. After two days of investigation, we obtained a criminal complaint against Maze. He was arrested at the courthouse and spent the weekend in jail.

On the ensuing Monday, we met with Pillersdorf, Maze, his wife Beth, and several others in an office in the courthouse before trial. There we hammered out the details of a plea agreement. Maze would plead to several vote-buying charges and obstruction of justice, and we would drop this new charge of jury tampering.

ONE OTHER ASPECT of the case bears mentioning. We had spent some time during recesses, over lunch, and in the evenings preparing to meet and refute Maze's defense to the obstruction of justice charges that resulted from his in-office discussions with Tammy Manley. In the opening statement Roach had laid out for the jury that Maze was simply acting like any ethical lawyer in his advice to Manley regarding how to defend the charges against her. He seemed to imply that it was the defense attorney's job to help the defendant come up with a good story. We couldn't let that impression hang in the air. Some misguided jurors might believe that to be the law. We wanted an expert in legal ethics to get on the stand and emphatically testify that what was reflected on the recordings was not ethical conduct, nor typical or reasonable attorney behavior.

Professor Bill Fortune, an expert on legal ethics, especially criminal defense ethics, was just up Limestone Street at the University of Kentucky's law school. We provided him with the transcripts of the recordings and gave him the backstory. He was appalled at Champ's conduct and agreed that we needed to refute that this was just normal lawyer advice. He even said we didn't need to pay him an expert witness fee. He considered this a public service to his profession. I would have loved hearing that testimony in court. But when Fortune appeared as scheduled, we had just taken a guilty plea from Maze and the trial was over.

We had two other trials that arose from the Bath County investigation. In March, Walter Shrout was convicted by jury of vote buying. Chuck Hart was later tried and convicted of jury tampering related to the snow day shenanigans. Interestingly, just before testimony was to begin in his trial, Hart attempted to contact a juror on his own case. Judge Hood allowed us to put that into evidence as relating to a *consciousness of guilt.* I recall the look of outright incredulity and outrage on the face of one female juror when that evidence was introduced. Hart was easily convicted.

Thus, I spent over a year and a half wherein most of my time was on Bath County matters. It was rewarding, but I was glad when it was over.

Everett Daniel Beverly

An Innocent Man

In the case of Everett Daniel Beverly, I convicted a factually innocent man. To this day I cannot fathom how a person could be so unlucky regarding the alignment of evidence against him but still be innocent. The circumstantial evidence of guilt was strong.

On Saturday, March 30, 1996, a state probation and parole officer in Hazard, Kentucky, opened her morning *Lexington Herald Leader* newspaper while enjoying her morning coffee and read about a bank robbery that had occurred on Friday afternoon in Lexington. The article included a bank surveillance photo of the robber. The parole officer was startled. The photo seemed to her to depict a felon under her supervision, Everett Daniel Beverly. She immediately recalled an incident from the day before that reinforced her opinion.

Around four or five o'clock that Friday afternoon, Beverly, who was on parole for theft-related offenses, showed up at her office, unannounced and unscheduled. He flatly stated that he wanted to have his parole revoked and return to prison to serve out his sentence. (This is not an uncommon sentiment among parolees who vehemently resent the oversight and scrutiny that comes with parole.) He said, "I'm sick of this parole, reporting, and everything. I just want to serve out." The parole officer said she could not seek to terminate his parole without a proven violation. She thought that, at the time, the encounter was odd.

Looking at the photograph of the bank robber in the Lexington newspaper, the parole officer immediately thought, *That's Everett Beverly.* The timeline made sense. The bank robbery occurred about noon in Lexington, which would be consistent with Beverly having time to travel the two to three hours from Lexington to Hazard after the robbery. She also believed that a necklace seen on the robber in the photo was the same as the necklace Beverly wore the day before when he came to the office. It made sense to her that the bank robbery incident could have prompted Beverly to decide that he wanted to get off parole and serve out. This opinion was reinforced when she read that the robbery failed because of an exploding dye pack.

As it turned out, the teller who was confronted by the robber had the forethought to place a dye pack in the money bag. This device is designed to explode a few minutes after a robbery, spewing colorful ink all over the money and the robber—essentially rendering the money unspendable and the robber easily identified. The money bag began to smoke as the robber ran away, and he threw it in some shrubs; all the money was recovered.

Beverly's parole officer believed that the failure of the robbery attempt prompted Beverly's visit to the office, seeking termination of parole. She immediately began her own investigation, prior to notifying Lexington police of her suspicions. First, she called Beverly and asked him to come into the office for an interview. Beverly denied that he had robbed the bank and insisted that he had not been in Lexington on the day of the robbery. This was important because Beverly had a parole condition that required him to obtain the approval of probation and parole if he traveled outside of Perry County.

The parole officer decided to challenge Beverly's story. She called his girlfriend, who obviously was not aware of Beverly's parole conditions. She informed the parole officer that, yes, she, some friends, and Beverly had traveled to Lexington the previous weekend for a getaway mini vacation, where they stayed with some mutual friends who lived there.

At this point, realizing that Beverly had lied to her about being in Lexington, the parole officer called Lexington police. The ensuing investigation was revealing. Interviews of those individuals who accompanied Beverly to Lexington revealed that they had traveled there on Thursday night and bedded down at the home of a friend from Hazard. They all agreed that Beverly was present with them for the entire visit except for a period on Friday between about 11 a.m. and 1 p.m.—when the robbery occurred. Beverly had borrowed a car to go buy cigarettes. At least one of these Beverly friends identified the T-shirt being worn by the robber as being one she had seen Beverly wearing in the past.

Another aspect of the bank photo added to the circumstantial evidence against Beverly. It appeared that the robber was missing a portion of his ring finger on the right hand. Beverly was, in fact, missing a portion of that same finger. What are the chances that another person, not Beverly, had that same deformity?

MY COLLEAGUE BOB Rawlins joined me on the case. In meeting with the assigned FBI agent, Jim Riley, we all agreed that we needed to supplement the evidence. We wanted more than the grainy surveillance photo and the opinions of those who viewed it as depicting Beverly. Admittedly, Beverly's squirrelly behavior on the same day of the robbery, his lack of an alibi at the very time of the robbery, and the missing finger were a good start, but we wanted just that little bit more that cinched the proof. As it turned out we never got that.

We noticed that the robber in the photo wore a golf or baseball style cap with a certain corporate logo. We identified the corporation but could find no record of Beverly ever having worked there. We inquired whether those caps were ever given away at some company event. Maybe we could place Beverly there. There indeed had been a golf tournament where they were distributed, but we had no evidence that Beverly attended or even played golf.

We had some questions about Beverly's whereabouts in the days leading up to the robbery. We decided to take a somewhat unusual and awkward course of action—visit the home where he lived with his mother and brother and interview the mom. Maybe they would consent to a search of his living area in the home to look for the clothes matching those worn by the robber. (Clearly, when Beverly visited his parole officer that day, he was not wearing the clothes in the photo.)

That trip to the head of a holler in Perry County provided some comic relief. If you've never been up in that area of Kentucky, you may not appreciate just how suspicious residents are about the comings and goings of strangers, especially those who appear to be government agents. Three middle-aged men in business suits, in a Crown Vic sedan, on the gravel roads sparsely lined with modest houses and cabins turned some heads.

At a local store we had gotten vague directions to the Beverly residence. But as we crept up the mountainside on the gravel road to which we had been directed, something wasn't right. We thought we had gone too far and hadn't seen the house described for us. When we saw three older men sitting on a pickup tailgate in a wide spot in the road we stopped and rolled down the window. The men glared suspiciously. "Can you gentlemen tell us where Everett Beverly lives?" Bob Rawlins asked. One of the three said in a country drawl, "Wayell, you take at little rite up 'ere around the corner and his house is up 'ere on the left." The other two men gave the one a look that said, "Don't cooperate with these city dudes." Rawlins asked, "So how far up that road does he live." Now chastened to be uncooperative, the one man said, "I don't know. I ain't been up 'ere in a while." Bob then quipped, "Well, tell me how far it was the last time you were up there. I'll assume it hasn't moved." He didn't answer but we got a good laugh.

We pulled up to the house, which was a very modest abode, and cautiously exited the car and approached. A man appeared at the door.

We asked to speak to Mrs. Beverly, the mother. A small, pleasant woman came out of the house. We introduced ourselves and asked to interview her. She was very agreeable. She invited us to sit on the porch and discuss the case. It was a late summer day. From the start she insisted that the man in the bank photo was not her son, Everett.

We were going through our list of questions we had planned to ask when, suddenly, the door to the house was flung open, and the man we had just met at the door emerged carrying a high-powered rifle. For a moment I thought we were dead. But the man, Everett's older brother, continued past us and walked briskly toward the back of the property near a wood line. Moments later there was a loud gunshot coming from that area. I saw Riley move his hand toward his pistol, which was holstered on his leg. Mrs. Beverly quickly interjected. "Don't pay any attention to the shootin'. He just went over there to shoot a hole in the septic tank to drain it." We got another good laugh. To this day I believe that the brother's little septic maintenance stunt was timed to send us a message that he didn't appreciate us going after his brother.

Nothing of value to our case came out of the interview. Mrs. Beverly said she had never seen the ball cap in the picture, nor any of the other clothing. She didn't feel comfortable letting us pry around Everett's bedroom without his permission, which we respected. Beverly had had his parole vacated because of the trip to Lexington and his lies about it and was in state custody at the time.

WE WENT TO trial with our largely circumstantial case. My closing argument essentially listed all the events and things that had to go the wrong way for Beverly that fateful day if he were in fact innocent. First, he looked enough like the robber for friends to have given their opinions that it was him. Second, he just happened to be in Lexington on the one day when the robbery occurred. His friends said he left them to buy cigarettes right about the time of the robbery. Third, he was missing a portion of his finger, the same finger as the robber. Fourth, he showed up at his parole officer's office at a time that could not alibi him. He lied about going to Lexington. He had on what looked like the necklace worn by the robber.

To make matters worse for him was his testimony. He denied that he was the robber, but he just didn't have that disbelief and indignation in his voice and demeanor that one would expect from a person wrongly accused of such a crime. The jury deliberated for several hours before informing the court that it was deadlocked. The judge sent the jury back to deliberate further in hopes that they could reach a verdict.

After a short additional period the jury reached a verdict. Apparently, there had only been one or two hold outs for not guilty. They now agreed with the majority to convict. I noticed that as the verdict was read by the clerk, one woman on the jury was crying. She clearly was uncomfortable. She must have been a holdout.

ABOUT SIX MONTHS after the trial, in the spring of 1997, I was having lunch with some colleagues and FBI agents when one of the agents mentioned to me that their office had received a strange call from an FBI office in Alabama.

Alabama was in the process of taking information from an arrested bank robber, who, to gain leniency, was telling about the dozens of other robberies that he had committed across the Midwest. One of those was at the bank in Kentucky that Beverly was convicted of robbing. Alabama wanted to know if Kentucky had an unsolved robbery matching the description. The answer was no, but we had a solved robbery that seemed to match—the Everett Beverly case.

I called Jim Riley. He had already spoken with Alabama, and yes, it did sound like the same robbery—especially because the confessor was saying that he dropped the money when a dye pack exploded.

Riley suggested that when he got a block of time he would go to Alabama and interview the guy for more details. I immediately said no; someone needed to do a thorough interview right away. Now that we had been put on notice of a possibility that we convicted an innocent man, each day we delayed in exploring that would be held against us in court someday.

Riley made that trip to Alabama the next day. He came back to Kentucky with a detailed account from the confessor of his movements and activities leading up to the Lexington robbery. The man considered himself to be a professional bank robber who carefully planned each one, and he had a prodigious memory about the circumstances of each robbery. He told Riley about getting off I-64 at a certain exit where certain businesses were. This was the North Broadway exit right near the bank in question. He spoke of driving around, casing the bank the day before the robbery. He said he checked in to a particular hotel under a particular alias. He remembered that after checking into the hotel he went to get a haircut. He remembers where the hair salon was in relation to the hotel. He said the woman who worked on his hair had mentioned being married to a Kentucky state trooper. He and the stylist chatted about chili recipes and made other small talk. The confessor was not missing any portion of a finger, but a close look at the photo of the hand was consistent with that finger being shrouded by the way he was holding the money bag. If that finger had been exposed in the photo it would have exonerated Beverly.

Upon returning to Lexington, Riley meticulously corroborated every detail of the confessor's story—the hotel, the alias, the hair stylist, the state trooper husband, and the chili recipes. There could be no question now but that the confessor was the robber, not Beverly. We checked prison records just to be sure that Beverly and this new guy had never crossed paths in prison. The concern was that maybe Beverly had put the guy up to confessing. But even that would not make sense because his detailed story about visiting Lexington would be unsubstantiated if that were the case.

I called the office of Charlie Gore, Beverly's defense attorney. I was going to give him the evidence we had uncovered and tell him that I would not oppose a motion to release Beverly on an appellate bond until the court could consider whether to vacate the conviction. I learned that Gore was on vacation and, as a solo practitioner, he would not be able to draft a motion until he returned. I decided to file the motion myself. It was the first time I had practiced defense law in years.

DESPITE THE EVIDENCE that I laid out in my motion, Judge Forester was skeptical. He instructed the government to produce the Alabama confessor in his courtroom, along with Beverly. The judge wanted to hear from the horse's mouth himself. In the meantime, Beverly would be released on an appellate bond.

We had that hearing a week or so later. The real robber took the stand. The first thing he did was apologize to Beverly for the mix up. He told the same story as before. The judge was satisfied and granted the motion to vacate. Mrs. Beverly was at the hearing, and she got some pleasure out of, "I told you so. I knew that wasn't my boy." But she was very gracious about it.

Sometime after the trial, our office received a Freedom of Information (FOIA) request from Beverly's new attorney, Ned Pillersdorf of Prestonsburg, Kentucky. Ned, who I have known since we were public defenders in the state system together in the '80s, had a great reputation as a representative for the oppressed and downtrodden. It would be well within his wheelhouse to file a lawsuit against the government generally, and any member of the prosecution team particularly, if he could establish that we had deliberately or even with a careless disregard for the truth, falsely convicted Everett Beverly. The FOIA request sought every speck of documentation related to the Beverly case—reports, correspondence, emails, texts, documents, statements, and so forth.

Pillersdorf got all the information he sought, but we never heard anything as a result. I assume that upon reviewing it he concluded that we had done nothing wrong. His client was simply the victim of a series of circumstances and events that lined up against him one day. I believe our quick response to new evidence to spring Beverly as soon as possible was a testament to our good faith.

Anytime an innocent person is wrongfully convicted it is a tragedy. But the extent of the effect on Beverly is not what it would be to a person with a clean record. After all, the day after the robbery Beverly was begging to be sent back to prison. And he was revoked for lying to his probation officer. The time he served on the federal sentence could be applied to his backup state time.

In later years, the experience of this case provided a lot of lunchtime banter in the office. Occasionally, I would be asked to recount the events to a person who had not heard them. I would then say something like, "Anyone can convict the guilty. It takes a real prosecutor to convict the innocent."

Randy Thompson II

Trying to Pave the Way to Victory

I am fond of Knott County, Kentucky, and its many interesting stories and people. I started making periodic trips there in the 1990s to visit my disabled brother who was a resident of the Caney Creek Rehabilitation Center in Pippa Passas. I would drive down narrow, dangerous country roads with their instant-death steep drop-offs, gripping the steering wheel with both hands. After passing by the edge of the quaint downtown of Hindman, I would head out past the renowned Hindman Settlement School, then past Alice Lloyd College before reaching the Pippa Passas post office and the Caney Creek facility. A few miles farther down that road is the little town of Wayland with the boarded up old high school building where King Kelly Coleman set state basketball scoring records in the '50s, playing for the Wayland Wasps. Hindman is also noteworthy as the home of late US Congressman Carl D. Perkins, who served decades in Washington, beginning in the 1940s. Reminders of Perkins's service and influence are all over the little town. I didn't know that, at the time, Knott County would be the situs of at least two memorable cases that I would prosecute.

One case was Elijah Jacobs, a violence against women case which began in Wayland. The other was Randy Thompson, the county judge executive of Knott County, who I convicted of vote buying and misappropriation of county funds in 2008. A judge executive in Kentucky is the chief executive officer for county government.

IN THE EARLY 2000s, Randy Thompson was a gregarious, business-savvy radio announcer and popular personality in Knott County. He owned and operated a local radio station nicknamed the Killer B, and he was often on air, speaking to the residents of Knott County. As a registered Republican, Thompson was in the political minority in heavily Democrat Knott County. But Thompson had connections to well-placed Republicans across the state, and that would soon give him an opportunity to get involved in a big way in Knott County politics. That is because the governor of Kentucky at the time was a Republican, Ernie Fletcher, and there was an unexpected vacancy in the office of Knott County judge executive, one that Fletcher would fill.

Around this time, Democrat Judge Executive Donnie Newsome was convicted by our office (not me personally) of vote buying and sentenced to prison. In 2005 Fletcher appointed Thompson to serve out the remaining one year of Newsome's term, which would expire in 2006. Thompson quickly hired two cronies, John Mac Combs and Ronnie Adams, as deputy judge executives and placed another friend, Phillip Champion, in the position of foreman of the county road department. Thompson filed to run for election to his own term in the 2006 general election.

Thompson knew he had an uphill battle to win the election as a Republican, but he had the advantage of free publicity on the radio waves, and he came up with a brilliant campaign strategy. He would run, ironically, on a promise to clean up the Democrat corruption that had plagued Knott County. He also promised to improve the infrastructure of the county, especially roads that needed paving and graveling.

One of Thompson's first official acts was to convince the county fiscal court to issue a $1.5 million bond offering, the proceeds of which would be earmarked for blacktop. He also found surplus local funds and state funds. In all, he had $2 million dollars to spread blacktop around the county. Thompson, Champion, Ronnie Adams, and John Mac Combs directed the county's usual blacktop contractor, Mountain Enterprises, to blacktop both private drives and county roads. Mountain Enterprises abruptly quit working for the county, quietly announcing that they didn't want to be part of the diversion of county blacktop onto private property.

To replace Mountain Enterprises, Thompson hired a small-time local paver, Randy Campbell, to do the work. A meeting was held, and the Thompson group got a commitment from Campbell to pave precisely where he was told to pave by Adams and Champion. He was also told that, when he paved a private driveway, he should make up a fake receipt or invoice to falsely show that he was paid by the owner/resident for the private blacktopping.

At least one employee in the road department publicly voiced his concern about the private blacktopping. In addition, he had noted that county gravel was being similarly diverted to private property. Finally, one county employee, Randy Gayheart, was building bridges on private property and was being paid for the construction with county funds over and above his normal salary.

Word of the misuse of county funds found its way to the regional news media. A reporter started asking questions, especially at the fiscal court meetings. The county attorney, fearing he might be blamed for missing county funds, asked Thompson to certify in writing that all the blacktop and gravel that had been distributed was done for a public purpose. Coincidentally, around this time, the Kentucky auditor of public accounts concluded an annual audit of Knott County finances and found that much of the aforementioned blacktop funds could not be accounted for, because the paver was not recording exactly where, and how much he was paving.

This report made its way to the Kentucky attorney general's office, the state police, and an FBI public corruption task force, and a criminal investigation was begun.

Mark Hopkins was a state trooper who had been assigned

to the public corruption task force and the Knott County matter. Mark worked several cases with me over the next few years, and he became one of my all-time favorites. He was a hard worker with great investigative instincts and techniques. For weeks in 2006 and 2007, Mark scoured Knott County doing interview after interview and taking photographs of dozens of private driveways that sported new blacktop. He brought the case to our office, and we used the federal grand jury to assist in the investigation. We had some relevant federal statutes for the facts Mark was developing.

Mark had found that some of the individuals who received blacktop on their driveways had promised to vote for Randy Thompson as a quid pro quo, a violation of the federal vote-buying statute. The diversion of county blacktop, gravel, bridge building time, and materials violated a federal statute.

AN OFFSHOOT OF the Thompson investigation, involved the father-daughter duo of Hoey Dobson and his daughter Tammy Brewer. Tammy was an employee in Judge Thompson's office, and she lived very close to her father, Hoey. Mark Hopkins noted and photographed the driveways of Tammy and Hoey because they were newly paved. When questioned by Mark, Tammy said that, yes, Randy Campbell did pave her driveway, but it was a private job that she paid for out of her personal funds. She said she had a receipt for the payment, but she would have to look for it. Several days later, Tammy produced a handwritten receipt, but it was made out to Dobson. Campbell told Mark that the receipt was a fake, that he had been asked to prepare that by Ronnie Adams.

Tammy Brewer was called to testify at a grand jury proceeding, and she recounted a false story about paying for blacktop. Mark then interviewed Dobson who said he didn't know anything about the blacktop nor the receipt. Thereafter Dobson was called to the grand jury where he tried to corroborate Brewer's story. Suddenly, he remembered everything. Both Brewer and her father were indicted for perjury, and conspiracy to commit perjury. Both were convicted at trial that was conducted during the pendency of the related Thompson case.

I felt sorry for Tammy. She was offered immunity from prosecution if she told the truth. But she had some misplaced loyalty to Thompson and fell on the sword for him, bringing her elderly father to prison with her. I believe her receipt of the blacktop was unrelated to the election, that it was just a bonus as an employee. But her perjury and obstruction of justice was of no benefit to Thompson. To the contrary, we later introduced the perjured testimony as evidence of the case against Thompson. It was proof that the defendants had a consciousness of guilt because they orchestrated the fake evidence to cover their crime.

IN THE FALL of 2007, the grand jury indicted Thompson, Adams, Champion, and Combs in the scheme to distribute county property and to buy votes. Thus, began months of legal maneuvering and motion practice, culminating in a six- or seven-day trial. Attorney Kent Westberry and a couple of associates from a firm in Louisville represented Thompson, and several local lawyers represented the other three defendants. Among those was the colorful attorney, Larry Webster. I still chuckle at some of Larry's lines during the trial, like when he said at the beginning of his closing argument, "I've got a lot of points to make. I feel like a mosquito at a nudist colony. I don't know where to start." Later, he told the jury, "To make a long story short—if it's not too late . . . "

The case was hard-fought by the defense attorneys who argued that all the blacktop, gravel, and bridges were provided for some *public purpose* and therefore did not constitute a misappropriation of county property. The unstated, yet advanced by subtle insinuation, message was the "everybody does it," or "that's just the way we do things up in these mountains" defense. I was well aware of the culture surrounding government and elections in Eastern Kentucky.

Incumbent candidates often openly use their authority to confer benefits on voters around election time. A person with a large family might be given a county job with the understanding that the family would vote a certain way. I had one case where a small-town mayor threatened people in public housing, controlled by the city, with eviction if they didn't vote for her. And gravel was always a big deal around election time.

I filed a pretrial motion and obtained a court order to preclude the defense from making the argument, or introducing evidence, that other administrations or other counties do the same thing. But I knew the defense attorneys would still try to plant that seed in the jury's collective mind.

The argument was made that a certain road was blacktopped because it allowed the public to access an old cemetery. A bridge was built to allow a bus to pick up children on the other side of the creek. Another person's driveway was paved because it made it easier for the school bus to turn around. Someone had a chronic illness and might need an ambulance someday. A road had been treated as a county road for years and the new blacktop was just a needed upkeep.

One defense witness had received free blacktop and testified as to the reason it was justified as being for a public purpose. On cross-examination I asked why he felt it was all right for his driveway to be paved when his neighbors didn't get theirs done. He said something like, "I think if you all had left him alone, he would have eventually paved everyone's driveway."

Another issue that arose during this trial explores how much a court can limit a criminal defendant's ability to speak publicly about his case, the court, or witnesses, without infringing upon his First Amendment right to free speech. Recently, former President Donald Trump, who as a criminal defendant at the time, appealed a gag order from a DC-based trial court that barred certain kinds of speech believed to be injurious to the fair adjudication of charges.

After the first or second day of our trial, word came to me that Randy Thompson was speaking on his radio station after the trial each day, wherein he discussed and criticized the trial proceedings and testimony. I asked the court to preclude him from discussing the case on public airways. Jurors commuting from the courthouse might inadvertently hear the comments.

It never occurred to me that a First Amendment argument might have merit. I was used to trial judges have complete power over the conduct of trial participants that might influence the jury. But we never took up the issue of the legitimate scope of a gag order because defense attorney Westberry, after conferring with his client, informed the court that his client would voluntarily refrain from such conduct. He believed that the optics of such a performance was not good for his client.

ALL FOUR DEFENDANTS were convicted of at least one count of the indictment. Thompson was sentenced to forty months in prison, and the other three defendants received lesser sentences. All were allowed to remain free pending appeal. But the case was about to take another turn that would extend the length of the appeal.

Several months after sentencing, the defendants filed a motion for a new trial, alleging that prosecutors had violated their ethical obligations by not disclosing evidence that many of our witnesses—specifically those that had received free blacktop—had been granted immunity from prosecution. Such grants constitute material that can cast doubt on the credibility of the witness's trial testimony. The allegation arose from the fact that agents informed witnesses who received free blacktop that they would not be prosecuted if they told the truth. That informal assurance was made again by me when the witness appeared to testify at the grand jury. The motion was bizarre in that, again, the immunity grant was right there in the court transcripts provided to the defense. Ultimately, the motion was unsuccessful, but it did require extensive litigation that prolonged the proceedings. It was at least three to four years after trial that Thompson and the others exhausted their appeals and reported to prison. Thompson continued to serve as county judge all that time.

LET ME GIVE you a short humorous postscript to this case. First, some background. Two years before the Thompson trial, I moved into a log cabin on six wooded acres on a dead-end road in the boonies of Anderson County. That road was paved but in grave need of repair. Potholes were everywhere, and the surface was cracked and uneven. There were only a handful of houses on that mile and a half of road, so I guess there wasn't enough political heft there to make my neighbors and me a priority when it came time to lay blacktop on the county roads. But that didn't stop us residents from mentioning our need to our magistrate or the county judge executive when we saw them. Nevertheless, when I left for a full week in Pikeville that summer to try the Thompson case, I had lived on that road for over two years, and the road had not been touched.

So, as I was turning onto my road late that Friday afternoon, having just convicted a county judge of using county blacktop to buy votes, I couldn't believe my eyes. Our road was now surfaced with the most beautiful smooth blacktop you could ever imagine. It was so thick I was fearful of dropping a wheel off the side of the road. I could not believe the coincidence. After two years, the county chose the week of that trial to pave my road. I was glad I had never promised to vote for someone in exchange for the blacktop.

Milby And Coffman

The Great Oil Scam

I learned a lot about the development of oil and gas wells in Central Kentucky during my career as a prosecutor. Or should I say, the shady and fraudulent form of that industry. To understand the story of Gary Milby and Bryan Coffman, an introduction to the industry is helpful.

In theory, there is a legitimate method of privately funding the drilling of oil wells. It goes something like this: An entrepreneur wants to drill oil wells, but not with his money alone. So, he uses the *oil program method.* He buys mineral rights to a specific parcel of land, usually one that he has been examined by a geologist in the past, and an opinion rendered that it contains substantial deposits or pools of oil.

He estimates what it will cost to drill, say, three wells on a portion of that land. Let's say its $100,000 per well, or $300,00 for the project. He estimates that it will cost another $100,000 to bring all wells online. So, he wants to raise $400,000 to begin drilling.

He incorporates the project as a limited liability corporation (LLC), and names the project something catchy like Solid Gold Number One, LLC. He sets aside several other three well project areas and names them Solid Gold numbers Two, Three, and so forth. He divides each project into ten shares and offers shares to the public at $40,000 per share. The investors receive a prospectus and offering documents, spelling out their rights and obligations. When the project is sold out, the drilling begins. As oil and gas are produced and sold, the owners of the shares divide the proceeds *pro rata*—in proportion to their share of the project.

This form of oil production works fine when there are sufficient oil reserves in the ground to cover the cost of production with money to spare as profit. But you can see how quickly this all becomes fraudulent when an oil producer misrepresents the likelihood of striking oil, the amount of expected production, and the cost of production. I saw numerous cases over the years that involved unscrupulous oil men who would secretly describe the scam among themselves as "making my money above the ground."

In other words, they made money by pocketing the investment dollars, going through the motions of drilling, and then apologizing for the paltry production or dry holes. Once their track record of minimal production was revealed, they changed company names and moved on to look for new victims.

Gary Milby, from around Campbellsville, Kentucky was one of these shady oilmen. He had spent years in the oil fields, so he knew the lingo. He had an "aw shucks" disarming manner that potential investors found reassuring. He often wrapped his sales pitches in religious messages, proclaiming how God had blessed him financially (untrue) and now he wanted to give to others by producing oil for them—in large quantities. He professed to have an uncanny ability to know where the oil was, and he wrapped that in a quaint little term that mocked real science—*close ology*. He said he knew how to go onto plots of real estate where productive oil wells were drilled in the past, and by putting new wells near by the old sites he could tap into the same pool of oil and hit gushers.

That was pure fiction. In fact, the opposite was true. Oil deposits in Kentucky are small pools in fractured limestone. Gushers are extremely rare, and the proximity of old wells militates against new production. But Milby could make you think you would be wealthy in a matter of weeks. He promised levels of production that were off the charts unrealistic, according to experts. He lied to investors about how he was going to spend their money. He hid from investors the regulatory actions taken against him and his companies in other states, and he failed to disclose that he had taken bankruptcy a few years before. Instead, he said he was a very wealthy oil tycoon. He flat-out made-up stories about investors who had gotten filthy rich by investing in his oil projects.

MILBY OPERATED UNDER the name Mid-America Oil, Inc. for several years in the early 2000s. He raised millions of dollars, but no one made anything close a full return on investment. Almost all investors lost the lion share of their money. As regulators closed in on his operation, Milby changed his business organization to Global Energy, Inc. And somewhere along the way he developed a relationship with a Lexington lawyer, Bryan Coffman. Coffman became the manager/lawyer for Global Energy, and he helped set up a business facade designed to give Global an aura of legitimacy.

Canadian investor Victor Tsatskin eventually became a coconspirator. At some point Tsatskin realized that he had been scammed and would lose his money, and he wasn't happy. He came to Lexington and somehow extracted from Coffman and Milby a share of their business.

With Tsatskin's assistance, Milby and Coffman decided to change their business model. Instead of relying on Milby to make the sales pitches, they would utilize a phone bank—robocalls—in Canada. But Milby had to train the callers on how to make a convincing sales pitch. In a video-recorded training session in Canada, which we subsequently obtained, Milby conducted training. But he used an alias at the training. He was now Jerry Miller. Later, this dynamite evidence would be presented to a jury—the fake Jerry Miller teaching callers to make outlandish claims designed to fool future investors.

Over a three- or four-year period, Milby raised approximately thirty-six million dollars from hundreds of investors. Investors all over the country became concerned when the oil and money did not flow as promised. By 2007, many investors had reached out to securities regulators and law enforcement offices. But the real clincher occurred when a number of investors saw an MTV episode of *My Super Sweet 16*, a reality TV show displaying the lavish birthday parties that wealthy families hosted for their children. That episode showed Gary Milby showering his daughter with a helicopter ride, a BMW, and other expensive gifts. In the episode, Milby takes his daughter to an oil field and shows her oil wells. She says "I love oil. It buys purses, shoes, and everything." At another point, when noticing the pungent odor of oil she exclaims, "It smells like money, Daddy!" The investors were livid. Their money was paying for that party.

THE CASE CAME to the attention of securities investigators in the Department of Financial Institutions (DFI). Investigator Chad Harlan became the face of their office in the investigation, one of many cases we worked together over the years. Inspector Marni Gibson was a vital participant. DFI attorney Christy Lewis became a special assistant US Attorney to help with the investigation and subsequent trial. Roberta Bottoms and the Postal Inspection Service joined the team. A colleague, Rob Duncan, was assigned to assist me in what was expected to be a difficult investigation and trial. Rob was primarily a drug prosecution attorney but was seeking trial experience, as he was a fairly recent addition to our office. Duncan later became the US attorney in our district.

Early in the investigation, we had what can be described as a turf battle with the US Attorney's Office in Nashville. We learned that the Mid-America phase of Milby's business was and had been under investigation by that office. A very active FBI agent was having trouble getting the prosecutor assigned to the case to move it forward toward indictment. We had an idea. We could ask them to stand down in favor of a single, overarching conspiracy case in Kentucky that covered Mid-America and Global Energy. Instead of framing and charging it as two separate conspiracies, we would argue, persuasively based on the evidence, that it was really one conspiracy with members moving in and out.

In 2009, we traveled to Nashville and met with the FBI agent there and the prosecutor. The prosecutor was not at all receptive to our plan. He said that he was going to indict, regardless of what we did. We returned to Kentucky and placed the case on the next grand jury schedule and prepared to indict. Out of the blue, Tennessee prosecutors indicted the Mid-America scheme the day before we were to present in Kentucky. We indicted as planned and the race to trial began.

For months, the two federal cases moved along parallel tracks. However, at some point one of the two would disappear, by operation of law. That's because we had charged the same conspiracy, though ours was broader in scope. If Tennessee got to trial first, their trial would mean that double jeopardy would prevent us from proceeding against Milby a second time. We pressed on, confident that we would be able to get to trial before Tennessee. They just didn't appear to be that much invested in the case.

The indictment charged four individuals with fraud and money laundering—Milby, Coffman, Tsatskin and Coffman's wife Megan. The latter had handled many of the financial transactions, which were alleged to constitute money laundering.

Shortly after indictment, a memorable event occurred during a meeting we prosecutors called a *reverse proffer* session. A little background. It is common for a defendant in federal court to seek leniency by offering to help the prosecution investigate and prosecute other individuals who they know have committed crimes. This is called providing *substantial assistance* to the government, and it earns the cooperating defendant a motion for a lower sentence than otherwise called for by the sentencing guidelines. In order to provide the government with an opportunity to evaluate the information and evidence the defendant can offer, a proffer session is scheduled. The defendant meets with agents and prosecutors and, in an off-the-record discussion, he lays out what he knows.

A *reverse proffer* happens when a prosecutor invites the defendant and his attorney to a meeting where the prosecutor lays out all the evidence and arguments that will be used to prove the defendant's guilt. The object is to convince the defense that going to trial is a fool's errand, and that the better course of action is to negotiate a plea agreement. We had such a session with Bryan Coffman, his wife Megan, and their attorneys at my office not long after indictment.

Bryan Coffman was represented by a renowned defense attorney Steve Romines, who had cultivated a reputation in Central Kentucky for aggressive criminal defense in high profile cases. He approached cases with a take-no-prisoners attitude. Plea bargaining was not his strong suit. We butted heads at the beginning of the case, but over time I think we developed a mutual respect.

After listening to Postal Inspector Roberta Bottoms methodically outline the evidence against the Coffmans, and to me make what essentially was a closing argument, the Coffmans were unmoved and visibly defiant. Romines professed to be unimpressed with the presentation. The three indicated there would be no deal. I don't recall her exact message, but Inspector Bottoms zeroed in on some aspect of the case and said something that Romines obviously believed was criticism of his representation, perhaps to the effect that he was not serving the best interest of his client. Romines exclaimed, "Fuck you, Roberta." I thought she was going to shoot him. At that point I wouldn't have objected.

I asked Romines to step out of the meeting room. I said, "Steve, you need to really look at this evidence. Coffman is facing a very long prison term if convicted. What we are offering will result in about a seven-year sentence. If convicted at trial, he could receive twenty or more years. Our evidence is overwhelming. I will convict your client at trial with one hand tied behind my back." Steve replied something like, "The Coffmans have a lot of fight in them. They want to take this to trial. I will not get in the way of that. If I plead them guilty, I don't get my name in the paper. If we go to trial and we lose, that's expected. Nobody can fault me for going to trial. If I win, on the other hand, I'm a hero."

So, we had to try the case.

A CENTRAL PART of our proof at trial was the testimony of the victim investors. They told of the sales pitches they received from Milby, with the glowing reports of abundant oil and money. They spoke of the excuses for delays when the promises did not materialize. They introduced offering materials with claims that other witnesses proved were false. They all testified that they lost almost all of their investment. A few received some paltry sums from oil sales.

One victim witness was especially memorable. Eric Taylor (no relation to me) was a feisty, fiery, and pissed-off victim who had organized an email support group among the victims, wherein they traded stories and evidence. He and this group were instrumental in helping us assemble victim evidence, and boy was he ready to raise holy hell at trial. He wasn't about to be intimidated by the in-your-face" cross-examination of Steve Romines.

The cross-examination of Eric Taylor quickly deteriorated into a shouting match, with each participant cutting off the other. Taylor wasn't going to listen to Romines' suggestions that he had been a negligent and careless investor. He interjected non-responsive testimony about things Milby had done to influence his investment decision. Repeatedly, Judge Caldwell interjected herself into the process, calling out both participants. Finally, her patience exhausted, she sent the jury out of the courtroom and read both individuals the Riot Act.

When the trial resumed, the judge had stationed two US marshals in prominent positions in the courtroom. The rest of the cross-examination was mild by comparison to the way it had started. At the conclusion of the day's proceedings, Romines said, "Judge, I was wondering, were those marshalls for me or the witness?" Judge said, "Both."

We called as an expert witness, a geologist from the Kentucky Division of Oil and Gas, the agency that keeps records of oil and gas production in the state. He refuted Milby's claims of large oil reserves in Kentucky, and especially his claim termed *closeology*. He said the Kentucky limestone structure was fractured and could not collect large pools of crude oil. He told the jury that Milby's past production history involved small amounts of oil, not the prolific production Milby claimed.

We called a financial analyst to show where the money raised by Milby was spent. A large portion was spent on personal items by Milby and Coffman. It was not held in escrow as claimed, and it was not spent as promised solely for the drilling and related expenses.

Bryan Coffman professed to be just a lawyer representing a client of whose criminal activity he was unaware. That has some surface appeal, as Coffman did draft documents and conduct office business and rarely met the victims or made sales presentations. So, what we had to establish, beyond a reasonable doubt, was that he knew of the fraud, approved it, and facilitated it. We did this in several ways.

We retained an expert witness to address directly Coffman's claim of just being a securities lawyer for Milby. Professor Manning Warren from the University of Louisville law school provided very helpful testimony about a lawyer's duty and obligations when representing a client who is issuing offering materials like a prospectus or investment agreement. It is not enough to just draft the documents, Warren testified. The lawyer's duty is to conduct *due diligence* to ensure that representations made about the investment are true, and that all relevant representations are made. Coffman's professed ignorance of Milby's business was not a reasonable or ethical representation.

We continued our focus on Coffman's culpability with witness/victims who had had conversations with him. Several victims had contacted Coffman when they began to suspect things were amiss with their investments. They had been led to believe that Coffman was holding their money in escrow until it was needed for drilling. The presence of an attorney in the business was comforting to them. Surely, a lawyer would not jeopardize his career by helping commit fraud. But, when asked about their money and the bona fides of the business, Coffman vouched for Milby's great track record of production (a lie), and he did not inform any victim about regulatory actions against Milby for which he was the attorney of record. He did not tell them about Milby going bankrupt a few years earlier.

A salesman for Milby complained in a letter to Milby about what he was seeing out in the field in terms of wild—unsubstantiated claims and promises. Milby asked Coffman to respond to the complaint. Coffman chastised the salesman for complaining and told him he should get back to bringing in the money and quit whining. We introduced that letter into evidence.

A very incriminating piece of evidence against Coffman was a video-recorded interview the DFI did of Coffman in the early days of the investigation. Coffman feigned ignorance of anything of substance about Milby's business. He would say things like, "I *think* they are headquartered in the Bahamas" when he was the one who went to the Bahamas to set it all up. He claimed he didn't know much about Milby's past. He was just an hourly fee attorney providing legal services to Milby's company. Coffman's lavish spending traced to the victims was especially damning. He had purchased a $1.5 million yacht and hired a captain.

A key witness against Coffman was the Bahamian Arthur Chase.

He testified to Coffman coming to the Bahamas and establishing their shell corporation. In the aforementioned DFI interview, Coffman had denied knowing Chase. Getting Chase to Kentucky for the trial was a challenge. He initially refused to cooperate, and we had no subpoena power to compel his attendance, but we started a mutual legal assistant treaty (MLAT) to compel his deposition in the Bahamas. Finally, he relented and agreed to attend and testify.

We introduced a video of the aforementioned Canadian sales training where Milby introduces himself as Jerry Miller. At one point in the presentation, Coffman is seen moving behind Miller as he spoke. So, he knew Milby was using an alias, and of course he knew why that was needed. Victor Tsakskin worked out a deal with us, in conjunction with prosecutors in Canada. He would plead guilty to fraud charges in Canada and receive a lenient sentencing in exchange for him agreeing to come to Kentucky to testify against Coffman and Milby. At trial he described conversations he had with Coffman about how best to structure the scam. I do not believe that Coffman's guilt was a close question for the jury.

The jury obviously had trouble with the case against the wife, Megan Coffman. The grand jury had indicted her because she was the person who conducted substantial financial transactions that we alleged were designed to facilitate and promote the fraud. But apparently, the jury had a reasonable doubt about her knowledge and intent and acquitted her.

Coffman and Milby were convicted and sentenced to twenty-five and twenty years, respectively. Romines approached me after sentencing and said, "You told me months ago you would convict Coffman with one hand tied behind your back. Well, looks like you did it. I want you to know this is the longest prison sentence any client of mine has ever received."

A nice postscript was that this case was profiled on the CNBC television series *American Greed.* Roberta Bottoms and I were interviewed and filmed discussing various aspects of the case.

LD (Lost Dog) Ridgeway

Panty Man Bank Robber

It was the spring of 1996 and LD Ridgeway, a man in his fifties with no close family and who had a disability was at his modest home just outside of Sandy Hook, Kentucky. Strangely, LD was his given name. It wasn't L.D., as if short for Larry David or Loren Donald. That's what his momma named him. But the locals often called him Lost Dog, which seemed an apt moniker. He generally had no plans or ambitions. He just lived.

LD was one of those eccentric characters who is seen and known by sight to everyone in a small town. He often wandered the streets of Sandy Hook, exchanging pleasantries. He would cash his disability check at the Sandy Hook Bank even though he had no account there. He was a cash only type of guy. He was considered harmless and likable by town folk.

It was check day (when the government check arrives), and LD had company. Some local layabouts had shown up to sponge off LD. They encouraged him to cash his check and spend a substantial sum on liquor and beer. As the spirits flowed there on LD's porch, and the boys exchanged tall tales and laughter, LD commiserated that he had spent too much of his check on hard drink for those boys and might not have enough left to eat all month. One of the boys jokingly told LD that he should supplement his income by robbing the Sandy Hook Bank.

After the boys left, LD apparently took to heart what the one fellow had said. He retrieved from the house a pair of women's panties (no clue where he got them) and an old toy cap pistol that looked very much like a real gun. He walked the short distance to the Sandy Hook Bank and as he entered placed the panties over his head, with his nose in the crotch area and his eyes looking through the leg holes.

LD approached the teller counter. All the tellers were now wide-eyed as this panty man crossed the lobby. LD stepped up to one of the ladies, placed his toy gun on the counter and said in his distinctive voice, "Give me twenty thousand dollars." The teller calmly responded, "LD, you know we don't have that kind of money up here."

"Well, shit," LD replied. Then he turned, left the bank and went home.

It was only a matter of minutes before the sheriff's cruiser pulled into LD's driveway. LD was on the porch, just sitting. The sheriff casually got out of his car and approached LD. He queried, with incredulity.

"LD did you just try to rob the Sandy Hook Bank?"

"Hell no."

"Well, the girls at the bank told me you came in there with panties on your head and had a gun."

"Hell, it were just a toy gun."

"LD, get in the car."

The Elliot County sheriff arrested LD for attempted robbery, but then, as was customary in those days, turned the case over to the FBI for federal prosecution. Whenever the bank in question is FDIC insured, as almost all are, the federal government has jurisdiction over the crime as well. I was assigned to prosecute the case in federal court.

I knew from my first reading of the police report that there was going to be an issue as to whether LD was legally sane and competent to stand trial. But I had to get the case started with a grand jury indictment. I presented the evidence in Ashland, Kentucky and an indictment was returned.

At his arraignment, I moved the court for a psychological evaluation. LD was sent off to a medical facility run by the United States Bureau of Prisons for the evaluation. I sent the evaluating doctors all the paperwork and reports in my possession. They spent the next month or more testing LD, observing his interactions with people and interviewing him.

I was not surprised when I received the formal written report from the medical facility. The opinion of the reporting psychologist was that LD was not competent to stand trial. He could not understand the nature of the charges, nor sufficiently participate in his defense. He could not understand and appreciate the role of the judge, the prosecutor, and his defense attorney. Most importantly, the psychologist opined that LD's condition was static and permanent, meaning that this was not a case where, with a period of treatment, he could be restored to competency. He truly was a Lost Dog, or, as our judge, Henry Wilhoit, once said to a defendant, "Son, you really are a lost ball in high weeds." (Judge Wilhot played a lot of golf.)

As required by law, we had an evidentiary hearing to make a formal finding on the issue of competency. Sometimes this issue is hotly contested with evidence adduced by both sides. Here, however, I did not feel the need to cross-examine the psychologist, and I told the defense attorney that he didn't need to call him. I wasn't going to challenge his opinion.

The defense did call to the stand a local female resident from Sandy Hook who knew LD well and could give the judge LD's background and living situation. Most notably, she testified that if the court would release LD to her, she would supervise him going forward to ensure that this behavior, nor anything like it, would happen again. She discussed the probability of initiating a guardianship proceeding in state court so someone could manage LD's affairs.

The law technically requires that upon a finding of incompetency, the defendant is committed to the bureau of prisons (BOP) for mental treatment to see if he could be restored to competency. If not, the government prosecutors would work with local authorities to institute state guardianship proceedings. But Wilhoit was a very practical judge who did not elevate form over substance. I informed him that the government would dismiss all charges, with prejudice, if the court wanted to bypass the commitment to BOP and release LD to the care of this volunteer from Sandy Hook. And that is what happened. So that was the end of my LD Ridgeway case. I often wonder how his life turned out when he returned to Sandy Hook.

I'll add here a little humorous postscript to the case. On the morning that we were scheduled to have the competency hearing, I left my home in Jessamine County to proceed to federal court in Lexington. As I left my subdivision, someone had posted a large cardboard sign on a light post that read, *LOST DOG* with the usual photograph and description. I got a good laugh out of that coincidence. Was this some kind of message to me from the gods? It made for a good story to share with my colleagues.

Daniel Lubowa

The Grifting Missionary

In early 2001, a thirty-something-year-old African man by the name Mark Phelps (at least that's what he said) called the chair of the Mercer County Baptist Association, Pastor Larry Redding, and asked for an audience. Phelps said he was an undercover missionary from Uganda who was spreading the Gospel in his native country and in Sudan by heading up a US-based organization called Grace Ministries. There was a sister organization located in Uganda. The goal was to raise money and donated goods in America and send them to the Uganda ministry. The money was to be used to sponsor new churches and pastors, and clothing was given to poor Ugandans.

Phelps had a silver tongue. He so impressed Pastor Redding that he immediately agreed to seek an audience for Phelps at many Baptist and other churches in the Mercer/Boyle County area. Over the next several months, Phelps spoke at numerous churches about the poverty in Uganda that he was fighting. He said that Christians in Africa were subverted by the spread of Islam. They had to work secretly at times to avoid being attacked, even killed. He told graphic stories about the violence there, including the time a man sitting next to him in a service was shot and killed.

Many who heard Phelp's spiel were impressed by him and greatly moved by his cause. People said he made them want to sell everything they owned and give him the money. Church people held fundraisers, clothing drives, and provided two donated used cars. A cargo shipping container was placed in a church parking lot to be filled with donated items for eventual shipping to Africa. Thousands of dollars were raised and sent to Grace Ministries in Rochester, Minnesota. Phelps was usually taken to dinner after these church talks. He was even a guest in the homes of church people. He was truly liked and admired by these generous folks. That is, until the truth began to trickle in.

IN EARLY SUMMER that year, Pastor Redding received a call from the Baptist Association in the Louisville area who said that Phelps was actually a man name Daniel Lubowa. He was not a missionary, though his father was. He had learned the ways of mission work by growing up around it but had no real connection with the mission field. Lubowa, he said, had been through numerous other communities like Mercer County all over the South. He used the same alias and modus operandi. The clothing was not going to people in need directly. It was being sold out of stores owned by Lubowa. Lubowa owned a hotel and fancy cars. The Ugandan national police had investigated the scheme there and concluded that there was no true mission.

As part of the scam, church members had been on trips to Uganda where they were going to see the churches and schools they had ostensibly been donating to build. They reported back that Phelps would always have an excuse or explanation why they weren't seeing anything tangible. Lubowa had lied to them about the cost of their plane tickets and lodging and greatly overcharged them. They paid to stay in a hotel that he owned. In short, the facade around Lubowa had crumbled.

Pastor Redding swore out a criminal complaint against Lubowa for theft. Local law enforcement continued their investigation. Lubowa's hotel room was searched. More details were discovered. Meanwhile the shipping container and all those goods remained in the parking lot of the church. Lubowa was jailed on a $25,000 bond. After a preliminary hearing where the above details were provided to the court, the case was bound over to the grand jury for possible indictment. Commonwealth Attorney Richie Bottoms, my good friend and former colleague with the Kentucky public defenders, had only thirty days to indict or Lubowa would have to be released. But he knew the feds were doing their own parallel investigation, and that the federal courts had bigger hammers and more investigative resources, so he agreed to step back and allow the case to go federal.

Chief postal inspector in Lexington, Lanny Miller, assigned Inspector Roberta Bottoms to the case. I was assigned to prosecute. In early August, just before Bottoms's thirty days expired, we took the unusual step of obtaining a criminal complaint against Lubowa. If there had not been time restraints, we would have taken the case straight to the grand jury. We traveled to Rochester, Minnesota, and obtained a search warrant on the premises of Grace Ministries. We found, essentially, a largely vacant room with miscellaneous records. There were no employees on site. We conducted some interviews of former employees and learned that Lubowa had been abandoned by everyone who had worked for him because of the sloppy way he handled money and for his failure to account for donations. We arranged to have the shipping container moved from the church parking lot to the parking lot at the postal inspectors' office in Lexington.

In September, we indicted Lubowa in federal court on mail and wire fraud charges. But we still had more investigation to conduct. We found witnesses in Uganda who knew Lubowa and his background and established through a Ugandan police officer and others that there was no real ministry. We located church people who had traveled to Uganda on the sham trips. We examined bank records to track the flow of money and could show that the funds were used personally by Lubowa. The case looked like a slam dunk for a conviction.

Surely, Lubowa would see the handwriting on the wall and plead guilty. But Lubowa must have been delusional. He insisted to his appointed counsel that there was some sort of cultural misunderstanding that made what was legitimate mission work look like fraud. There would be no guilty plea.

THE TRIAL OCCURRED in early February 2002 and lasted four days. Witnesses included several of the duped church people who donated, some acquaintances of Lubowa from Uganda, and the Ugandan police investigator who helped during the investigation. We had photos of the donated items, bank records, financial analyses, and video tapes of presentations made by Lubowa at various churches.

I recall a humorous event during the trial. A Ugandan man who was to testify to Lubowa's background had just walked into the courthouse the morning of his scheduled testimony when suddenly a February snow squall of giant flakes beset downtown Lexington. The man suddenly turned ran out the front door into the street and held his cupped hands out to catch the falling snow. He was beaming from ear to ear and even yelped a few times. He marveled at this fluffy, floating substance in the air. He said he had always heard about and seen pictures of snow but had never seen or felt it in person. It was a poignant moment in his life. Unfortunately, it would not be a memory of long duration.

In one conversation with this man while he was in town, he told us that his willingness to come testify against Lubowa was not without risk to his personal safety. Lubowa had associates there who were not above using violence against those that crossed them. Our witness would have to be careful when he returned. And, unfortunately, we would not be able to offer any kind of protection, like we would if he were living in the United States.

His fears were prophetic. We got word, not long after the trial, that the man had eaten something at a gathering one evening and immediately went into convulsions and died. No doubt he was poisoned. It was sobering news.

Silver tongued Lubowa could not resist the opportunity to convince the jury that we were wrong about him. He took the stand, most likely against the advice of defense attorney, Kevin West. Lubowa had an answer for everything. It didn't pass the smell test, but it was well-delivered. My cross-examination was probably overdone and overly dramatic. There was so much to work with. Example: Lubowa had testified about the board of directors of Grace Ministries, giving the impression that it was more than the shell company. On cross I said, "You mentioned the board of directors of Grace Ministries. Who are the current members of the board of directors?" He said, "Me." The jury returned a verdict of guilty on all counts after forty-five minutes of deliberation.

After trial, Inspector Bottoms tackled the formidable task of disposing of the hundreds of items in the shipping container. One day she called an all-hands-on-deck sorting and moving operation. Attorneys, agents, and support staff came together and unloaded the container. I don't recall now where it all went—I think the Salvation Army or Goodwill took the clothes—but it was a monumental task. It wasn't in any of our job descriptions, but sometimes you just must get your hands dirty.

Darlene Dedman

I Am My Own Grandma

Over the years, I prosecuted several individuals whom I described as *system gamers*, people who manipulate the facts and stories of their lives to obtain government benefits. An example would be a businessman who puts his company in the name of his wife to qualify for disadvantaged business (woman-owned) preferences in obtaining government contracts. (The Tina Conner case, mentioned elsewhere, is a prime example). But Darlene Dedman was perhaps the most creative gamer I encountered.

My involvement in the case began when, in 2005, Dedman reported to the U S Department of Defense (DOD) that her adopted daughter, Nelva Holland, was defrauding the government by receiving her deceased husband's military survivor pension. The DOD assigned a criminal investigator.

Darlene Dedman reportedly had a difficult childhood. In 1983, at age eighteen, she sought to be emancipated from her parents and for some reason she was adopted by an older family friend, John Watson. Darlene later married and had children, and the family lived with Watson in Harrodsburg, Kentucky.

Watson was a Marine Corps combat veteran who was drawing a nice pension. Darlene became conversant regarding survivor benefits for veteran pensioners. She learned that as John's adult daughter, she was not eligible for those benefits upon his death. A surviving spouse, on the other hand, would qualify. Dedman started to hatch a new plan to obtain Watson's benefits upon his death when she met a long-lost cousin, Nelva Holland, at a family funeral. They struck up a friendship resulting in Nelva residing with Darlene, her husband, their kids, and Darlene's adoptive father, John Watson. Nelva wanted to attend nursing school but learned that she was required to be covered by a health insurance policy to do so. Darlene decided to adopt Nelva to qualify her as a dependent on her husband's insurance. At this point, Nelva was legally Darlene's daughter and John's granddaughter.

Darlene mentioned to Nelva that she was trying to come up with a way to draw Watson's survivor benefits upon his death. One day, after an argument with Nelva, she kicked Nelva out of the house. But after cooling off a bit, she offered Nelva a deal. "You can come back here if you agree to marry John Watson." Darlene knew that if the two remained married for over one year, Nelva was entitled to draw those benefits for the rest of her life. But the deal was going to be that, while the pension was going to be in Nelva's name, the check would be deposited in Darlene's bank account, and Nelva would only receive a small portion.

Nelva agreed to marry John, who was many years her senior. The marriage was going to exist only on paper, a secret that would be acknowledged only when it was time to draw the pension. In 1997, John, Darlene, and Nelva made a trip to Arkansas to see other family members. While there, Darlene arranged for the two to be married by a justice of the peace. Nelva had just married her grandfather. She was now her own grandmother. She also was her mother's stepmother. This all made my head hurt.

A LITTLE OVER a year into the sham marriage, John Watson died. Darlene reported the death to the DOD and put together the paperwork for the claim for Nelva. As planned, Nelva endorsed the checks and Darlene got the money. Things went along swimmingly for the next five or six years. Then in 2005, Darlene's son accused Nelva of molesting him. Nelva denied it, but Darlene pressed charges. Nelva moved away, but not before telling Darlene that she was now going to keep the checks that were in her name. That would prove to be a bad move for all involved. Darlene decided that she couldn't let Nelva profit off the scheme that she had crafted. She reported the sham marriage to the DOD. She lied and said she had only recently learned of the marriage and that Nelva was receiving a survivor's pension. That story was easily refuted with the bank records, Nelva's testimony, and Arkansas marriage records that showed Darlene as a witness to the wedding ceremony.

Nelva and Darlene were indicted for conspiracy to defraud the DOD, and Darlene additionally was charged with lying to an investigator. Nelva agreed to plead guilty and testify against Darlene. Darlene was defiant and decided to make us prove the case at trial. Her defense was that Nelva had done everything on her own and without Darlene's involvement. She deviated from the story she told the DOD agent to one where she knew of the marriage, but that she only recently learned that under Arkansas law, it was illegal to marry your adopted granddaughter. We called neighbors to testify that they never knew of the Watson-Holland marriage, that the two did not publicly hold themselves out as husband and wife. It didn't take long for the jury to convict Darlene, and she was sentenced to twenty-seven months in prison and ordered to pay $200,000 in restitution to the DOD. Nelva received three years of probation.

THOUGH THE FACTS of the case are unusual and interesting, it was the legal issues that arose on appeal that made this case stand out even more. We almost lost the case on appeal, with a two-to-one vote for affirming the verdict. First, there was the legal issue surrounding the use of the sham marriage theory by the prosecution. We had indicted using parallel theories. One was that a marriage on paper only, designed to obtain government benefits, is, in and of itself, fraud. The court of appeals held that a sham marriage is not illegal, unless it is spelled out in the statute covering the government program at issue. For example, the immigration statutes prohibit paper marriages entered into just for the purpose of legalizing entry into the country. Immigration officials are authorized to go behind the facts of the marriage to see if it is genuine. Not so with the statute governing military pensions.

What I learned was that Congress decided on a length of marriage requirement—one year—to screen out fraudulent marriages. Once that year has elapsed, the new spouse is entitled to the pension even if there was never any intent to live as spouses in the customary understanding of that relationship. The rationale for this is that it would be too time-consuming and intrusive to investigate marriages for authenticity.

Fortunately, we had another theory of the prosecution—the marriage was illegal under Arkansas law. Arkansas's incest and marriage statutes voids marriage to one's grandchildren including those adopted. Therefore, Nelva swore on the claim forms that she was legally married to her adoptive grandfather, Watson. That was a lie, and she was not entitled to the pension.

However, there was a problem within this theory as well. We had to prove that Nelva's statement was made with knowledge that it was false or that she turned a blind eye to what was true. Two appellate judges relied on the *willful blindness* argument to uphold the verdict. A dissenting judge reluctantly would have overturned the conviction, despite Darlene's obvious attempt at a scam, because he said there was insufficient evidence that Darlene had any inkling that the marriage was unlawful under Arkansas law. The majority said that Darlene's scheming behavior evidenced a reckless disregard for whether the marriage was lawful.

Now here is the real irony: Under Kentucky law, John and Nelva's marriage would have been valid. Kentucky only prohibits marriages involving certain levels of consanguinity—meaning blood kin. Watson and Holland were not blood relatives. So, the very act of choosing Arkansas as the venue for the wedding—obviously designed to hide the marriage from the public—was Darlene's undoing. I guess this comes under the rubric of poetic justice.

ONE OTHER LESSON that came out of the appeal concerns the rule governing the process by which the jury is advised of the content of state laws, like Arkansas. I asked the trial judge to take judicial notice of Arkansas law and instruct the jury that it says marrying your granddaughter by adoption is void. Judicial notice, however, is reserved for evidence or facts, not statutes. The court must instruct the jury on all the relevant law. So, the judge should have placed what Arkansas law says about such marriages into the jury instructions. Though we used the wrong process, the court held it to be a harmless error. Bottom line: In Kentucky, you can be your own grandma.

Dr. Roger Browne

The Oxy Express

Drug prosecutions have long been a major part of the life and focus of most US attorney's offices. To give you an idea of the scale of this effort, the criminal section of our office in Lexington was divided into the drug section and the general crimes section. The drug section was staffed with several prosecutors and their assistants who devoted all their time and effort to this area of the law. These prosecutors developed close working relationships with DEA agents, tirelessly working beside them, pursuing drug cartels and gangs from around the country that had tentacles into our district. They were experts on the complex federal drug laws and the ever-changing illegal drugs du jour. They spoke a special language. This was truly a specialty, and one that I was not a part of, with a few exceptions.

I prosecuted several drug charges that arose incidental to some other crime I was pursuing. If a felon in possession of a firearm was found to have drugs, we would add that charge to the indictment. However, if the suspect was part of a larger network of drug dealers being pursued by the DEA, we would refer the matter to the drug prosecutors. But in 2007, by happenstance, I backed my way into a major drug investigation and prosecution. That case was significant to me because I learned so much about the drug culture that arose from the proliferation of pain-killer medications, especially OxyContin, that created a crisis in Eastern Kentucky.

FOR SEVERAL MONTHS in 2007, I worked on a currency counterfeiting conspiracy in the Ashland, Kentucky area. A network of local drug addicts was printing twenty-dollar bills and passing them at local stores and other businesses. It was fairly unsophisticated operation, and we quickly infiltrated the group and shut it down. I was working with a Secret Service agent and a small contingent of police officers from the small Greenup County town of Russell. Detective Tim Wilson was my primary contact with that police department. We developed a close working relationship and friendship.

Most of the counterfeiters plead guilty, but not John Riggs, a former standout athlete in the Ashland area. During trial preparation I decided I needed to meet in person with one of the cooperating counterfeiters who had agreed to testify against Riggs. She couldn't come to my office for the interview because she was incarcerated in a facility many miles away from Lexington. So, Tim Wilson and another officer picked me up in Lexington and we drove to the distant facility for the trial preparation session.

On the road, Wilson began to discuss a frustration he was having with an ongoing investigation. I believe Wilson and other Russell officers were part of a drug investigation task force in that area called FADE (Fivco Area Drug Enforcement). The task force had developed a case against a group of local individuals who were purchasing large quantities of prescription pain killers from pill mills—so-called pain clinics—in southern Florida. A brief back story is helpful here.

Kentucky had just gone through the OxyContin crisis, where the very pure form of oxycodone was hyped and pushed by Purdue Pharma. Doctors were incentivized to prescribe heavy doses on a repetitive basis. Many people were addicted and traveled from doctor to doctor across the state to obtain additional and redundant prescriptions. The addicts took some of the pills and sold the rest to finance the next round.

Kentucky had addressed the problem in part by establishing a digital reporting platform for doctors and pharmacists called KASPER (Kentucky All Schedule Prescription Electronic Reporting). The providers of narcotics now had to report to the state, by name of the recipient, each prescription. Investigators had a database from which they could identify addicts, pill mill doctors, and dirty pharmacies. This changed the landscape for everyone. Addicts couldn't doctor shop within the state any longer. Doctors could not prescribe large quantities of pills. And thus arose the Oxy Express—my name for it.

Florida had very lax drug distribution laws and no platform for reporting like Kentucky's KASPER. I'm not sure who first started the game, but it took off like a wildfire. It worked like this. An enterprising drug dealer in a community like Russell would enlist haulers or mules to travel to Florida—as many as they could get in a car or van—to seek out prescriptions for Soma, Xanax, and oxycodone. The drug dealer would fund the expedition. The mules would relate made-up symptoms to a compliant doctor who would prescribe a month supply of all three drugs. Everything was paid for in cash. No insurance was used.

Some of these mules were addicts, others were just making money. Once back in Kentucky the drug dealer would give addicts some of the drugs and pay in cash those who were not addicts; there would be lots of drugs left over for him to sell on the street. The mules would make numerous trips each month. Some of the addicts couldn't resist taking large quantities of drugs in the car on the way home. Interstate I-75 developed a reputation for overdose deaths by travelers back to Kentucky.

Detective Wilson and FADE had developed an informant who was part of the local Oxy Express network. He had made recorded phone calls, allowing officers to diagram the network and its constituent parts. They knew who was going to Florida and when. They knew who the local head of the snake was—the person funding the network. They knew which clinics in Fort Lauderdale were dirty. They even had recordings between the informant and a dirty doctor in Florida, where they discussed the next trip and the load of Kentuckians that were coming. FADE had even sent undercover officers to the Florida clinic where they photographed automobile license plates from Kentucky and other Appalachian states in the parking lot. Wilson told me he couldn't get anyone on the federal level to show interest in the case. He had called DEA in Florida, but to those guys this little enterprise was not of great significance. They were working on stopping multimillion-dollar drug smuggling schemes from Central and South America. They weren't impressed by a bunch of hillbillies and their prescription meds. Tim didn't believe he had the jurisdiction or the resources to go after the doctors or clinics in Florida.

I was impressed by the work Detective Wilson described and his passion for doing something about the problem. I told him that if we could establish that the dirty doctors were part of a conspiracy to transport unlawfully distributed pills from Florida to Kentucky, we feds would have jurisdiction to prosecute that conspiracy, doctors and all, in our district. I said I would take Wilson's case back to the office and see if I could get our drug section to open a case and get the DEA involved on our end.

The head of the drug section at the time was my good friend, fellow golfer, and fellow biker, Kevin Dicken. Kevin immediately jumped on the case with both feet. Before long, Wilson, Kevin, the Lexington DEA, and others were putting together a case that would take down the pill mills that were sending their poison to Eastern Kentucky. I told Kevin I had developed a keen interest in the case and would like to tag along as a second chair.

Over the next few weeks, the agents and officers developed more evidence against Dr. Roger Browne and his clinic. A plan was developed for a raid and arrest. We would travel as a group to Fort Lauderdale. Additional surveillance of the clinic would establish that our Kentucky addicts were continuing to patronize the clinic. The informant would make additional phone calls advising Dr. Browne of the next wave of patients. They would discuss matters that could prove that Browne knew he was prescribing to Kentucky addicts and that he was turning a blind eye—if he didn't know for certain—that the symptoms were false, and the drugs improperly prescribed. The informant and undercover officers would pretend to be drug seekers, providing us with testimony about the scant or nonexistent medical examination that preceded the prescription.

Once in Fort Lauderdale, we met local DEA agents, and they provided us with an office to work out of while we prepared for a search and arrest. That office had decided that our case was meritorious and provided excellent assistance while we were there. Kevin drafted a very detailed affidavit in support of a search warrant and arrest of Dr. Browne. We were warned by a local prosecutor that the magistrate we would present the warrant to was a stickler for detail and that we better have our facts straight before submitting the affidavit to him. That proved true; we had to submit at least two revisions before he signed the warrant.

We then prepared to conduct the search. This was going to be fun. Agents and officers were to be staged at various positions around the outside of the clinic. Several undercover officers, deputies from Russell, were going to go inside the clinic and pose as patients. Once they were seen by Dr. Browne, they were to signal to the entry team and the raid would begin. That would consist of entry with guns drawn. (I sometimes wondered if that wasn't overkill in this situation, but you never know what a desperate drug addict will do when he thinks he's going to jail.) Everyone would be put on the floor. Then one by one, patients, staff, and doctors would be interviewed. Most significantly, we had authority under the warrant to pull a large sample of medical files, and any file that pertained to a Kentucky resident. As it turned out, over 500 files on Kentucky patients were seized. All were to be analyzed to establish the pattern of visit, cash, and prescriptions.

No sooner had the undercover officers entered the clinic then they signaled that the raid should commence because they had been "made" by some of the patients in the lobby. They were recognized as cops from back home and patients began to freak out and leave the clinic. The officers jumped into action and prevented a mass exodus as the entry team came rushing in. Once the premises was secured, Kevin and I were summonsed, and the interviews and record selection began.

It was a long day. We interviewed and collected records up into the night. Kevin left to obtain a supplemental search warrant for some item that we had not known to cover in our initial warrant. I believe Kevin even had to get up early the next morning to meet the magistrate for yet another warrant. We were all exhausted by the work, but it was satisfying. I had finally seen the inner workings of the drug unit in full display.

Back in Kentucky, Dr. Browne and about ten other individuals were indicted for an interstate drug distribution scheme. Ultimately, all plead guilty. Browne was sentenced to three years in prison.

Leonard Lawson

The Acquittal

In early 2008, my office phone rang and my friend, FBI Agent Clay Mason, asked, "Are you sitting down?" I said, "Yes, what's happening?" By the tone of his voice, I knew that he was on to something big. He said he had just concluded an interview with an employee of the Kentucky Transportation Cabinet (KTC), Jim Rummage, and what he learned was explosive. And that was the beginning of probably the most notorious, laborious, and most disappointing case of my entire career.

Clay Mason, for several years, though assigned to the FBI resident agency in Lexington, managed a satellite office in Frankfort, the state capital. There he developed working relationships with many state government officials. He was available to listen to any whistleblower who suspected public corruption. Many people knew of his presence, and he was often provided potential leads for prosecution. (In a regrettable move, the FBI later closed that office.)

Clay and I already had worked several cases together, most notably a scam run by a group of vanity publishers who took money from aspiring authors to publish their books but never publishing them. We had a great working relationship, and he frequently called to chat about some legal issue (Clay was a lawyer himself), and he brought cases directly to me for prosecution. This KTC matter was one such referral.

In Kentucky, the construction and maintenance of state highways and roads are the responsibility of the KTC. It is a huge department with hundreds of employees, and it doles out millions of dollars per year for road construction and repair. Very little of this construction work is done by the KTC employees. Private companies are awarded contracts for the projects.

These highway contracts are very much coveted by the contractors across the state. To give everyone a fair opportunity, a bidding procedure was established. When a road contract is ready for bidding, contractors registered with the state receive notice of the project and a detailed description of the requirements and specifications for the job. Contractors interested in the job submit secret, sealed, written proposals, and their bid. A committee of engineers within KTC conduct a public meeting to open the bids and award the contract. In order to assess the feasibility of the bids, a cabinet engineer prepares a secret document called the *engineer's estimate.* This is a detailed itemized calculation of what the project is expected to cost in materials and labor. The project is supposed to be awarded to the lowest bidder unless, based on the engineer's estimate, all bids are too high or unreasonable.

Anytime a large amount of government money is up for award, there's the potential for fraud or corruption. For years, suspicions of graft, cronyism, and political gamesmanship surrounded the KTC. Highway contractors would financially back a political party or candidate in exchange for the hope of obtaining highway work. Contractors have been known to collude and agree which contractor would bid on which project—an antitrust violation. It was suspected that political operatives would place their thumb on the scales of the bidding process to direct contracts to their favorite contractor.

ONE OF THE largest, and undoubtedly the most politically active and powerful Kentucky contractors was Leonard Lawson and his company, Mountain Enterprises. Lawson was shrewd when it came to business, with a rag-to-riches story. He started as a construction laborer in Eastern Kentucky and ultimately becoming a wealthy broker of power, money, and influence in Kentucky politics. He hedged his bets and often contributed to both Democrats and Republicans. He knew all the governors and all the transportation secretaries.

In the 1980s, Lawson pleaded guilty in federal court to bid rigging, and he was the subject of at least two other federal antitrust investigations that never went to indictment. His name was familiar to me when FBI Agent Mason brought me this new case. In fact, a few years prior, Lawson approached me as I ate dinner in a hotel restaurant in Pikeville and discussed a case I was prosecuting against another local business executive, Ross Harris. Lawson was very friendly and expressed support for the prosecution.

In 2008, Steve Beshear, a Democrat, replaced Republican Ernie Fletcher as governor. Beshear had been hearing the stories about the corruption in the KTC and vowed publicly to clean up the state transportation agency. He reached out to a retired state senator Joe Prather to be his transportation secretary and encouraged him to investigate the rumors and allegations and take the appropriate corrective action.

In the weeks that followed, state investigators began interviews and audits within KTC looking for any evidence of corruption—bribes, kickbacks, bid rigging or the like. This caused high anxiety among those in the cabinet whose consciences were not clear. One such employee was Clay Mason's interviewee, Jim Rummage.

Rummage was a mid-level manager within the KTC. He had become close to Bill Nighbert, the Republican cabinet secretary under Gov. Fletcher. Rummage did not have the authority to make substantive decisions within the cabinet, but he was in a position to see them made and had found himself complicit in what he knew to be wrongdoing. When the investigators began snooping around, he convinced himself that it was only a matter of time before his complicity in crimes was uncovered. He was especially afraid that those with power would make him the scapegoat. He decided to take preemptive action, hire an attorney, and tell all. He might still be in trouble but at least he would have grounds for receiving leniency. He told Clay Mason the following story.

Rummage said he had become the go-between for Secretary Nighbert and Leonard Lawson in a bid-rigging scheme. It started when Nighbert directed him one day to go obtain the engineer's estimate for an upcoming project and deliver it to Leonard Lawson at Lawson's house. The theory was that Lawson could use this secret engineer's estimate to determine what he needed to bid to win the contract. Rummage called Lawson at a phone number provided by Nighbert, and a meeting was arranged. Rummage drove to Lawson's vast estate outside of Lexington and gave him an envelope containing the estimate. Lawson showed Rummage around his home and the two engaged in small talk. As Rummage was leaving, Lawson slipped a wad of cash into his shirt pocket. Rummage didn't count it until he was alone. It was $5,000.

This process was repeated several times. Each time Rummage received $5,000 cash. On one occasion Lawson went to a freezer in his garage and retrieved frozen fish wrapped in paper and labeled with a magic marker. He gave it to Rummage, telling him that this was fish he had caught while deep sea fishing in Florida. On another occasion he met and briefly spoke with Lawson's wife.

If Rummage's story was true, both Nighbert and Lawson would be guilty of federal crimes. First, there was the illegal diversion of property (the engineer's estimate) from a state agency (the KTC) that annually received large sums of federal funding. Then, if we could find where Lawson had given Nighbert something of value for the engineer's estimate, that would be bribery. And, of course, there was a conspiracy to commit federal crimes.

FOR THE NEXT few months, Clay and I attempted to corroborate Rummage's story. Most notable were a series of recorded phone calls we had Rummage make to Leonard Lawson. The pretext was that Rummage had been approached by investigators and asked about certain contracts and had made statements that lead Rummage to believe that they already knew a lot about Lawson getting the estimates, and that he had some involvement. He said he had consulted with a lawyer and had been advised to cooperate. He was inclined to do just that but wanted Lawson to know before he went forward with the plan. In essence, he was telling Lawson, "They know about the estimates and the money you gave me, and I'm going to have to expose you."

On the tapes, Lawson never admits to receiving the estimates or giving Rummage money. In fact, he specifically denies it but he strongly advises Rummage to keep his mouth shut, saying things like, "The only way they can prove anything is if you admit it." He said the worse thing I ever did in my life would be to cooperate with the police and plead guilty. He offered to pay for Rummage's attorney, even trying to steer him away from the one currently representing him and hire him one who would work with Lawson's attorney. Once he said he hoped Rummage wasn't recording their conversation. In my opinion, the conversations were very corroborative of Rummage's story. This was not the way Lawson would interact with someone making up a story that implicated him. He certainly would not be a logical person from whom Rummage would seek legal advice. Lawson would have blown him off immediately if there were no prior collusion between the two.

Another corroborative item of evidence was Rummage's banking habits during the period he said he was receiving the cash from Lawson. We had asked Rummage what he did with all that cash. We were hoping he had promptly deposited it in the bank, where there would be a paper trail. But he said he just spent it on daily expenses. He used cash for groceries, gasoline, and hardware store as he didn't like to use cards. He said his bank statements would reflect that he regularly withdrew several hundred dollars of cash at a time to carry around with him. Then, for the period during which he was supposedly receiving cash from Lawson there would be no such withdrawals. And he was right. To me this was powerful corroboration. And then there was the package of fish. In passing, Rummage told us he still had one of the packages of fish Lawson gave him at home in his freezer. We obtained that fish, photographed it and its wrapper. This corroborated his story about visiting Lawson's home. You just can't make up something like this.

Rummage said that during the month or so before he came forward, he had become so anxious he couldn't sleep or eat and had lost a ton of weight. We were able to document that with medical records. And then there was the absence of any motive to falsely implicate such powerful people and incriminate himself in the process. In short, I felt we had a strong case—but ultimately a jury disagreed.

WE INDICTED BOTH Lawson and Nighbert on the previously mentioned charges. Thus, began over a year of very contentious pretrial practice with a battalion of very expensive and thorough lawyers from Barnes and Thornburg in Indianapolis, as well as several Kentucky lawyers. My colleague and friend Kevin Dicken joined me as cocounsel, but we were a small team compared to our opposition. I know defense counsel often lament the enormous resources of the federal government, but in this case our resources paled in comparison to those of the defense. Lawson funded everything. Through back channels we later learned that he spent over $10 million on the defense.

Every aspect of the defense received top dollar. An expert analyzed the probability, based on statistical theory, of whether Lawson's bidding on the contracts in question comported with him having access to the estimates. They did mock trials to see how average citizens off the street viewed the case. They had one lawyer who came to trial just for the jury selection. They had a jury selection expert to listen to juror responses to screening questions (*voir dire*) and opine on their political or philosophical leanings. They had done social media analysis of the jury pool. They studied the political donation history and other political activity of potential jurors.

During the trial, Lawson rented out an entire floor of a nearby boutique hotel for the trial team. The hotel provided them with a dining room and full dinner each evening.

After the jury acquitted both defendants of all charges, Kevin and I did some postmortem analysis. How could twelve people listen to those incriminating tapes and agree to acquit. I now have an opinion of what happened. I begin with an overheard conversation. As I was leaving the courtroom to return to our office in the courthouse, I passed a reporter calling in the verdict to his office. One of the jurors was standing a short distance away, probably waiting for a ride home. The reporter said in a loud voice, "They were found innocent." The juror defensively blurted out, "They were found not guilty. They weren't found innocent. There's a difference."

She was right. And for her that distinction was comforting. I later mentioned that exchange to the reporter in question. He explained that he clearly understood the difference between not guilty and innocent, but that he intentionally used *innocent* because of another instance where he called in a not guilty verdict and the person on the other end of the call misunderstood him and published the verdict as guilty. In any event, that juror's exclamation told me that the jury probably believed there was a crime, but for reasons other than the evidence, they would not convict—calling it reasonable doubt.

Weeks later, Clay Mason reported back to me the results of a conversation he had after the trial with another juror. He had seen the man in Frankfort in one of the state office buildings and briefly discussed the case. The jury did not like Jim Rummage. I got the impression that the juror was trying to say they didn't believe him, but

I now think they didn't like the case, the prosecution, and the forces behind the prosecution.

IN MY OPINION, the trial was, for this jury, evidence of a politically motivated prosecution. The end of the Fletcher administration was controversial and contentious. Republicans alleged misconduct by the opposing party, feeling set upon by ambitious and opportunistic Democrats. Ultimately, it resulted in Fletcher being a one-term governor, and the Democrats taking the governor's office. Republicans believed their people had been mistreated. Nighbert was Fletcher's chosen secretary. Beshear had vowed to clean up after Nighbert. Joe Prather was Beshear's guy.

This case against Nightbert looked like Democratic forces were continuing to pile on the Republicans. The political overtones of the case were exacerbated by the witnesses called to testify. We called Governor Beshear to the stand to testify to a phone conversation he had with Lawson when he took office. Beshear said he had heard that Leonard Lawson was saying that Beshear and company would not give him a fair shake. Beshear called Lawson to assure him that he would be treated fairly. Significantly, Lawson then told Beshear that there was an employee in KTC, Jim Rummage, who was a good man and needed to be promoted. David Williams, one of the top Republicans in the state senate, also testified. Nighbert had worked for Williams immediately after stepping down as KYT secretary and before taking a position with a Pikeville business affiliated with Lawson. This was part of a string of dots we connected to show how Nighbert was rewarded by Lawson for giving him the engineer estimates. The defense elicited favorable testimony from Williams, who testified that he had never seen Nighbert do anything improper. Again, the case sounded like a Democrats vs. Republican affair.

Transportation Secretary Joe Prather also testified about how when he took office Nighbert met with him and said, "If you want to succeed as secretary you have to have a good relationship with Leonard Lawson." I have to interject here a humorous anecdote from Prather's testimony. He was being cross-examined by one of the defense attorneys who kept trying to get him to agree to the premise of leading questions. Prather kept correcting the attorney and his premise. Finally, Prather shook his head, "There ain't no taters where you're digging."

The perception that politics permeated this case, I believe, was shared by Judge Karl Forester, a Republican appointment to the bench. At several junctures, Judge Forester subtly communicated his dislike of the case to the jury. I think Forester's perception contributed to several very squirrelly evidentiary rulings that put before the jury irrelevant information that was prejudicial to the prosecution. It contributed to an unspoken argument that the case was politically motivated, the prosecutors were unprofessional, and that Jim Rummage might be part of some kind of sinister plot. I have no doubt that the jury selection team for the defense vetted jurors for their political leanings—Republican, you're on, Democrat, you're off.

JUDGE FORESTER'S DISLIKE of our case was evident even during opening statements. I began reading to the jury excerpts from transcripts of the recordings that we intended to introduce. These were sections I believed were most incriminating. Without any objection from the defense, the judge cut me off in mid-sentence and said, "No, you will not read transcripts to the jury in opening." I had to regroup and reorganize my thoughts to continue. Then in his opening, the defense attorney used a power point presentation that contained excerpts from different pieces of evidence that they believed would be introduced. The judge allowed that.

The court's ruling about a certain recording of the prosecution *work product* was mystifying. Before each recorded phone call between Rummage and Lawson, the prosecution team of attorneys and agents would brainstorm how Rummage should begin his conversation with Lawson. In other words, we were coaching him on the pretext for the call. We wanted to maximize the possibility that Lawson would make incriminating statements. This is a very typical and acceptable investigative procedure.

In one of the calls to Lawson, Rummage was told to call a lawyer who worked for Lawson, and he was provided the phone number. After hanging up with Lawson, and before placing the call to the lawyer, we had a planning session for the call to the lawyer. Unbeknownst to all of us on the team, a tape recorder happened to be recording during that planning session. I don't recall what exactly we told Rummage to say, but it was some story that I knew would be reported back to Lawson—something to the effect that Rummage was going to cooperate with the authorities, despite Lawson's wishes to the contrary. As is my inclination, I made a graphic and ribald observation. "I bet that will pucker his ass." The reference was to Lawson's ass, but at trial the defense would argue that I was trying to set up an innocent lawyer.

There is nothing about that planning session that was remotely relevant to the guilt or innocence of Lawson. The content of the actual pretextual calls was the relevant evidence. But the court bought the defense argument that somehow the planning session gave meaning to the pretextual call. I believe that the court let it in because it made us look bad.

Letting our planning session be captured on a recording was our first mistake. We compounded that by failing to carefully check what was being handed over to the defense in discovery. The planning session recording was accidentally mingled in with the relevant recordings. When I discovered this, I requested that it be returned. It clearly was not discoverable under any theory. The defense refused and advanced their argument that the recordings showed that the prosecution trying to frame an attorney for Lawson. The judge agreed.

WHEN JIM RUMMAGE had finished his testimony one day he was escorted by an FBI agent out the back door of the courthouse to avoid the press. As he was getting into the agent's car, he and the agent shared a humorous moment, and a reporter snapped a picture of Rummage laughing. The picture appeared in the Lexington paper the next day. The newspaper article was just reporting that Rummage had testified and made no reference to the picture being relevant to Rummage's credibility. But the defense pounced. The court granted the defense request to introduce the photo, over our objection, as evidence that Rummage was not truthful, that this whole trial was just a joke to him. Another bizarre ruling.

When the case agent, Clay Mason, was testifying he was deflecting defense questions that had faulty premises, and thus could not be answered with a yes or no. He would explain and qualify his answer, as he should. After a few of these exchanges, Judge Forester snapped at Mason and barked, "Just answer the question!" Here was the judge exhibiting to the jury his displeasure with the government's chief investigator.

One of the counts in the indictment involved Nighbert receiving a bribe from Lawson for his provision of the engineer's estimate. The bribe compensation consisted of a job given to Nighbert by a company partially owned by Lawson, Mountain Enterprises. Nighbert was paid a handsome salary and provided a new Toyota Avalon for *consulting*. We showed the paychecks going into Nighbert's account, but there was absolutely no evidence that he did any work for the compensation. The judge directed a verdict of not guilty on this count. The jury should have been given this for consideration. The ruling was that we had no evidence that Lawson was a part of this arrangement. It's as if the judge had never heard of circumstantial evidence. I don't think this jury would have convicted on that count, but the act of dismissing the charge outright was just more of an indication of the judge's bias.

I've been involved in several cases where I believed the presiding judge exhibited undue displeasure with defense counsel or the defendant. Sometimes I think judges don't realize the effect this can have on a juror. Typically, this works in favor of the prosecution. Here, it went the other way.

This was a grinding case with an unhappy ending for the prosecution. But I have no regrets about bringing it. Former FBI Director James Comey used to refer to prosecutors who will not try a case they aren't guaranteed to win as the "chickenshit club." This case needed to be tried. It shone a light on the coziness between the KTC and Leonard Lawson, even if it did not result in his conviction. *The Herald Leader* captured that sentiment in an editorial and cartoon which read, *Business As Usual* in reference to the verdict. Kerry Harvey, a state cabinet secretary while the Lawson case was being tried, told me the prosecution had a deterrent effect on those in state government because of the evidence of cronyism and politics in contracting that was reported. That is why this case was important.

Richie Farmer

The Unforgettable

Of all the cases I handled over my career in criminal law, the Richie Farmer prosecution seems to be my signature case in the sense that more people—colleagues, childhood buddies, family and so on—know about my involvement and have mentioned it to me. It is nowhere near the most complicated and time-consuming case I've worked, nor one of major societal importance. It was just a media darling. It's a former Kentucky basketball star who rose to political prominence only to fall from grace.

Richie Farmer was well known in the state of Kentucky beginning in the late 1980s. He was a prolific high school hoops scorer, leading Clay County High School to a state championship and another title game. He scored over fifty points in the championship game. He was recruited to play basketball at the University of Kentucky at a time when the university was at rock bottom because of a recruiting scandal and NCAA probation.

Rick Pitino had been hired to replace Eddie Sutton, but he did not have the usual five-star athletes from across the nation because none of them wanted to come to a school prohibited from postseason play. But to his credit, Pitino recruited a team of all-state Kentucky high schoolers who would go on to punch above their weight and make a name for themselves as the *Unforgettables*—Deron Feldhaus, John Pelphrey, and Richie Farmer, along with Sean Woods from

Indiana. Pitino would take that team to an SEC regular season championship one year and almost to the Final Four, with the help of Jamaal Mashburn, the next year. Those guys truly were unforgettable in the way they breathed life into a lifeless Kentucky fan base.

Some years after playing for Kentucky, Richie Farmer decided to capitalize on his fame and name recognition and run for state agriculture commissioner. Could there be a better name for that position than Farmer? Because the position is of only moderate influence and importance, Richie had no problem coasting to an election victory in 2003. He was reelected to another four-year term in 2008.

Farmer was in over his head. He had no executive experience, and he had an oversized sense of entitlement. He believed that because of who he was he should be able to enter a commercial establishment and receive practically anything for free. Rumors and stories began to flow about the many abuses of his power and position.

There were stories about him having state employees build an outdoor basketball court at his private residence. He allegedly had new flat-screen televisions placed in his office so he could follow March Madness basketball. He had the state put his entire family up in a hotel in Lexington during the state tournament under the guise of running a Kentucky Proud promotional booth there. We later were told of instances where Richie would take a group of friends to a restaurant in Lexington and walk out without paying.

Most egregiously, when Kentucky sponsored a regional conference for agriculture commissioners, he ordered Kentucky-made rifles for all the commissioners and added extra ones to the order as gifts for his family and friends, all at government expense. He once went to an ATV store in Eastern Kentucky and left with a vehicle— *forgetting* to pay for it. He was going through a divorce and placed on the state payroll his girlfriend who seldom came to the office or did any work. Adding to the concerns were stories of a pain-killer addiction that stemmed from an old sports injury. Witnesses told us of wasted days and nights where Richie could not function because of his drug-induced stupor.

When Farmer's term of office expired in 2013, he was succeeded by James Comer, who later became a US congressman. Comer immediately addressed the rampant rumors about corruption in the commissioner's office by requesting an audit of the office. Kentucky State Auditor Adam Edelen uncovered extensive evidence of corruption, and his report was referred to the Kentucky attorney general's office (KAG) for criminal investigation. At or about the time of this investigation, the Republican candidate for Governor, David Williams, selected Farmer as his lieutenant governor running mate.

KAG conferred with the FBI and a decision was made to take some of the allegations federal. I received a call from the state investigators and was asked to take the case. Special Agent Ken Kirk was assigned as well. We began the grand jury phase of the investigation. I recruited a new, very capable prosecutor in our office, Andy Boone, to join me on the case. Over several months we interviewed numerous witnesses who laid out convincing evidence of Farmer's outsized sense of entitlement and graft. We eventually indicted Farmer for theft from a state agency—the Department of Agriculture—that had been federally funded.

I fully expected a brutal pretrial motion practice from the defense and ultimately a protracted jury trial. Farmer's lawyer, Guthrie True, was a seasoned trial attorney who did not shy away from trials. I was fully aware of the perception of some in the community and state that this was all one big political witch hunt. This false impression was the product of the political environment in Kentucky at the time. Attorney General Jack Conway, a Democrat, was going to run for governor. The US Attorney was Kerry Harvey, a Democrat. So, to some, this had the feel of politics—Democrats trying to eliminate a rival Republican.

One day while the case was making its way through the court system, I received a call from Larry Forgy, a prominent Republican in Lexington. Larry was a former candidate for governor himself and well known for his outspoken candor. I had become acquainted with Larry during the trial of Leonard Lawson and Bill Nighbert. Forgy disliked Lawson, believing Lawson had cost him the governorship some years earlier. Larry had attended Lawson's trial every day and often provided encouragement during the trial. But on the day of this phone call, he was blunt. I should not be prosecuting Farmer for what was described in the indictment. He said, "Ken, I've supported you in several cases, but this one is just not right. Richie's not doing anything different than what goes on in Frankfort every day." I told Larry we would have to disagree on this one and we left it at that.

Apparently, Farmer did not have the stomach for a protracted period of negative press with the potential for a significant prison sentence. In short order, we began plea negotiations and ultimately reached a deal.

The day of the guilty plea in Frankfort, press from all over the state assembled outside the federal courthouse. They were wanting a statement from the US Attorney's Office about the case and the proceedings. I had in our office a somewhat negative reputation for being a press hound, meaning that I enjoyed making statements to reporters. The joke was, "Don't get between KT (nickname) and a camera, you'll get run over." But our office policy was for assistant US attorneys to make a no comment when a microphone was put in our face. I hated this policy as I thought we were doing the citizens' business, and we should address them. But I had begrudgingly begun to abide by the policy and expected to do the same that day.

To my surprise, the word came from the office that Kerry Harvey was approving me giving a public statement on camera to the press lingering in front of the courthouse. I think Kerry knew that this case was important to me and he wanted me to have that closure. I appreciated the gesture. And so that is what happened. I made a statement to about twenty or more reporters and camera people outside the courthouse. My little speech expressed regret that someone who had achieved so much and who had so much potential had fallen so far. That little speech made the evening news across Kentucky, which is why so many of my friends and family identify me with this case.

Motorcycle Theft Case

Soft Tails and Fat Boys

In early 2013, David Grise, the first assistant US attorney in Lexington, appeared in my office doorway with one of those, *I need a favor from you* looks on his face. "What are you doing in March," he asked. "I think you're getting ready to tell me," I replied.

Steve Smith, a prosecutor in the London satellite office, had a major trial scheduled to begin in March. It was a case that had lingered far too long, with many delays and plea negotiations. It needed to be tried, now. But Steve was experiencing some health issues and was going to take a leave of absence. If humanly possible, someone needed to take over the case and try it as currently scheduled. I was going to be that person.

Fellow prosecutor Erin Roth was assigned to work the case with me. I had never tried a case with Erin, but this one proved that we were a good team. We would handle several more cases together over the next several years. Each of us sought out the other when we needed cocounsel. Our first case together proved complex and interesting.

In the mid-2000s, a coalition of insurance companies, law enforcement officials, court clerks, and others in the eastern part of the country, became aware of a suspicious pattern of motorcycle titling, especially in Ohio and Kentucky. These bikes looked to have been Harley Davidsons that were rebuilt with after-market parts and did not bear the vehicle identification number (VIN) placed on them by the original manufacturer.

Former KSP officer turned vehicle identification expert, Bill Riley, teamed up with experts from Harley Davidson and other experts to investigate these bikes. The suspicion was that the bikes were stolen and then modified by removing the parts that bore VIN and other identification to avoid detection.

Investigators traced the recently titled motorcycles back to specific thefts. First, they identified all the bikes titled by a group of suspects, including Jason Chapman, Christina Bannigan, and Shon Fields. From the public records they could identify the current owner of the motorcycle. Then they located that owner. Using secret industry records that revealed hidden identifiers on the bike, or using manufacturers' paint codes they could identify the original bike and its VIN number.

The next step was to run the VIN numbers through national databases, like National Criminal Identification Center (NCIC), to determine whether a bike with that VIN number had ever been reported stolen. Around fifty such reports were discovered. Each person who reported a theft was interviewed. Officers requested photographs of each stolen bike, and the owners were asked to identify modifications, accessories, or damage to the bike that could corroborate that the bike in question was, indeed, stolen.

Once officers connected a specific stolen bike to one of the newly titled bikes, a very unfortunate event occurred. The authorities went back to the new owners and gave them the bad news. "That beautiful bike you just purchased is stolen. We have to take it with us." Thus, there were innocent victims on both ends of these events—the original owners and those who bought the stolen bikes. The recovered bikes were placed in a warehouse for storage pending further investigation, charges, and trial. The ownership of each bike was ultimately sorted out among insurance companies, new owners, and original owners.

In 2011 our London office indicted ten individuals for conspiracy, interstate transportation of stolen property (ITSP), and money laundering. The ITSP charge is self-explanatory, but the money-laundering theory was unusual. Money laundering is defined as a financial transaction involving the known proceeds of a *specified unlawful activity* (SUA), done to conceal the source of the funds. ITSP is a statutorily listed SUA, and the motorcycles were deemed to be the proceeds thereof. Another statute provided that titling a vehicle constitutes a financial transaction. So, the theory was that the defendants laundered the stolen bikes by modifying and titling them.

Investigators were able to flip several of the thieves, including Christina Bannigan and Shon Fields. Christina very thoroughly and methodically told of the sophisticated operation of the theft ring headed up by Greg Chapman (who died before being charged) and his son Jason Chapman.

The team would target annual motorcycle rallies like those in Myrtle Beach, South Carolina, Sturgis, South Dakota, and Florida. Members of the theft ring would travel to the event and stay in hotels. For a day or two they would ride around town scoping out dead spots in camera fields and other places where they could successfully steal bikes. They looked for bikes, almost always Harleys, that they could start with a pair of vice grips or channel locks. Sometimes women involved in the scheme would lure a male biker into a bar for drinks, distracting him, while other members of the group stole his bike.

The stolen bikes were loaded in trailers and transported to Ohio, where they were stripped of identifiers and modified with after-market parts. The modified bikes were titled in Ohio or Kentucky under the pretense that they were kit bikes (bikes assembled by individuals) or wrecked bikes that had been rebuilt. Most of these were then sold to John Slusher in Pineville, Kentucky and Richard Meade, Mark Justice, and George Ferguson in Ashland, Kentucky. These individuals then sold them to the public through their existing commercial establishments. The theory of the prosecution was that these *fences* knew the workings of the theft conspiracy and facilitated it by providing a market.

FELLOW PROSECTOR ERIN and I had only a few weeks to prepare for trial. We divided the labor to accomplish all we needed to do. The days were long, and free weekends were nonexistent. By the time the trial had rolled around, in March 2013, many of the defendants, especially the theft-ring members, had pleaded guilty. Left for trial were three fences in the Ashland area—Meade, Ferguson, and Justice. Their defense was simply that they did not know that the bikes they purchased and then resold were stolen. Our evidence needed to show that they either knew they were stolen, or that they turned a blind eye to what was obvious.

Justice's attorney was his longtime friend Garis Pruitt. I was told by a colleague that Pruitt had been a well-respected advocate in his day but now seemed diminished. His antics provided many laughs for Erin and me as the trial progressed. In opening statement, Pruitt was pooh-poohing the government's evidence and theories and loudly announced, "The government's theory is a *Fig Newton* (instead of *figment*) of their imagination." Erin looked at me and whispered, "Did he just say Fig Newton?" I was trying to suppress laughter but nodded in the affirmative. When we got a break, we all just guffawed at the slip—or was it a slip? One day during the trial, one of our witnesses was describing the loading and moving of motorcycles off Justice's property and transporting them to another location. Pruitt suddenly jumped up and boomed, "Objection!"

"Approach the bench," Judge Van Tatenhove ordered. "What is the basis for your objection?" he asked Pruitt. "It's not true!" Pruit exclaimed. The judge got a quizzical look on his face. "I don't think that is a basis for an objection to this testimony," the judge said. But Pruitt persisted. "Judge, there's no evidence that these bikes were ever at my client's place." The judge replied, "This testimony *is* evidence of that. Objection overruled." Erin and I just shook our heads and later we shared a good laugh.

Pruitt also was in the middle of a controversial twist in the evidence, which, in my opinion, reflected either incompetence or dishonesty. Critical to our case against Justice was the fact that a motorcycle that he claimed was wrecked and rebuilt was unsupported by any bill of sale or other documents that should have existed if Justice's version of events were true. I had made that point in opening statement, and it had been mentioned several times during the trial.

We were confident that the defense had no such documents because we had not received any such papers from the defense. A defendant, through counsel, has a duty to turn over to the prosecution—after receiving the prosecution's documents—any evidence it intends to introduce at trial.

On the witness stand, Justice magically produced a bill of sale or related document and claimed to have provided them to his attorney many months ago. We went sidebar with the judge and objected to the breach of the *reciprocal discovery* obligation. Pruitt claimed that he had not realized the significance of the documents when given to him, and only in the last day or so had found the documents. Out of an abundance of caution, Judge Van Tatenhove allowed the documents into evidence. These documents appeared to me to be fakes and forgeries of recent manufacture. They reflected some private transaction and could not be obtained from a public record. I accused, through my questioning, Justice of fabricating evidence to meet the challenge I had laid down in opening.

In retrospect, the judge's ruling inured to our benefit. The jury had already heard about these documents and excluding them now could be perceived as the government thwarting the accused's right to defend himself. It was much more powerful that we could just use the highly suspicious documents as evidence of what prosecutor's call *consciousness of guilt.* Whenever a defendant engages in conduct that is deceptive or obstructive—such as making a false exculpatory statement or introducing a fake document or alibi—the jury can infer that he did so because he knew he was guilty.

Judge Van Tatenhove is well known for his creativity in handling the presentation of evidence. He is not a slave to tradition or protocol. (In a subsequent case, he agreed to take the jury by van to a remote crime scene, at my request.) If a litigant proposes a better way to get evidence before the jury in a more understandable way, he is all ears.

Crucial to this prosecution was the jury's confidence in our experts who would trace these rebuilt bikes back to stolen Harleys from Sturgis or Myrtle Beach bike rallies. We wanted the jury to see real motorcycles and have the experts point out relevant parts. We did not want to rely on photographs.

The judge authorized two unusual procedures in this regard. The first was that we brought a huge motorcycle into the courthouse, up the elevator to the courtroom, and down the aisle where it was parked in front of the jury box. Our Harley Davidson expert then educated the jury on the parts of the bike that would be discussed during trial. The jurors hung on his every word, and some leaned over the rail to get a better look.

The second procedure involved moving the trial from the courtroom to a jury room on the first floor where we could stage most of the stolen and recovered bikes that we had in a warehouse. Different counts of the indictment were based on different motorcycles recovered. Each motorcycle was assigned its individual number—bikes one to sixty, say. So, we wanted the specific bike in question in front of the jury as officers discussed it. It would have been a Herculean and time-consuming task to bring the bikes up an elevator one by one as they were discussed. So, the bikes were brought to that large jury room where each was quickly available to roll over to the jury box when its turn was up.

The judge set up this makeshift courtroom with the same physical footprint as the real courtroom: The judge's bench, the jury box, the witness stand, and counsel table were in their respective positions. The procedure worked quite well, and we were grateful to the judge for accommodating our presentation of evidence.

During this case, Erin and I learned more about motorcycles, especially Harleys, than we ever wanted to know. We learned the different styles and names—Fat Boy, Soft Tail, Road King, Dog. These made for hilarious plays on words—not always acceptable in polite company. We learned that owning and riding a Harley is a lifelong dream and practice for many men and women, and the theft of their bike can be a traumatic event. This isn't just a means of transportation. It is a signature, an expression of individuality. Owners customize their Harleys with accessories and personal art. This proved useful in identifying stolen bikes.

George Ferguson's attorney, Jeremy Clark, provided some comic relief prior to and during his closing argument. Clark was a friendly man and a pleasure to work with and against. The day before closing argument, as is customary in such cases, counsel alert their opponents to any demonstrative exhibits they intend to use during the argument that they think could elicit an objection. This is to provide the opposition an opportunity to assert an objection outside the presence of the jury, and it serves to avoid an interruption in the flow of the argument.

Jeremy provided us with a large, blown-up photograph of jelly doughnuts. Yes, jelly doughnuts in a motorcycle theft case. We were dumbfounded and amused. What could possibly be the relevance of jelly doughnuts? We discussed moving to preclude use of the photograph, but we were eager to see how he was going to work that into the case. We did not see any harm in this.

Jeremy displayed the photo for the jury to see. Then he pointed to the doughnuts and said, "You can't tell from the outside of a jelly doughnut whether the filling is grape, cherry or cream." He said his client, Ferguson, was dealing with jelly doughnut motorcycles. They looked great on the outside, but he had no idea what was inside of them. He said the government witnesses had the advantage of taking them apart and seeing inside. Ferguson was relying on what he saw on the surface, his lawyer contended.

I guess the doughnuts impressed the jury. They acquitted Ferguson. (Actually, we believed that Ferguson came across as a likable pawn of Justice and Meade. He just blindly followed them and should not have been lumped into the same category as the two.) The next time I encountered Jeremy in a case I asked if he was going to use the jelly doughnut argument again. We had a good laugh.

MEADE AND JUSTICE were convicted, and their sentencing was scheduled for several months later. But the sentencing proved to be an elusive event because of the insertion into the case of a new attorney for Meade, Katherine Macpherson from Michigan. She filed something seldom seen—a motion for arrest of judgment. Therein, and in subsequent pleadings, she made many untrue allegations of prosecutorial misconduct, and twisted arguments about the law. Thus began a couple of years of seemingly endless litigation, at the district, circuit, and supreme court levels. Motion after motion, *interlocutory appeals*, petitions for *writs of mandamus* and prohibition, petitions for *writs of certiorari*, and motions to reconsider. Each of her pleadings was more bizarre than the last. She said she was mourning the death of actor Robin Williams; she mentioned something about a Navy SEAL; she went on about how the US Supreme Court justices were in danger, and on and on. It was truly out there. At one point we put on a motion to have her held in contempt of court for lodging demonstrably false allegations about the judge and prosecutors, without offering any evidence in support. Ultimately, her pleadings were all dismissed, and we withdrew our motion for sanctions as unnecessary piling on.

More than two years after conviction in 2015, Meade and Justice were sentenced. Justice received eighteen months and Meade twenty-four. The judgment, conviction, and sentence were upheld on appeal. The case was not final until 2017, over six years after indictment.

Wendell Keith Hall

Bribery in the Mountains

One day in June 2012, Lexington Herald Leader politics reporter John Cheves published an article outlining a recent investigation by the Kentucky Energy and Environment Cabinet that raised eyebrows among those of us who investigate and prosecute public corruption cases. It involved a state representative from Pikeville, W. Keith Hall, who was also a significant coal operator. Hall also had a history of legislative ethics issues, which made him subject to increased scrutiny by law enforcement and administrative investigators.

The investigation was initiated by a phone call Hall had made to cabinet engineers, complaining that he was being shaken down for money by a state mine reclamation inspector. He said Inspector Kelly Shortridge was threatening to issue trumped-up citations for reclamation violations, or even shut-down orders, if Hall did not pay him. Hall said he had already given Shortridge significant amounts of money—"He likes the Benjamins"—but Shortridge wanted more.

Shortridge was interviewed by reporter Cheves for the article and denied any threatening, but curiously, said tauntingly, "If Keith Hall says he's paid me money, I wonder what he paid me for. Could it be something illegal?" This all sounded like a dispute between a briber and a bribee, with the briber racing to be the first to complain publicly. It was a case our office might be interested in pursuing. Soon after the article was published, investigations began in the US Department of the Interior, and the Kentucky Legislative Ethics Commission.

I called John Cheves and asked to see his underlying evidence for the story. He was very cooperative. My office reached out to the FBI, which assigned Special Agent Jim Huggins to the case. I opened a case in the US Attorney's Office and asked my colleague Erin Roth to join me. The US Department of Interior, which is responsible for federal surface mine reclamation, assigned Inspector Laura Hast. Our investigation initially revealed that Hall had numerous coal mine leases in Eastern Kentucky, and Kelly Shortridge was, in fact, the state mine reclamation inspector assigned to periodically inspect Hall's mines. In 2011, Shortridge's supervisors removed Shortridge from Hall's mines because it had become apparent that the two had become chummy, to the point that Hall tried to use his position as a legislator to have Shortridge promoted. Shortridge's removal so enraged him that he threatened workplace violence, resulting in his suspension for fifteen days. We suspected that Hall had been bribing Shortridge to give him a pass on reclamation violations, or perhaps to give him advanced notice of inspections so that he could make corrections or other moves to avoid citations. Both sides in this cozy arrangement between operator and inspector seemed to have the propensity to push the boundaries of the law and ethics.

IN ANY POTENTIAL bribery case, tracing money flow is vital. So, we sought the assistance of a financial expert. FBI analyst Tressa Whittington was assigned the case, and that was a godsend, as she methodically blew the case wide open. Her job was to analyze financial and banking records of the targets—Shortridge and Hall—to identify specific transactions that could represent bribe money moving. Oftentimes, subjects disguise the payments using shell corporations or straw persons to avoid leaving an obvious and incriminating money paper trail. So, Tressa had to look behind the transaction to see if it could be disguised bribes.

The first step in the financial analysis was to identify any bank account that could have been used to pay the bribe—that is, any account for which either Shortridge, Hall, or even their spouses, had signature authority. Tressa would use several different data platforms to identify accounts, such as FinCen, Accurint, or LexisNexis.

We compiled a list of relevant bank accounts and sent grand jury subpoenas to the respective banks requesting any and all bank records for any account associated with the target. There were a lot of them as Hall had numerous businesses, each with its own account. Tressa began to see a repetitious type of transaction that piqued her curiosity. Checks were being written off various Hall-owned businesses payable to some entity called DKJ Consulting, Inc., with a memo line denoting *consulting*. She looked up the company in the publicly available records of the Kentucky secretary of state and learned that the incorporator and owner was the wife of Kelly Shortridge. Further investigation revealed that Ms. Shortridge did not have a history of any kind of consulting experience, nor any skill that would benefit a coal company, so these transactions were believed to be a disguised conduit of Hall's money to Shortridge.

We conducted numerous interviews of Hall's current and former employees and developed testimony that Hall had asked various individuals to pay bills for Shortridge, for which Hall would reimburse them—another common method of disguising bribes. Especially helpful to the investigation was Hall's ex-wife, Stephanie. She was quite the character. You've heard the saying that "Hell hath no fury like a woman scorned."

Keith and Stephanie Hall divorced soon after Stephanie received a text message from Keith that was meant for Keith's mistress. At the time, Keith was staying in Frankfort for the legislative session while Stephanie was running the businesses in Pikeville. The message said something about how good it was last night and expressing his love for the mistress. That ended the marriage, but not before Stephanie drove several hours to Frankfort and trashed Keith's office for his staff to see. When Keith next returned to Pikeville, he had to retrieve his personal belongings and clothes out of the yard, all in view of neighbors.

Stephanie was eager to help with the investigation, and she told us about the methods Keith used to doctor business records, especially how he used the term *consulting* on checks. She explained that the checks to DKJ were not for actual consulting—although she didn't know in real time that these went to Shortridge.

We put together a timeline that showed the relationship between the payments to Shortridge and the dates of Shortridge's inspections of Hall's coal mines. We lined up experts to visit Hall's mines and note obvious violations that should have been cited by Shortridge. The expert would convey what an honest inspector would have done based on the obvious violations. In other words, certain violations, such as mining off the permit site, were impossible to overlook.

In the fall of 2014, we indicted Hall and Shortridge. The former was charged with bribery and the latter with bribery and several other charges. Shortridge pleaded guilty before trial and agreed to testify against Hall. We fretted about how he would come across to the jury. He had such a lousy record as an inspector, and during his cooperation prior to trial, he had told us several different versions of the same story. Each time we had to disclose the discrepancy to his attorneys, the father-son team of Brent and Bryce Caldwell. We learned of another scam he was perpetrating regarding solicitation of money under false pretenses that also had to be disclosed to the defense. At one point I said to Brent Caldwell, "That Shortridge sure is full of truth, because none has ever come out of him." In the end we felt Shortridge had to testify to demonstrate how he had turned a blind eye to mine violations in exchange for bribes.

Hall's defense was that, while it is true that he gave money from time to time to Shortridge, those funds were out of friendship, actual consulting, or part of a legitimate business arrangement. He said he never intended to induce Shortridge to ignore violations. He didn't know it was improper to give money to friends just because they inspected his mine. He pointed to many other people he had helped over the years. He had crocodile tears and his voice cracked when he told of how he had helped kids in need in Millard, Kentucky.

Erin dismantled Hall on cross-examination. Hall didn't have good answers to why, if he thought the payments were proper, he went to such extremes to hide them. At one point Erin demonstrated that Hall was performing, not testifying. She asked him something to the effect, "Mr. Hall, did you pay other mine inspectors to forgo violations?" In obviously feigned self-righteousness and indignation Hall retorted forcefully, "No, I am insulted that you would ask me that! I have never paid off a mine inspector."

In closing, I highlighted the implausibility of Hall's claim that he didn't know it was improper to do financial and business deals with his mine inspector. "He wants you to believe that this educated, experienced state representative and coal operator, had no idea that it is improper for the inspector and the inspected to be in bed together. Everyone here knows that doesn't pass the smell test." Hall was convicted by the jury in less than two hours of deliberation.

THE PROSECUTION TEAM had paid up rooms in Pikeville for that evening because we were prepared to come back the next day for continued deliberations. The deliberations being brief, and it being late afternoon when the verdict was announced, we decided to stay in town, have dinner, and unwind. The team of me, Erin, paralegal Mandy Poynter, Hast, Tressa and Jim Huggins had become close during the case we had a wonderful evening of storytelling, recounting the humorous events of the trial, and general merriment.

Keith Hall was sentenced to approximately seven years and was allowed to stay out of prison on bond pending his appeal. His conviction was upheld, but we were not finished with him. Months later, I received a call from an investigator for a WCI company. He said, "Mr. Taylor, I understand you were the prosecutor who convicted Keith Hall a while back." I confirmed, and he said, "You want another crack at him?"

Apparently, while Hall was awaiting trial in the above case, he was committing WCI fraud. One of his companies that sold a liquid treatment for coal that reduced dust, was asked by another company with whom it was doing business to provide a certificate of workers' comp insurance. (Proof that his employees were covered by WCI.) Hall was not carrying such insurance, a violation of state law. To resolve this problem, Hall decided to fake and forge the certificates of insurance. It was brazen conduct from one already in the throes of a criminal prosecution.

Using some type of computer software, Hall was able to generate certificates that looked like the real thing. Then he forged the signature of a corporate official within the insurance company. We indicted Hall on mail and wire fraud charges, and capped that off with aggravated identity theft, which involves using the personal identification information of another person while committing fraud. That carried a mandatory two-year sentence to run consecutively to any other sentence received. Hall plead guilty to the identify theft and received two additional years of incarceration.

Rooster Risner—Salyersville

The Vote Buying Capital

It was business as usual in Magoffin County in 2014—and that business was vote buying. In 2012 I had successfully prosecuted Salyersville man Randy Salyer for buying votes in the 2010 race for sheriff and other local offices. It was our belief that Salyers was a part of a vote-buying conspiracy headed up by the sitting county Judge Executive Charles "Doc" Hardin. We had hoped to flip Salyer against Hardin, but he dutifully stood trial, kept his mouth shut, and served a twenty-one-month sentence. When released, Hardin hired Salyer to be the deputy county judge executive. I guess it pays to be loyal.

At that time, I was a member of an informal task force led by the Kentucky secretary of state (SOS), and composed of prosecutors, law enforcement agencies, and other government entities that monitored election statistics. One of those statistics was the number and percentage of the votes that were absentee ballots. Historically, absentee ballots were the most abused method of voting, and when the numbers were exceptionally high, vote buying might be afoot.

When I received a report from SOS following the primary and then the general election cycles that year, Magoffin County was at or near the top of all counties for absentee ballots cast. A typical percentage was around 2 or 3 percent, but Magoffin came in over 15 percent.

Absentee ballot purchasing was the desired method of vote buying by the fraudsters in Magoffin County. Vote buyers would pay voters to apply for, and deliver to them, an absentee ballot. The fraudsters had the vote seller sign the absentee ballot documents before mailing it into the county clerk.

Our team of investigators from the FBI and the Kentucky Attorney General's Office put in motion our proven investigative plan. First, we obtained the names of all persons who voted absentee in Magoffin. We shared the list with trusted sources and concerned citizens who were complaining about absentee ballot fraud, and they told us who on the list was a likely ballot seller. People knew that Joe Blow was regularly unemployed and generally apathetic about life and would not have made the effort to vote on his own. His sister Jill Blow was a drug addict and always trying to make a quick buck. With a list of likely sellers in hand, we formed interview teams from both state and federal agencies and did as many simultaneous interviews as possible. Agents informed the Joe Blows that we were not interested in prosecuting them. We were after the buyers, and the political bosses who formed, funded, and directed the vote-buying scheme. This technique is surprisingly effective. Around fifteen to twenty witnesses admitted selling their absentee ballots and told us who bought them and how the process unfolded.

Our next step was to approach the money handlers to attempt to identify the organizers. This is typically less successful than flipping the sellers. Of the seven or eight middlemen we confronted only one, Scotty McCarty, came clean. McCarty told us an eye-opening story of historical corruption in the polls of Magoffin County. Before relating that story, I'll describe persuasive analysis of the vote totals done by FBI financial analyst Tressa Whittington, which we used to corroborate McCarty's testimony that the absentee vote-buying scheme was responsible for turning election results in favor of vote-buying conspirators.

A slate of candidates had pooled money and resources, and

engaged jointly in vote buying, as a way of getting more bang for their buck. McCarty told us that the slate in 2014 was Doc Hardin for county judge executive, Rooster Risner for magistrate, and Rene Sheperd for county clerk. When a ballot was bought, the buyer would vote all three candidates. Tressa compared the percentage of votes for each of these three candidates for election day and absentee voting.

Tressa reported that on election day Hardin received 46 percent of the votes, but his absentee count was 69 percent. Risner had 50 percent on election day and 76 percent by absentee ballot. Shepherd had 51 percent election day and 78 percent absentee. Tressa also analyzed other non-slate candidates in Magoffin and a nearby control county and confirmed that the percentages of live and absentee votes were similar. With basic math, Tressa showed that had Hardin and Risner received the same percentage of absentee votes as they did election day votes, both would have lost their elections.

SCOTTY MCCARTY, OUR key witness and informant, had been a basketball star at Magoffin County High School. Judge Doc Hardin had taken an interest in Scotty and was very friendly with him even after he graduated. One day in 2002, Hardin called Scotty into his office and gave him a thousand dollars and told him to find people who wanted to sell their vote. Scotty paid fifty dollars for their absentee ballots. Thereafter, Scotty was "in the fold," as he put it, of the vote-buying group, and he told us about his activities in 2006, 2008, 2010, and 2012, as background for what transpired in 2014. The methods differed somewhat from year to year depending on the slate of candidates and other vote-buying participants. Scotty told of one election where he was a poll worker and had control of a device that allowed him to activate the voting machine before each voter entered the voting booth. He was instructed by candidate Rooster Risner and others to vote often during the day but to keep track of the number. Scotty placed pennies in one pocket, and each time he voted he would move a penny from one pocket to another. At the end of the day, he had voted sixty times.

When the polls closed, and before taking the results and ledger to the clerk's office, Scotty stopped by Gary Risner's house, where Risner forged in the poll book ledger the signature of sixty registered voters who had not voted that day. In another election, Risner sent a person to Scotty at a voting station with a blue ticket in hand. After Scotty voted, he would give the person a red ticket to take back to Risner for payment. According to Scotty, the consistent members of this fraudulent scheme were deputy county clerk Larry Shepherd, Gary Risner, Randy Salyer, and the head honcho, Doc Hardin.

Unfortunately, when conducting the investigation and preparing an indictment in 2014, the statute of limitations had expired for most of the conduct Scotty described. I considered charging it as a long-running conspiracy that started back in 2002 or earlier. But after closely reviewing the facts, I didn't believe there was enough evidence of ongoing activity to support that tactic. It looked more like separate conspiracies, though similar in scope, for each election cycle. And, regrettably, for 2014, Scotty didn't have any real interaction with Doc Hardin, so I did not seek to indict Hardin. We indicted Scotty, Gary Risner, Larry Shepherd, Tammy Jo Risner, and Mason Daniels.

A very important part of our evidence involved one Jamie Gibson, a Salyersville resident who was a felon and could not vote. He was also an active drug user and would frequently get so high that he would forget what he had said and done. So, he started to secretly video record transactions and conversations on his cell phone so that he could review them when he was sober. One day during the election campaign, Gibson met with Rooster Risner and told him that he had people lined up who wanted to sell their votes. Gibson got in a truck with Risner and switched on his video. He captured their entire conversation—most of it was just sound, as the phone was in his pocket, but a few frames captured pictures of Risner in the truck.

Risner could be heard telling Jamie that he would have to personally meet the vote sellers. He told Gibson, "Now don't say anything about this. We don't want to wind up in court and all that bullshit. We don't want to go to the penitentiary." FBI Agent Ken Kirk obtained this video form Jamie, and it became a great trial exhibit. Risner's goose was cooked when it was played to the jury, but like Randy Salyer before him, Risner kept his mouth shut and took a proverbial bullet for Doc Hardin.

OUR TRIAL EVIDENCE consisted of the persuasive testimony of McCarty, the testimony of thirteen voters who had sold their absentee ballots or who were paid to allow Shepherd to vote for them in the voting booth, testimony from Jamie Gibson along with the playing of his video, and the vote analysis of Tressa Whittington. All defendants were convicted except for Mason Daniel. Rooster Risner was sentenced to just under two years, Tami Jo Risner received a one-year sentence, and Larry Shepherd received just over two years imprisonment. McCarty received a misdemeanor conviction as a reward for his cooperation. There were major legal challenges to whether our evidence could be used in court, and the case was heavily appealed. In the end, convictions were upheld.

While we never made a case against Doc Hardin, at least he finally lost the election. I suspect that his name being mentioned at trial so often, and in a negative light, had something to do with his defeat. And, perhaps, just maybe, vote buying stopped in Salyersville. But maybe not.

Walter Wayne Brown and Winona Cox

Cherokee Nation

In my career I encountered a significant number of legal kooks and nut jobs. These are individuals who embrace pseudo-legal beliefs about the law and society. Included here are the tax protestors who argue that the national income tax laws were never ratified by Congress and therefore they don't have to pay taxes. More recently, the sovereign citizen movement has promoted the belief that the federal government is illegal and that the individual is sovereign and beyond the jurisdiction of the courts and the law. But the most memorable and amusing experience in this genre of defendants involved my encounter with the common law husband and wife duo Walter Wayne Brown and Winona Cox.

The story began in 2014 when my colleague Neeraj Gupta opened a tax fraud case against Winona. She had submitted false income tax returns, seeking refunds for taxes supposedly withheld for four calendar years in the first decade of the 2000s. This was known as the 1099 OID scam, which was popular among tax cheats at that time. Here's how it worked: We all know that the IRS requires persons or businesses that pay money that is taxable to third parties who are not employees, to report the income on Form 1099. There are several different types of 1099s. For example, independent contractors receive a 1099 from every company for whom they worked instead of a W-2. Banks report your annual interest income on another type of

1099. A lesser-known form in the field of finance is the 1099 OID. The initials stand for original issue discount. Certain bonds are offered to the public for an amount less than the face amount. For example, if you purchase a bond with a face value of $200 for $150, you can cash the bond at the end of the stated term for $200, making a profit of $50 over the life of the bond. But the federal government doesn't want to wait the five or more years for the bond to mature to receive its share. It requires the bond issuer to amortize on paper the amount of interest that is accruing each year and report that as income to you on a form 1099 OID. But, unlike a typical 1099 form, the bond issuer is required to withhold taxes from this income and submit it to the government.

Cox generated, and sent to the IRS, 1099 OID forms on behalf of a fictious bond issuer that purported to show that thousands of dollars of taxable interest had accrued on bonds in Cox's name, and that thousands of dollars had been withheld and sent to the treasury. Then, on her personal tax returns, she claimed thousands of dollars of fake deductions and exemptions that erased any tax liability. Thus, she claimed that she was entitled to a refund of the taxes withheld.

In most instances, these returns were flagged by the IRS as suspicious, and no refund was paid. There were so many of these flagged returns at the time that the IRS investigators just put them in a file to review later. But amazingly, someone approved a refund of more than $60,000 for one year. When the error was discovered, attempts were made to recoup the money, but Cox transferred all her real estate and cars to others and plead poverty. That's when IRS criminal investigators came looking for her.

My colleague, Neeraj, obtained an indictment against Cox charging a count of making a false claim against the government for each of the tax returns and a count of obstructing an IRS investigation. Soon thereafter, the weird legal claims began. Cox, or someone on her behalf, began to file some crazy motions and notices, which Neeraj shared with me. We had good laughs, and, at some point, Neeraj asked me to come join him on the case so I could enjoy the circus.

After Cox's arrest, but before her initial appearance and arraignment, Walter Brown filed a long notice and motion seeking to dismiss the indictment. The pleading was captioned, IN THE TRIBAL COURT OF THE ANIYVWIYA GRAND FIRE COUNCIL FOR THE CHEROKEE NATION OF INDIANS. The heading referred to "The Great two row 'Wampum Belt' of Peace and Friendship Among Nations." The body of the motion contained a lot of legal analysis of Indian rights under various treaties and stated that Winona Cox's case was being transferred from federal court to the Cherokee court. It was signed by Judge Navin-Chadra Naidu. At arraignment, Magistrate Judge Wier dismissed the motion because Brown was not a lawyer.

Following a dispute with her appointed lawyer, Rachel Yavelak, Cox sought to substitute new counsel, Wegani Anisahoni, supposedly a tribal law advocate. Neeraj did some internet research and filed a notice informing the court of his findings. The so-called tribal advocate, Anisahoni, was an alias used by another oddball, Regan Dwayne Reedy, an anti-government individual who had sued President Obama and others for some grievance and called himself the "the living Aboriginal being." Neeraj told the court that his research revealed that the Aniywiya Cherokee tribe was comprised largely of Caucasian individuals and was not one of the listed federally recognized Cherokee tribes. Judge Hood denied the request for the Cherokee lawyer to take on the case and ordered Cox to find a real lawyer.

Shortly thereafter, Cox filed a notice that she wanted to hire one Jennifer Pawlowski from California. She began her notice "I, Jean (her middle name), have reviewed several attorneys . . . " and she believed this was the one she wanted, but there was no notice from the attorney or entry of appearance. She wanted a continuance of two months to get this lawyer up to speed. Judge Hood denied the motion for more time and set the trial for mid-April.

I wasn't overly surprised when on the day of trial Cox was a no-show. Cox's initial lawyer, Yavelak, told the judge that she had met with Cox the day before and that she had a witness subpoena served on Cox's husband, Walter Brown, who also did not appear. Warrants were issued for Brown and Cox, and the jury was dismissed. A quick investigation by the IRS agents revealed that Brown and Cox, the day before trial, had left their Lexington home in the hands of a friend and left for places unknown.

SEVERAL MONTHS LATER, US marshals in South Florida located Brown and Cox residing with several supposed Cherokees in a suburban house. The couple was transported back to Kentucky where we obtained an indictment for failure to appear and conspiracy to obstruct justice. Now we were going to have two trials. One for Cox on the tax matter, and one for both Cox and Brown on the failure to appear. But the situation only became more unpredictable, as Brown's behavior grew increasingly erratic and disconnected from reality.

Brown announced at his arraignment that he did not recognize the court's jurisdiction to try him, so the judge entered a not guilty plea on his behalf. Brown's court appointed counsel Matt Malone apparently didn't live up to Brown's expectations, because a few days before trial Brown notified the court that he had fired Malone and wished to represent himself. The day before trial Judge Hood conducted a hearing to determine whether Brown was legally competent to represent himself. That hearing was a hoot, as Brown was barely comprehensible. He said the court was one of admiralty and therefore had no criminal jurisdiction. He said he wanted to represent himself *"pro se in vitus,"* whatever that means. The court, he said, was committing a felony by putting him in admiralty jurisdiction, and "that flag that's flying right behind you, that's an admiralty flag of the United States." Judge Hood denied Brown's request to represent himself because he was not capable of presenting a rational defense, and, because his request was untimely.

Cox was convicted of all counts in the tax case and a few weeks later both Brown and Cox were convicted of all counts in the failure to appear indictment. None of that was unexpected. It was like shooting fish in a barrel. They simply had no defense.

Shortly after his conviction Brown filed in the record a pleading entitled *Writ of De Novo*—something no one had ever heard of. It was an incomprehensible rambling missive, but Judge Hood directed the prosecution to respond, probably with a smile and tongue firmly in his cheek. Ultimately, he would order that the pleading be stricken from the record. I decided to have a little fun with the matter.

The pleading from Brown was based on the writings and teachings of David Wynn Miller who had developed something he called *parse syntax grammar,* which was a new language that he claimed was the only true language and would allow tax protestors and other anti-government persons to successfully defend criminal cases. (YouTube clips of Miller's seminars are still online). At one pretrial conference Miller appeared in our court but Judge Hood made it clear to all that Miller would have no speaking role in the proceedings. Here is the somewhat mocking response I filed:

"The defendants have filed a pleading which they label a *Writ of De Novo*. The Court has directed the United States to respond. After carefully parsing the grammar and syntax of the defendants' pleading, it is apparent that no one in the office of the US Attorney has the intellectual faculties to respond to the substance of the pleading. The document and its attachment reflect the deranged ramblings of the infamous David Wynn Miller, self-professed genius, federal postal judge, and king of Hawaii. The pleading does not appear to allege any deprivation, seek any relief, or cite any authority—at least not in a language known to the government. The pleading is a nullity."

Cox was sentenced to thirty-six months in prison and Brown to sixteen. I believe this should have gone the other way. I believe that

Brown controlled Cox and put her up to all her crimes. Cox died of cancer while serving her time. Brown served his sentence, and his supervised release was moved to Florida. In 2021, Brown and another man were arrested for impersonating US marshals in Florida.

John Westine

The Recidivist

John Westine was a real piece of work. In my career I never witnessed a more prolific financial criminal, the most brazen and unrepentant scammer one can imagine. Let me clarify. There are two kinds of persistent scammers. One type makes no bones about it; they admit they are scammers, but refuse to change, and seek out their next victim at any opportunity. The other type always professes some rationalization—implausible though it may be—for their scheme and claim the allegations of fraud are the result of a misunderstanding. Westine was of the latter type.

When Westine came across my radar screen in 2014, I had no idea that the man we were pursuing had only recently been released from prison after serving twenty years for fraud, arising from a scheme to sell interests in oil and gas development programs. Remarkably, he was using almost an identical method to sell fraudulent interests in oil and gas production. It was déjà vu. The same aliases, the same practice of using shell companies and changing names when the law focused on him, the same excuses for inability to produce the promised results.

It started when financial analysts with our office analyzing bank reports from the Northern Kentucky area noticed that one Michael Hicks was opening bank accounts, depositing money of suspicious origin, and then wiring the money to a bank in California. Camera footage at ATM machines at the California bank showed John

Westine withdrawing large sums of cash. The Kentucky DFI entered the investigation and determined that the money being generated was from the sale of unregistered securities, a violation of state and federal law. DFI had begun to receive numerous complaints from investors in Westine-related companies about misrepresentations and deception in the selling of interests in oil and gas production projects.

Postal Inspector Roberta Bottoms traveled to California to gather evidence of Westine's activities. She obtained those video recordings of Westine withdrawing cash that was traceable to the oil and gas scheme. DFI Investigator Marni Gibson analyzed dozens of bank records reflecting the movement of investor money to Westine and his associates. She would take an investment check provided by a victim, examine it to determine where it was deposited, then obtain the records for that bank account. There she identified other investors and reached out to them. This process was repeated until she had profiled the entire financial picture. It was determined that Westine and others had fraudulently obtained around $3 million through three distinct, yet related, phases of a fraud scheme. The evidence demonstrated that Westine would operate through a set of companies and associates until the law closed in, then transition to other named companies and associates.

When we had put together a good deal of evidence against several individuals, we approached Michael Hicks in Northern Kentucky to confront him about his handling of the proceeds of fraud. He quickly agreed to cooperate, but he minimized his knowledge and involvement. He claimed that he was doing Westine, his half-brother, a favor by handling the money, but that he had no idea he was aiding and abetting a fraud scheme. Nevertheless, he agreed to assist in the investigation by making discreet, recorded phone calls.

We obtained an indictment against Westine, placed it under seal, and arrested him. Then we had Hicks make a call to a coconspirator and Westine associate, Henry Ramer, to discuss the arrest. The result was very incriminating to Ramer and Westine. Ramer had directed

Hicks to take all available money out of the bank and send it to him. Ramer said, "I am the boss now." He expressed no incredulity regarding the arrest of Westine, nor any surprise as to the allegations of fraud in the indictment.

Our investigation revealed that the scheme was a classic oil and gas fraud scam. Westine would buy old oil and gas leases for pennies, because they were essentially worthless, and generate fake reports and records, giving the impression that they were sitting on large reserves of oil. He used fake engineer and geologists reports to the same effect. He elicited the assistance of a Kentucky wildcat driller, Mark Cornell, and convinced him to sign a document containing a guarantee of seventy-five barrels a day of oil per well—an outlandish claim. He put all these materials together into prospectuses and used them in sales pitches to potential investors. These were sent by mail to investors across the country, thus implicating the federal mail fraud statute.

Westine used four or five aliases at different times during the scheme. He was John Ross, Michael Fairchild, James Harmon, and others. Emails we obtained by search warrant reflected that he and Ramer would discuss which of these identities he should use in any particular meeting with investors or investigators.

Investors told us about trips they took to Kentucky to see the wells when they began to question the lack of oil production they had been guaranteed. Driller Cornell would take them around the oil fields and show them wells that were just stage props—old wells that had little if any production. But Cornell would tell them that a big oil strike was imminent, and he would provide them with a Ball jar of oil as proof that the oil really existed.

Assistant US Attorney Neeraj Gupta volunteered to second chair the case with me. He was hungry for trial work, and he was an excellent addition to the team. He wanted to learn from my experience, and he contributed enormously to the brainstorming, strategizing, research, and other trial preparation. It was the beginning of a series of cases we tried together. When he was more experienced and had his own significant caseload, he would ask me to join him for trial. It was a great working relationship.

When arraigned on the indictment, Westine wanted to represent himself. He was a vexatious litigator throughout his criminal history, and he believed that he was smarter than any prosecutor or judge. He was well known for his frivolous lawsuits and motions, and he sued every warden he had ever known for violation of his rights. He claimed that every prosecutor was acting illegally and that all the charges against him were improperly brought.

Judge Van Tatenhove agreed to allow Westine to represent himself but appointed public defender Jeff Darling to act as a standby counsel—an attorney who could answer any legal questions Westine might have going forward.

Westine contended that he was truly trying to find oil for his investors, that he had never wished to defraud them, and that Cornell was the true culprit and the one who had made all the false representations to the investors. He denied that he used the aliases, or that these were real people, or that someone else had interjected these names in the case. It was truly a bizarre defense, but Westine was undaunted and seemed to enjoy the drama.

Humor was a substantial feature of the trial. One day, at the beginning of the proceedings, Westine told the judge that he didn't think he could go forward that day. He claimed that the night before, in his jail cell, another inmate played loud music all night, requiring him to put chunks of bar soap in his ears to mute the noise. But the soap got stuck and now he couldn't hear. The judge told Westine that we would proceed but that if he needed it he would provide Westine with earphones to amplify the sound. Then he said, "If it's any consolation, the prosecutor can't hear either." (That was indeed my reputation, as well as a fact.)

One morning, Westine appeared in his usual jeans, a button-down shirt, and a blazer. But this time he had a white pocket square protruding from the front blazer pocket. Upon close examination, the pocket square was made from toilet paper. We all had a good laugh. It felt like a fitting moment for someone who had mastered the art of deception. He wore it for the entirety of the trial.

A SIGNIFICANT WITNESS against Westine was the driller, Mark Cornell, who had entered a guilty plea and agreed to cooperate by testifying against Westine. The focus of Cornell's testimony was the seventy-five -barrel-per-day guarantee that had been so instrumental to the sales pitch. Numerous investors cited this guarantee as the primary reason they decided to put up their money. Cornell testified that he was simply presented the pre-drafted letter by Westine, and he signed it without any substantive discussion. In short, he was refuting Westine's defense that the driller, Cornell, was the real culprit and the true impetus behind the guarantee. Westine was claiming that Cornell had duped him as well.

The night following Cornell's testimony, DFI Investigator Gibson, looked back through the email traffic between Cornell and Westine. What Marni found was disturbing. The emails showed that Cornell had first proposed to Westine that the letter should say something like, "We'll do the best we can to find as much oil as possible," without making any guarantee. Westine replied suggesting that they needed the seventy-five-barrel-a-day figure and a guarantee. He further suggested that if Cornell was not willing to sign such a letter, he would look for another driller who could. Cornell relented and agreed to sign.

This evidence was no less damning to Westine than Cornell's testimony. It showed Westine was the mastermind behind the guarantee, and it showed he knew the figure was simply made up, but it also demonstrated that Cornell was minimizing his role in the origins of the guarantee letter. The defense could argue that if Cornell lied about his role in the scheme, his testimony couldn't be trusted regarding other aspects of the operation.

It was clear to me and Neeraj, that left uncorrected, Cornell's trial version of events would constitute a *Giglio violation* now that we knew the truth. (The prosecution must disclose any evidence in its possession that could call in question the credibility or motives of a witness.)

Before the jury came back to the courtroom for a new day of testimony, I asked for an audience with the judge. I explained that overnight we had discovered email evidence that contradicted Cornell's testimony in a significant respect, and that we would like to recall Cornell immediately to correct the record. Judge Van Tatenhove readily agreed that we needed to do that.

When he was back on the stand, I treated Cornell as an adverse witness—meaning I could impeach him using leading questions. I first laid the foundation for my cross-examination by asking him to confirm what he said on the stand the day before. Then I asked him if he had said the things in the emails. He professed not to remember the emails, so I displayed them on the overhead screen for everyone to see and we walked through them one by one. Of course, Cornell had to admit that he was indeed involved in discussions concerning the contents of the guarantee letter. As noted, it still looked very bad for Westine, but this process confirmed for the jury that the prosecution was honest and trustworthy. Despite the initial concern, the event was beneficial to the prosecution. Westine was convicted of all counts after a relatively short period of jury deliberation.

Cornell wasn't finished with his efforts to torpedo our case against Westine. Unbeknownst to the prosecution team, a civil branch of DFI was investigating complaints from investors about another oil and gas scheme in Central Kentucky at the same time as the Westine trial was being conducted. This investigation was pointing to Mark Cornell as the principal actor in a fraud scheme that looked almost identical to Westine's operation. If Cornell was involved in fraud at the time of his testimony, and if that was known to the prosecution, we would be, again, under the Giglio obligation to provide the evidence to Westine to use to impeach Cornell.

Long after the conclusion of the Westine trial—and a subsequent trial of a coconspirator Henry Ramer—the Cornell investigation came to the attention of the prosecution team. Victims of the Cornell scam had called our office after reading in the paper about Westine's involvement with Cornell. There we learned of the Cornell investigation and obtained whatever information we could from the DFI civil investigators. I could see a problem on the horizon. Both Ramer and Westine would, upon learning of this new information, claim they had been denied material that impeached Cornell's credibility.

We sent a notification to defense counsel for Ramer and Westine outlining the new evidence against Cornell. We filed a notice of the same to the court in which we argued that this new evidence should not disturb either verdict because it would not have changed the results at trial. Understandably, the defendants filed motions for a new trial. The court held a daylong hearing in which numerous witnesses from DFI, agents, and I testified. We laid out in brutal detail the timeline of our evolving knowledge of the parallel Cornell investigation. Judge Van Tatenhove denied the motions for new trial in a very long and well-reasoned opinion, agreeing with us that the information was not unlawfully withheld, and that Cornell had been so thoroughly impeached by both sides in the case there was no reason to believe that this material would have changed the verdict. In other words, Cornell was not essential to prove guilt in either trial.

Westine received forty years in prison. Judge Van Tatenhove noted that Westine was articulate, presented well and was not a dangerous criminal from a violence standpoint. "But you're just a thief," he said, "and justice calls for a very lengthy sentence. I believe this forty-year sentence is the longest imposed in any of my cases."

I can't begin to describe the number and nature of the motions and pleadings Westine filed in the years since his most recent conviction. He has been the subject of special status orders in both the district court and court of appeals (called a *vexatious litigator* designation) whereby his filings are screened by law clerks for frivolousness before being accepted for filings in the record. However, it doesn't seem to have slowed him down. When I retired in 2022, there were Westine motions pending, and I've learned since that more were filed in 2023. I recently learned that Westine died in custody in February 2025. I'm happy that John Westine is no longer my concern.

David Giles

What's That Smell?

One day in the summer of 2015, I was reading Lawrenceburg, Kentucky's weekly newspaper, the *Anderson News*, when a particular story piqued my interest. The piece was more in the nature of an Op-ed column by the editor of the paper describing a trip he had taken to the scene of a raw sewage dumping on a creek hillside in nearby Tyrone, Kentucky. There, he witnessed the remediation efforts of a private company, hired by the Kentucky state environmental disaster department as it attempted to vacuum up the stinky mess on the banks of Wildcat Creek.

I read with interest his recounting of the gag-provoking stench and the remnants of toilet paper and tampons that covered the hillside. He was bewildered, saddened, and angry by the realization that there was someone in his county who thought it was okay to dump an estimated thousand pounds of excrement into a pristine rural creek that was a tributary of the Kentucky River, which is the source of potable water for many Central Kentucky cities.

As a ten-year resident of Anderson County, I was very familiar with the many beautiful, meandering creeks and streams that permeated this rocky and rolling county. I lived just half a mile from Hammonds Creek, and only yards from an unnamed creek behind my cabin, which I called a flash creek because the only time it carried water was during the flash flooding that comes with torrential rain. I loved the scenic topography of Anderson County and was disgusted, like the editor, that someone would so horribly pollute it.

The editor went on to discuss the evidence the local sheriff had gathered regarding the incident, which pointed to a David Giles from Versailles as the culprit. There were no eyewitnesses to the dumping, but a local resident—who can be described as a *nose witness*—had followed his nose in a chain of events that produced substantial circumstantial evidence of guilt. Little did I know as I read the account that within two years I would try that case in federal court in Frankfort as a violation of the Federal Clean Water Act.

After reading the piece in the *Anderson News*, I quickly forgot about the dumping. The scene of the crime, Wildcat Creek, was at least five miles from where I lived, and I had never been there. It wasn't on my way to anything in my normal travel and routines, so it was out of sight and out of mind. I figured the culprit, Giles, would face misdemeanor illegal dumping charges, which seems like a slap on the wrist for the severity of the crime. But it wasn't in my professional area of concern or jurisdiction. What I was not familiar with at the time was the federal law dealing with polluting something called *the waters of the United States.*

Without getting too technical, the Federal Clean Water Act makes it a federal crime to discharge a pollutant, which certainly includes raw sewage, from a *point source* (too technical to discuss here). Just accept that a sewage pumper truck is a point source into a navigable stream or a tributary of such. I was unaware that the Kentucky environmental agency that conducted the cleanup had contacted the US Environmental Protection Agency (EPA) and their criminal investigators to see if this polluting event violated that act. After careful consideration of the evidence and facts, the EPA concluded that there was a federal violation and opened an investigation. Ultimately, the federal investigators reached out to the US Attorney's Office in Lexington for a prosecutor to be assigned to the case. But that was not my area of expertise in the office, so no one even mentioned the new case to me.

ONE DAY AT the office, I passed a man in the hallway who was wearing a sheriff's uniform, and I immediately recognized him. It was Anderson County Chief Deputy Sheriff Bryan Taylor. I first met Bryan several years prior during his investigation of a couple of burglaries at my cabin. He had identified and arrested the culprit and even recovered some stolen property. I had spent a significant amount of time with Bryan during that investigation and considered him a friend.

Bryan said he was there meeting with the prosecutor on a federal dumping case that originated in Anderson County. When he told me the nature of the case, the old piece I had read in the paper came rushing back to my memory. Because of my keen interest in Anderson County, and because the prosecutor he named, Erin Roth, was my great friend and colleague, I knew I had to join her on this case.

I immediately went to Erin and asked if she would like me to help. She was more than pleased. Erin was our office's specialist on environmental cases. She was already well-versed on the federal law in that area. I, on the other hand, had to study up on the Clean Water Act. Together we drafted an indictment and presented it to the grand jury. Soon we were preparing for trial in what would be a very technical, expert-laden area of the law.

As the case proceeded through the court system, Erin became pregnant with her second child, and her due date landed close to the trial date. She stayed involved during the entire preparation phase, fully aware that she wouldn't be able to attend the trial itself—a tough reality for any prosecutor. It's like going through grueling basketball practices knowing that you will not play in the actual games. Still, Erin was a trooper, and together we assembled the pieces of a persuasive case.

The little town that time has forgotten, Tyrone, sits alongside the Kentucky River, east of Lawrenceburg. It has only a handful of residents and very little commercial activity. Tyrone is not on the way to anywhere else, so its only visitors are those who live there or have a reason to visit someone there. I had never been there before joining this case.

Tyrone sits at the level of the Kentucky River but is surrounded by steep hillsides. At one end of Tyrone is Wildcat Creek, which traverses down the hillside and empties into the Kentucky River. Beside it is Wildcat Road, which is one lane in spots and climbs up the ravine, ending on US Highway 127 outside of Lawrenceburg. On one side there is a steep drop-off into the creek, and on the other is a wooded hillside. Essentially, Wildcat Road was carved out of that hillside. Often, when cars meet going in opposite directions, someone must back up to one of several wide spots and pull over to let the other pass.

THE INVESTIGATION STARTED one hot summer night near dusk. A resident of Tyrone was returning to his home at the lower end of Wildcat Road from US 127, as was his custom. (I've forgotten his name, so we'll call him James). The man was a lifelong resident of Tyrone and had a reputation for being an unofficial guardian of his beloved Wildcat Creek, which unfortunately attracted illegal trash dumpers because of its remoteness. James grew up playing, swimming, hiking, and camping in and near Wildcat Creek. It was a part of who he was, and one thing that angered him immensely was someone dumping their old refrigerator, furniture, or bags of garbage over the embankment toward the creek. He had had several confrontations with dumpers over the years and was diligent about getting things cleaned up whenever the dumping occurred.

One night, as he rounded a curve near the top of Wildcat Road, he noticed a large sewage pumping truck trying to turn around in one of the pullover wide spots in the road. It was unusual to see such a large truck on that road, and he thought it strange that it would turn around, rather than continuing up to Highway 127. James continued down Wildcat Road toward his home. Suddenly, as if hit by a wet towel in the face, James began gagging with the pungent smell of raw sewage. Each breath brought a new wave of nauseating stench as he drove faster to get beyond the smell.

When he reached the bottom of Wildcat Road, the stink was still strong but at least tolerable enough for him to pull over and assess the situation. He later testified that he realized exactly what had happened. That SOB in that sewage truck at the top of the hill had only minutes before dumped his entire load over the hill into the creek. The dump driver had been traveling up the road when he stopped, backed up to the edge of the road. After dumping, he apparently thought his only way out was to turn around and retrace his route. Had he continued up the road a little farther beyond the turnaround wide spot, he would have intersected US 127, and this case probably would never have been solved. This told James that the driver almost certainly was not a Tyrone resident.

James then knew that once he turned around, the dumper would be coming back down the road. James pulled his vehicle into a nearby driveway, turned off his lights, and waited. Sure enough, the truck passed James who fell in behind him. Apparently, the dumper realized he was being followed and sped up, but James stayed on his tail. The sewage truck took side streets in Tyrone and came to a stop in front of the home of a Tyrone resident.

David Giles, who was then unknown to James, got out of the truck as James pulled up in front of the house. "I know what you just did," James told Giles. "You dumped that shit over the hill." Giles denied the accusation, saying he also smelled sewage but that it must have been another sewage truck that he had seen on the road. He said he was up on Wildcat Road because he had a friend who lived there.

James stayed at the residence while he called the county judge executive, the sheriff's office, and anyone else he could think of. He was going to follow Giles if he tried to leave. Soon Deputy Bryan Taylor and some other officers were on the way to investigate. One officer went up on Wildcat Road where the stench was the strongest and located by flashlight what appeared to be tire tracks that indicated a large truck had backed up to the roadside overlooking the creek. This was the site of the release of the sewage. He also noted that the suspect truck had leaked oil just inside one of the wheel wells and he photographed the spill.

Deputy Taylor located Giles and James at the residence where the pumper truck was parked. Giles continued to deny involvement and gave the story about having been to visit a friend up the hill, who, as it turned out was not at home. (Actually, Giles did have an acquaintance up on Wildcat, which is probably how he came to know the road existed.) He said that the man and his wife at whose residence he was then standing, could corroborate that Giles had an empty truck earlier that day when he had visited. The two did in fact try to alibi Giles, but their stories had obvious discrepancies. Giles said he had been driving the sewage truck that day because he thought he had a contract with a Versailles orchard to pump out their septic tanks, but that job fell through, and he never had a load to dump that day. Deputy Taylor noticed that Gile's truck had an oil leak that corresponded to the location on the truck that was reported to him by the officer on Wildcat Road. With these facts, he had a strong circumstantial case.

Unfortunately, there was one significant problem with the investigation involving a line of defense counsel argument that is informally called *investigative things not done.* The officer who had gone to the dumping scene had reported the existence of clear tire tracks left by the dumping truck. I believe he had photographed them but for some unknown reason—probably a lack of resources in a small town—he had not done the more definitive thing of taking a plaster impression of the tire tracks for expert comparison with Giles's truck. The defense would have the benefit of the argument that the police could have solved the case conclusively. This can be a powerful argument in front of a jury.

So, it looked like we were going to trial with a he said, he said dispute between James and Giles, each corroborated to some extent by others or by circumstantial evidence. I kept searching my mind for evidence to strengthen our case theory.

ONE DAY ON my way home to my cabin, I thought it might be informative to see Wildcat Road and retrace the paths of James and Giles on the night in question. I drove to Tyrone and located Wildcat Road and traveled its entire length from Tyrone to US 127. I was completely blown away by what I saw. The idea that two such trucks could have passed each other on this road was unfathomable.

I conferred with Erin. She rode with me out to Wildcat Road, and after traveling its entire length, she agreed that we needed to find a way to put this sensory evidence before the jury. Our first inclination was to use a dash camera to videotape a car's trip up the hill. Deputy Taylor arranged that and produced a video that was somewhat helpful, but Erin and I agreed it did not have the persuasive effect of an actual trip to the site. It was then that I decided that the jury needed to see this road in person. This was a procedure I had never been involved in and would never be again—a jury view of the scene of the crime.

We filed a motion for a jury view wherein we set out the justification for this very unusual procedure. I knew that in Judge Greg Van Tatenhove I had the jurist in the district most likely to approve such a request. The judge was adventurous and innovative and seemed to relish going outside the bounds of normality when it made good sense. (This is the same judge in that motorcycle theft ring case who authorized Erin and me to roll into the courtroom for jury inspection dozens of actual recovered motorcycles.) After significant discussion in court regarding the logistics of such a field trip, he granted my motion. By the time of trial, the plan was set and ready to go.

During the presentation of the evidence, I used a hand drawn map to show the jury the location of different events. I labeled on my map the various sites one, two, three and four . . . etc . . . For example, site one was the driveway where James waited for the dumping truck to come down the hill. Site two was the location of the dumping. Site three was the wide spot where James saw the truck turning around. Site four was the house where Giles retreated after the dumping.

When it came time to execute the jury view, I was given permission by the judge to educate the jury on the procedure. We would travel to each of these sites in vans provided by the US marshals. Discussion of the case was prohibited during travel. At each of the designated sites, which had numbers visible corresponding to the map, the van would stop, and jurors would be allowed to exit and view the surroundings. Again, no discussion of the case would be allowed. The sole purpose of the venture was to put a visual image to the testimony that had been heard in court.

I believe that jury visit to Wildcat Road was extremely important in securing a conviction. Not only did it make Giles's story about a second sewage pumping truck implausible, but it also showed how the sewage made it into the creek because of the steep bank between Wildcat Road and the creek. One of the defense contentions was that Giles, if he was guilty of dumping, had not violated federal law because he dumped on the bank and not into the creek. But the law provides that dumping in a place where gravity takes the pollutant into the creek constitutes a discharge into the water. The trip also had the unstated effect of showing the jury how beautiful and precious such pristine locations are.

Attorney Rachel Yavelak put up a spirited defense using her undergraduate degree in microbiology, or something like that. Our expert testified to the bacterial count in the water above the dump site, at the dump site, and downstream from the dumpsite, drawing the conclusion that the bacterial measurements were consistent with sewage being dumped at the location. Rachel had an enthusiastic cross-examination of the expert about bacterial growth times and a lot that went over my head.

We refuted Giles' statement that he did not have a load of sewage on his truck that day. The owner of a local commercial orchard testified that Giles pumped his septic tanks that day, even describing the measured levels in the tanks before and after the pumping. This enabled investigators to estimate the amount of sewage on the truck that evening. So why did Giles dump the sewage on the hillside, rather than take the load to the Woodford County waste water treatment facility, which would have been the normal procedure? We can only speculate that it saved Giles time and money. The treatment facility charged a fee to dump. It was late in the afternoon when Giles finished at the orchard and dumping on Wildcat Road may have saved him a lot of time. In the end, the jury found Giles guilty of the federal offense.

Giles served several months in prison, but when he was released, he apparently returned to a lifestyle that was at the root of his criminal problems—drug abuse. He violated his supervised release by testing positive for drugs and was later saved from a fentanyl overdose by the administration of Narcan by law enforcement officers.

Ronnie Rogers

Another Oil Well Scam

One day in 2017, a man from London, England, David Parlons, called me at the office and began an hour-long conversation about what he described as an oil and gas production scam he had fallen victim to over the past couple of years. Parlons was the organizer and owner of a London-based firm called Kentucky Oil and Gas (KOG), which courted international investors interested in Kentucky oil and gas leases. Parlons said he got my name from some online research he had done, which revealed my history of successful prosecutions of such schemes.

Parlons was contacted after he placed international ads promoting KOG's business. A company called R&R, Inc. operated by Ronnie Rodgers was offering leases in Central Kentucky that promised to have large oil reserves. Parlons hired a Kentucky geologist to do due diligence, and the report Parlons received was promising.

Parlons traveled to Kentucky and had dinner with Ron Rodgers, his wife, and several of Rodgers's associates, including an attorney. Those associates gave glowing reports and vouched for the *bona fides* of Rodgers and his history of successful oil production. The next day the group traveled to the oil fields where Parlons was shown producing wells, the drilling equipment, oil pumps, and oil tanks. He was told that two promising leases owned by Rodgers and others were immediately available for purchase. It all sounded so profitable.

Parlons went back to London with a glowing report for his client investors. Over several weeks and months, Rodgers and Parlons negotiated an intricate business deal where Parlons would own the leases and Rodgers would drill the wells and get them up and running. Of course, this was going to be very expensive, but Parlons believed it was going to be very profitable as well. He sent a million dollars to Rogers from KOG investors. Parlons and his investors had been led to believe that they could expect a large return on their investment in a short period of time. However, as the months passed, they received very little money, but they did receive requests from R&R for more money to bring valuable wells on line. Parlons received excuse after excuse from Rogers about why he was not producing and selling oil.

Parlons hired lawyers and accountants to trace funds and to assess the status of the oil production. Their conclusion was that Rodgers and his group had defrauded them. They had been lying the entire time. In 2016, Parlons filed a lawsuit in federal court in Louisville against Rodgers and his company, alleging fraud and breach of contract, and he sought a criminal investigation by the US Attorney's Office in the Western District of Kentucky where most of the conduct occurred. He was working with prosecutors there but felt like they were not interested in taking the case.

Parlons emailed me a copy of the complaint he filed in Louisville. It was a very detailed and impressive document, and was supported by exhibits, affidavits, and attachments. I concluded that if these allegations were true, it was an indisputable case of fraud. I had seen this movie before in the Kentucky oil fields.

I ran the facts of Parlon's case past some colleagues, including my close colleague, Assistant US Attorney Neeraj Gupta, and my trusted sidekick paralegal, Rebecca Woolums. Both had the same reaction. Parlons sounds like he is promoting a scheme himself, they warned. There was just something about the story that caused their antenna to vibrate. Why would Parlons want to produce oil in Kentucky, as opposed to Oklahoma, Texas, or Alaska? There isn't enough oil in the ground here to make many people wealthy. Parlons had entered a very unusual contract with Rodgers whereby Rodgers was getting, in addition to the cash, thousands of shares of KOG stock. Parlons admittedly planned to take KOG public and sell stock at a high price, based on the promise of oil. The suspicion was that Parlons was engaged in a form of *pump and dump,* whereby the value of a company, and thus its stock, is hyped by fraudulent representations. Unsuspecting investors buy the inflated stock and the owner skips town with their money as the stock price falls to pennies on the dollar. This looked like a case of one scammer falling victim to another. We don't want to choose sides if that is the case. Though I shared their concerns, I wasn't ready to close the book on this case.

A few days later, following a meeting on another matter with representatives of the Kentucky DFI I recounted my conversation with Parlons to my good friend and longtime associate on oil and gas cases, Chad Harlan, a DFI securities expert. He informed me that DFI had an open case on Ronnie Rodgers for selling unregistered oil and gas securities in violation of an injunction they had obtained on Ronnie and his brother Ricky Rogers when they operated a former company called Rick Rod Oil, Inc. He gave me a quick overview of their investigation, and it confirmed that this was a potentially meritorious prosecution. I learned that there was probable fraud by Rodgers and others far more extensive and pervasive than the Parlons matter. Many individual investors from many states had complained to DFI about Rick Rod and its fraudulent solicitations. Despite qualms about KOG, I now saw this as a righteous effort on behalf of those small-time investors, and, after all, scamming another possible scammer was still fraud.[2]

In a telephone conversation with persons affiliated with our counterpart office in the Western District, I learned that the consensus there was that fraud could not be proven in this case because there

2 *Neither David Parlons nor KOG have been adjudicated guilty of any fraud. I relate suspicions herein which affected my evaluation of the case but do not make an affirmative statement.*

was drilling activity producing some oil. But I had learned that oil scammers go through the motions of drilling just to put that kind of doubt in the minds of prosecutors and investigators. Fraud scams are not always boiler room telemarketing operations where no product or service exists. Many scams involve some real thing for sale, but it's marketed through exaggeration and hype. If Rodgers was selling oil based on outlandish claims of future production, misrepresentations about his history, and a failure to disclose material facts, then that is fraud—harder to prove, but still fraud.

NEERAJ AND I traveled to Louisville to meet the attorney who filed the Parlons lawsuit, Michael Valenti. Valenti was a very reputable attorney who I believe would have done great due diligence before filing the suit. He was more than willing to help and opened his files to us.

With the help of DFI and the Postal Inspection Service we began a full investigation of what we would describe as an overarching fraud scheme that ran from 2007 to date. We were going to interview witnesses to the Rick Rod solicitation period and continue up to the present. We learned from numerous interviews that Rick Rod was indeed a scam—so many lies and omissions to induce the investors to part with their money and so much deception to avoid accountability.

Ricky and Ronnie Rogers were what is known in the oil business as *wildcatters*. These are typically individual, low-budget operations that drill one well at a time, then move on. They live in hope of hitting the big well and making a fortune. In 2007 or so, the brothers hit a gusher that produced over a hundred barrels a day, a huge output for Kentucky wells. The news of the strike was carried in newspapers all over the state. The event caused the Rodgers to envision a change in their business model. They were going to use their newfound success to raise money from investors and drill several wells at once. They used the newspaper articles to vouch for their claims of huge profits.

The chances of repeating their good fortune on any kind of regular basis was small and certainly not certain enough to guarantee a return on investment to numerous investors. But producing oil was not going to be the source of their income going forward. They were going to make their money *above the ground* with investor money.

The brothers opened Rick Rod Oil Company and sold oil programs, usually involving three or four wells in each. They claimed that it cost around $400,000 per program so they sold enough shares in the program to reach that amount. They mislead investors about how far along the drilling was and how much oil was being produced. When investors started asking questions, they responded with fake excuses and false explanations. Investors took their concerns to law enforcement agencies, who turned them over to the securities investigators at DFI. In 2011 DFI obtained an injunction against Rick Rod and the brothers prohibiting selling of oil investment securities.

After this, Ricky ceased his overt conduct in the scheme, as required by the injunction. Ronnie did not. He set up a company in Tennessee and continued to sell shares in oil programs under R&R. An attorney by the name of Hunter Durham, notorious in regulatory circles for his attempts to help oil drillers circumvent securities laws and regulations, fashioned paperwork that purported to make the oil investments not securities. But it was form over substance and they remained securities.

We discovered that many victims in the Rick Rod phase still had their email and text message conversations with Ronnie and Ricky, where so many provably false statements were made. But we had two big problems. Many of the individual cases of mail fraud against investors in Rick Rod were beyond the statute of limitations of five years. More problematic was that we didn't have venue to prosecute individual counts of fraud because that fraud occurred in the Western District of Kentucky, where the wells were located, and all the solicitations occurred. Individual counts of mail fraud must be prosecuted either in the district where the mail was sent or where received.

We decided to solve both our statute of limitations problem and our venue problem through the use of the law of conspiracy. The venue for conspiracy was in any district where any overt act in furtherance of the conspiracy occurred. By alleging that all of the Rodgers' scamming—whether through Rick Rod, R&R, or KOG—was one overarching conspiracy, the statute of limitations continued to run so long as the conspiracy continued. We could prosecute the entire period of 2007 to the present under one count of conspiracy.

For venue, we only had to show some overt act, in furtherance of the conspiracy, in the Eastern District of Kentucky. Here, we had numerous instances of R&R obtaining from a Kentucky agency in Frankfort, in the Eastern District, necessary drilling permits and licenses for their KOG operations, which qualified as overt acts. We charged a single count of conspiracy to commit mail fraud, wire fraud, and securities fraud. The risk with this tactic was that the jury would have nothing with which to negotiate or bargain among themselves. Prosecutors believe that jurors sometimes convict on some, but not all, counts as a means of compromise to reach a verdict. Here, it was going to be all or nothing.

For strategic reasons we decided to give the KOG portion of the case a minimal role. We wanted Parlons to be just one more victim, and to avoid any odor from the KOG business model creeping into our case. We had learned from our investigation that Rodgers was making somewhat credible claims that Rodgers and Parlons had a wink-and-nod relationship wherein they were both going to profit from the hyped stock value of KOG when it went public. Ultimately, we decided not to summons Parlons from across the ocean to testify.

(To be clear, neither David Parlons nor KOG have been charged or found guilty of any fraud. Any implication of wrongdoing or ill motives by Parlons or his firm are purely conjecture on my part.)

We made a difficult decision to forgo prosecuting Ricky Rodgers. We believed he had obeyed the DFI injunction and disassociated himself from Ronnie's operation. He sat down with us and provided some inside information that proved useful to our investigation, even though we decided not to use him as a witness at trial. Ricky did have criminal exposure for his involvement in Rick Rod, but his culpability was much less that Ronnie's. Ricky was the driller and Ronnie the salesman, and it was Ronnie's outlandish promises and predictions that was the essence of the fraud scheme. We believed, on balance, it was best to give Ricky a pass.

RONNIE RODGERS, THROUGHOUT the case, came across as a likable country bumpkin, but I believe much of that was for show. When he first got wind that there was a federal investigation involving our office, he called Postal Inspector Kyle Erhardt and insisted on having an audience with me and others. He showed up without a lawyer because he said he had nothing to hide. He was walking with a cane. He brought his wife, Melody, along and insisted that she sit in on the conversation. (I did have to question his judgment, however, because he showed up in Lexington Kentucky wearing University of Louisville Cardinal shorts.) He told us all about his three-year-old daughter who was the apple of his eye. His basic message was that he was truly trying to produce oil and that the investors were simply unrealistic in their expectations. We let him speak his mind, but we didn't develop any new evidence during the meeting.

At trial, the same old Ronnie Rodgers was present. Several times I had the awkward experience, during breaks in the proceedings, of standing over a urinal next to him. He always chatted me up and was very complimentary of my work, while insisting that his intentions were always pure.

The prosecution's case had to be like Chinese water torture for Rodgers and his attorney, Tom Hectus. We would put a victim on the stand and walk them through a long email string wherein the lies were told. Then we would introduce evidence refuting those lies. One big one he repeated with several victims as an excuse for not producing much oil was that he was traveling overseas. We called a witness from the US Passport Office to testify that Rodgers did not possess a passport.

We called expert witnesses to testify as to the outlandishness of Rodgers's claims of historical and future production. We proved that Rodgers had a substantial criminal record and did not disclose it to his investors. One or two investors had learned on their own that Rodgers had a prior conviction for solicitation of murder, and he lied in his explanation to them, saying that he had caught his wife in bed with another man and that he flipped out. In truth, he solicited the murder of an ex-girlfriend.

We brought in the financial analyst to trace the source of investor money and how it was used. We presented a chart showing that the money went into a business account and then was transferred into personal accounts that Ronnie Rodgers used to pay for his own expenses.

At the end of the government's proof, Rodgers was in that unenviable position that I saw many times in my career. Without him testifying he couldn't win, but if he did testify, he was sure to lose. Attorney Hectus probably advised him not to take the stand, but Rodgers wasn't having it. He wanted the jury to hear his side. He had obviously had a lot of time to think up responses to many of the points we were going to raise on cross-examination, and Hectus methodically led him through them on direct examination, but they were not credible.

One victim had introduced an email chain with Rodgers wherein he said he was tied up in Germany, which explained his lack of attention to the Kentucky wells. (I believe Rodgers thought this excuse made him look like a sophisticated world-traveler.) We had made a big deal out of this "lie" because he had no passport. Rodgers testified that this was all a huge misunderstanding. He explained that he uses the voice email function on his phone—dictating his response to an email sent to him. He had said he was in Germantown—a section of Louisville—and the transcription mistakenly said Germany.

The jury did not take long to convict Rodgers of the single conspiracy count. This brought us to the other drawback to the decision to proceed only with the one count. While his sentencing guidelines were higher, the maximum punishment for conspiracy is five years. The judge showed him a little mercy and gave him forty-eight months.

WAYNE WELLMAN

Obstruction of Justice and Perjury

In the summer of 2018, I was helping colleague Erin Roth prepare for trial in a case on the Pikeville docket. We had just finished a round of pretrial interviews of several witnesses who lived in the Pikeville area. We were having a nice lunch at a local restaurant when I noticed there was a new voice message on my phone. It was from a professional acquaintance, former prosecutor and then Fayette District Judge Julie Goodman.

As Erin drove us home, I returned the call and put Judge Goodman on the speaker phone. She explained that she had some information, which, as an officer of the court she felt she had an obligation to report to some kind of authority. She had obtained an informal eithics opinion that confirmed that she should report her suspicions of ongoing criminal activity. She knew I prosecuted public corruption cases and figured I would know where to direct her information and suspicions.

Her concern involved Lexington city politics and government, an issue that had been the subject of numerous *Herald Leader* newspaper articles in recent months. Lexington governance had been discussing for years the need to move from the cramped and outdated city hall building on Main in what formerly was the Lafayette Hotel.

The city had issued bid requests from area building contractors. Four proposals were received. Three were for new construction and one was for renovation and retrofitting of an existing, but vacant, building—the old *Herald Leader* building on Midland Avenue. The mayor had appointed a committee to review each proposal and rate them in terms of desirability, factoring in such characteristics as cost, location, parking, and accessibility to the employees and public. That committee had ranked the proposal by a local property maintenance and real estate development company, CRM, as the most desirable and recommended that the city council award it the construction contract. That proposal was to renovate the old *Herald Leader* building, and it was controversial among city leaders and the public. Many felt the building was too old, unsuitable as an office building, and was in a bad location.

In the days and weeks leading up to the scheduled vote on CRM's proposal, various members of the city council publicly expressed concerns about the proposal, and awarding the contract to CRM was by no means assured, based on the early statements of council members. Judge Goodman said she had spoken with Vice Mayor Steven Kay about the issue on several occasions and noted that he had recently flip-flopped from being opposed to the CRM plan to being one of its most ardent supporters. She had also learned that more than a dozen CRM employees of modest financial means had made the maximum donations allowed by law to the primary reelection campaigns of Vice Mayor Kay and Kevin Stinnett, who was running for mayor. These suspicious contributions suggested what we called a *straw contribution scheme,* whereby a wealthy donor evades the contribution limits by using other people to funnel money to a candidate. Had the principals or owners of CRM used this scheme to bribe Kay and Stinnett to vote for their bids?

Back at the office, Erin and I decided the issue merited a look-see, and that we would work the case together. We learned that Jacob Walbourn, an attorney, had been hired by a competitor of CRM in the bidding process to investigate potential pay-to-play scheme. He had combed through state contribution records and had put together a cogent circumstantial case that Kay and Stinnett were influenced by campaign contributions to vote for awarding the contract to CRM at an upcoming council meeting.

FBI Agent Jim Huggins was assigned the case, and we elicited the support of an excellent FBI analyst, Chris Darmand. He was a very intelligent man with whom I had worked several other cases, and I learned to confer with him about case strategy as though he was a fellow prosecutor. He always commanded a working knowledge of the cases and not just the financial aspects.

Chris obtained the campaign records from the KREF, which showed that CRM employees made maximum contributions. What he needed to confirm was that the money came from the management of CRM. To do this, we collected bank records for all the employees who made donations, as well as records from CRM itself, and its executives and owners. In short order, Chris put together charts and exhibits that detailed the money flow. All the employees who contributed to the campaign received checks from CRM-related accounts, or from its manager, Wayne Wellman's personal account, on the day of their respective contributions and in matching amounts. The next step would be interviews of donors to see if they would admit being *straw donors*, and, more importantly, if they knew anything about the donations being for the purpose of influencing the councilmen's votes.

The existence of the FBI investigation quickly became part of the rumor mill in Lexington as potential witnesses were interviewed and grand jury subpoenas were issued. Then, stunningly, at a city council meeting where the CRM proposal was scheduled for a vote, Steve Kay dropped his support of the proposal and refused to bring the issue up for a vote. We immediately suspected that this abandonment of the proposal was designed to show that CRM ultimately did not benefit from their concealed support of the councilmen. It would strip our case of jury appeal. Our investigation continued undeterred. If there was a bribery scheme or conspiracy, abandoning the plan in the face of a federal investigation would not be an ironclad defense.

THE ROUND OF employee interviews produced a mixed bag of results. Most employees denied they were reimbursed by CRM, but their stories were not credible. When confronted with a CRM check to them, contemporaneous with their contribution, they gave dubious reasons for having received the money: Cutting trees, doing Wellman's taxes, creating a website, cleaning houses, a loan, were some examples. It was just a coincidence, some said, that the payment coincided in time and amount with their contribution.

Some of these individuals did not even live in Lexington and would not be voting in the election they contributed to. Some were just getting by financially, and making a maximum contribution in a mayor's race from another town was preposterous. It was very clear to us that these stories were fabricated, and someone put them up to giving them.

All the employee donors were asked to donate by Wellman, who gave them the check in the same amount as their contribution At least two of the donors admitted they were reimbursed, and a couple more called us after the interview, recanted their story, and admitted being reimbursed.

When we served grand jury subpoenas on the CRM employees, we began to receive notifications from attorneys hired to represent them. I notified those attorneys (we later learned that everyone's attorney was paid for by CRM) that even if they had lied during FBI interviews (which itself is a crime), all would be forgiven if they told the truth going forward. Most of them recanted their false stories and implicated Wellman in coaching them to lie if questioned by the FBI. Wellman had gone to great lengths to thwart and obstruct our investigation.

No witness knew anything about a bribery scheme related to the contributions. Despite Wellman knowing that his employees had implicated him, at no time did he indicate that he was willing to plead guilty to obstruction or implicate candidates Stinnett and Kay. So, the bribery investigation hit a dead end. However, we launched a new investigation into Wellman for encouraging someone to lie under oath and helping them lie to the FBI. You may have heard the phrase, "The cover-up is worse than the crime." If Wellman had, from the outset, said, "Okay, you got me. I reimbursed the employees," and had he not put his employees up to lying, he would have faced a state campaign finance charge, but nothing federal. As it was, Wellman and two of his employees were convicted of federal crimes.

THE STORY OF one of the CRM employees who was charged and convicted is especially worth telling. (I will use a pseudonym here, Megan Wilson, because of privacy concerns). I don't believe I ever dealt with a more noncompliant and hostile witness. She had a chip on her shoulder, a total disrespect for legal proceedings and a completely misplaced cockiness. By her hairstyle, dress, bearing, and demeanor she sent a message that, "I'm a nonconformist and I ain't taking shit from anybody."

Wilson was a straw contributor. When the FBI interviewed her during the investigation, she told them a lie about the contribution and the reimbursement from Wellman. She claimed that no one asked her to contribute, she was not reimbursed, and no one told her to lie. The check to her from Wellman was compensation for having cleaned some houses he owned and rented.

As with the other contributors, we subpoenaed Wilson to the grand jury. I told her lawyer (again, hired by Wellman) that though I believed she had lied to the FBI and that I could indict her, I would forgive the lie and not prosecute if she told the complete truth to the grand jury and in all proceedings in the future. I was assured by her lawyer, Jarrod Beck, that she was prepared to tell the truth.

To my great surprise, Wilson told a grand jury a slightly modified version of the original lie. Before asking her any substantive questions, I informed her that we would extend total immunity to her if she told the truth. I asked if she wanted to accept that offer and she assented. I asked her if she was reimbursed for her contribution, and she emphatically said "no."

I was dumbstruck. The only change from her story to the FBI was an acknowledgment that Wellman had asked her to make the campaign donation. Again, she said that the alleged reimbursement check was for house cleaning. After a very contentious back and forth, wherein she was defiant, snarky, and even accusatory toward me and the prosecution, I paused, then said, "I need to advise you of a provision of the law governing perjury. By statute, a witness who has lied to the grand jury can return to the grand jury before the proceedings have concluded and absolve themselves of a perjury charge by recanting all false statements and telling the truth."

I advised her to step out of the room and consult with her attorney. She left the jury room with me, and I pulled Jarrod Beck aside and briefed him on the developments. After examining another witness, I spoke to Beck again. He said his client was ready to *clarify* things. Upon resuming the witness stand Wilson admitted she was reimbursed by Wellman and that the cleaning she had done was paid for by other checks. Her story still had some issues on the fringes, but at that point I was willing to forgo a perjury prosecution. It looked like she was a usable witness for any future trial of Wellman or others. But the story didn't end there.

I called Willson as a witness at a subsequent trial of Wayne Wellman. Outside the courtroom I spoke with Beck to see if he thought I would have any trouble with her comportment on the witness stand. He said she was ready to testify to the whole truth.

He was wrong. I did wonder why she refused to meet with prosecutors for our usual witness preparation sessions, but I did not see coming her total flip-flop. Sitting across the courtroom from her boss, Wellman, Wilson decided to give testimony in his favor. From the outset of her testimony, sparks flew. She went back to the voluntary contribution, no-reimbursement story. I confronted her with the transcript of her grand jury testimony. She told the jury she only said those things there because "It's what you wanted me to say," suggesting that I had coerced her to change her testimony.

I interrupted my direct examination by asking to approach the bench. You see, there is a provision in the perjury statute that gives prosecutors a very handy method of proving perjury under certain circumstances:. If a witness tells story *A* under oath at proceeding Number One, then tells story *B* at proceeding Number Two, and, if *A* and *B* are mutually inconsistent, at least one of them must be a lie, and the prosecution need not prove which one is a lie. Wilson had just done precisely that. Her second grand jury statement was mutually inconsistent with her trial testimony. I wanted the judge, out of the presence of the jury, to advise her of that provision of the law and that the current record established two inconsistent statements, thus establishing perjury. I hoped that such sobering advice might lead to her extricating herself from liability. To be sure, a perjury charge was already established, but I might have been willing to overlook it if she suddenly started telling the truth.

Defense counsel for Wellman, Kent Wicker, went ballistic. He accused me of trying to coerce Wilson to change her testimony to fit the prosecution's theory of the case. I didn't care at that point whether she changed her story. Her demeanor, contradictory versions of events, and the plethora of other evidence of the contribution-reimbursement scheme destroyed her credibility. But I wanted the record to be that, if she persisted with her perjurious conduct, it was with her eyes wide open to the legal risk.

Judge Van Tatenhove had another idea. We would take a recess and let Wilson's attorney advise her of all her rights and predicaments. After twenty or thirty minutes, the trial resumed. I re-asked the relevant questions, and what we got was a hybrid story. Wilson said she was asked by Wellman to contribute, she found a check for the same amount of her contribution on her desk about the same time, and she thought it was for cleaning. But in retrospect she could see that it was for reimbursement. On cross-examination, she came close to reverting to her false story. On redirect, she swung back to the truth, a bit. I knew at that moment I would indict her for perjury.

Wilson surprised us during Wicker's cross-examination with yet another false statement. Her attorney asked her whether she had witnessed a meeting one night at the CRM office between several employees of CRM. She acknowledged witnessing the meeting where she overheard a plan by a couple of our witnesses, who had just testified against Wellman, to change their testimony to frame Wellman.

Under questioning, Wilson claimed no one spoke with her or asked about the CRM employees meeting before trial. She said she didn't even know the meeting was even going to come up during Wellman's trail. But later in her testimony she admitted she in fact had discussed the meeting with Wellman's lawyer, Wicker. Again, we had two mutually inconsistent statements.

Several months after the Wellman trial, Wilson was indicted for lying to the FBI and for perjury. She filed a motion to dismiss, claiming that she was entitled to immunity because of the recantation defense, arguing that she had ultimately told the truth at both the grand jury and trial. Judge Karen Caldwell (different judge than presided in the Wellman trial), made short shrift of that argument, holding that it would be a nonsensical result that a witness could forever go from a lie to the truth and back with impunity. Judge Caldwell also noted that it was dubious that Wilson's testimony was a true recantation or that she ever told the complete truth.

Wilson finally accepted reality and entered a guilty plea. She was remarkably contrite, both during the entry of the plea and the sentencing. We agreed to probation. Though she had frustrated us and the process, she was a victim of Wellman's selfishness. He put her up to her crimes and she did not have the will to resist.

BACK TO WELLMAN. The trial was hard-fought. Wicker did a creditable job with what he had to work with. The proof of the conduct was overwhelming. Approximately ten witnesses testified to Wellman's reimbursement, his solicitation of their false statements to the FBI, and to the fabrication of documentary evidence. Most of the defense centered on legal issues like the scope of the FBI's jurisdiction to investigate, the definition of an *official proceeding*, and the *materiality* of witness's false statements to the FBI. Those were the kind of issues Wicker—a Harvard law graduate and former federal prosecutor—excelled at. Fortunately, his legal arguments, though facially interesting, failed in both the trial court and the court of appeals. Ultimately, Wellman was sentenced to a year and a day and a fine of $10,000. This reflected a downward departure from the sentencing guidelines, which Judge Van Tatenhove justified because of Wellman's history of community service and an outpouring of support from many in the community. Of interest here, Wellman later was convicted in state court of the illegal campaign finance charges.

Crypto Craig

Online Auction Fraud

This massive international fraud scheme, dubbed the "Alexandria Online Auction Fraud" or *Crypto Craig* case, can hardly be called one of my cases. I had a comparatively minor role in it next to my colleague in Lexington, Kate Dieruf (Anderson at the time) and Department of Justice trial attorneys from Washington, D.C., Frank Lin and Tim Flowers. However, I have many vivid memories from my involvement in the investigation and trial, and it is a case of significant societal import. The case was initiated by Kate in our office in 2015 and remained highly active when I retired in September of 2022. It had also generated several spin-off cases, likely to continue for years. I joined the prosecution team in late 2017 and by the time I left, between fifteen and twenty defendants had been convicted through guilty pleas or trials.

In late 2014, police in Ashland, Kentucky, were investigating a local man for fraud-related activity and conducted searches of his home or office. In hopes of gaining leniency for his cooperation, he said he could expose a fraud ring of enormous proportions. The KSP were invited into the investigation, and eventually the US Secret Service joined because of the technical and international nature of the scheme that this new informant described. I'll call him the CI for confidential informant.

The CI said he was providing money-laundering services for a group of scammers who were centered in Alexandria, Romania, and who were advertising for sale fictitious cars, trucks, trailers, campers, and the like on internet platforms like Amazon and eBay. American citizens would be fed sob stories by the fictitious posters of the ads explaining why they were selling the item at such a low price. For example, a poster claiming to be a soldier would say he just received orders to a foreign post, couldn't take his car, and needed the money immediately. The ads would contain stock photos of the fictitious item being sold that showed it in pristine condition.

The victim purchaser was instructed that the item would be shipped as soon as the purchaser paid for it by purchasing a prepaid credit card like Visa One Vanilla, a money order, or a wire transfer. Upon receipt of the payments, a Romanian scammer would send card codes to US-based associates, like the CI, who used it to create cloned or dummy debit cards that could be cashed out. The CI converted the cash to crypto currency, primarily bitcoin, and transferred it to the Romanians. Finally, the Romanians sold the bitcoin in Romania or Bulgaria for fiat (government issued) currency. Of course, the car, truck or trailer would never arrive, and the seller would go silent.

The CI showed the agents his encrypted email chats with the Romanians, proving that he had established connections to the scammers. The CI then began a long stint of cooperation and employment at the Secret Service office in Lexington. For the next two or more years the CI drew a modest salary and, while being monitored in real time by Secret Service agents, continued his collaboration with the scammers.

Using a CI in this manner is not without its critics. Law enforcement was allowing crimes to be committed, and victims defrauded, as the agents watched in real time. But, if the process allowed the agents to infiltrate the criminal organization and identify the players and their methods, they could bring the whole thing down, protecting many more future victims. The decision was made that the toleration of some bad to achieve a much greater good was defensible.

FOR OVER TWO years, Secret Service agents pored over chats and emails between the CI and the Romanian scammers, carefully putting real names and faces on the fake names or handles the scammers used online to hide their identity. To this end, the agents reached out to the Romanian national police who provided surveillance and assistance on the ground in Alexandria and Bucharest. The Romanian police became partners in the investigation and provided immeasurable value to the effort. Kate and a team of agents traveled to Romania to get a better understanding of the area and to meet with local police. In return, a group of Romanian officers visited Lexington several times to continue their collaboration.

The process of identifying the scammers by name was called *attribution*—attributing to a real person message details that would help us prove the crime. This was beautiful detective work. The CI became more and more friendly with his contacts, and he would discuss things in his life hoping to encourage the others to do the same. If a scammer said he had flown to Spain on say "last Tuesday," the information was given to the Romanian police who scoured airline records and identified a Romanian who flew to Spain on Tuesday. If a scammer said he was going to get married in Bucharest on June 3, the police would surveil weddings. Pictures were taken and sent to the agents in the states. The information was charted, and the chart grew day by day. Agents followed bitcoin transactions on the public ledger and identified the names of the owners of various addresses. (Bitcoin is not as anonymous as some think.)

Kate Dieruf, Tim Flowers, and Frank Lin worked tirelessly preparing dozens of requests for law enforcement assistance under the Mutual Legal Assistance Act treaty, called *MLAT requests*, we had with Romania. They studied up on the extradition process that would be used whenever indictments were obtained. The number of legal papers that team generated during the investigation was amazing.

Finally, in 2017 or early 2018, the team obtained an indictment of around seventeen Romanians and a few Americans, charging them with participating in a racketeering enterprise plus various counts of wire fraud and money laundering.

The indictment was sealed so that word of it would not be made public until the defendants were arrested and extradition procedures could begin. The risk that the Romanians would flee to avoid arrest was great.

Around this time, I was asked to join the prosecution team, largely because I had many complicated trials under my belt and the thought was that several of these defendants would eventually stand trial. As it turned out, we only had one trial of a Bulgarian money launderer named Rossen Iossifov. The other defendants entered into plea agreements and most agreed to cooperate in exchange for leniency in sentencing. For about three years I worked on this case, along with my other cases, as we slowly moved toward resolution of all the charges. At all times, Kate was the face of the case in our office, and I was on the fringes, but I learned a lot and had some interesting experiences.

SOON AFTER I entered the case, elaborate plans began for mass arrests in Romania, in conjunction with searches of homes, offices, phones, and computers. Our Romanian counterparts would lead the effort on the ground there in compliance with Romanian law. Kate had another round of seemingly endless document preparation, including more MLATs, search warrant applications, and arrest warrants. Plans for travel and lodging had to be prepared. We developed a detailed plan for examination of devices, such as phones seized during the searches. Finally, in December 2018 a team of dozens of Secret Service agents and prosecutors, including myself, descended on Bucharest.

It was truly a working trip with little time for sightseeing. I called the city "Bucha-no-rest." We set up shop in the US embassy there. Each day a bus transported the team from our hotel to the embassy. The day of the arrests and searches was long and hectic as teams of agents fanned out over Alexandria and Bucharest to execute both arrest and search warrants. The Romanian police lead the way to ensure that Romanian law relating to search and arrest were followed. The agents attempted to interview those arrested, but most declined. My job was to help catalog the phones and computers that were brought in from the searches and check them for compliance with search warrants.

The trip home was very memorable. We had seized many boxes of evidence, which had to be maintained under a chain of custody. It could not be sent home on commercial airlines, so the Secret Service decided to charter a private jet. It just happened that the Gulfstream was owned by Robert Kraft, the owner of the New England Patriots. It was determined that about eight people could ride back on the Gulfstream with the evidence. I was happy to be one of them. What a ride. We cruised for about nine hours at forty thousand feet, whisper quiet with no turbulence. The interior was designed for comfort with couches, tables, and lot of room for stretching out and napping, which most of us did at some point. The evidence was below in the cargo hold. We landed at a small airfield in Northern Virginia, which is used by the Secret Service, and unloaded the evidence onto a truck before traveling by car to Reagan National Airport for the return flight to Lexington.

For the next several months, Kate and her team engaged in extensive litigation extraditing the defendants from Romania to the United States. Once stateside, the defendants were arraigned, and defense attorneys were appointed. A few of the defendants retained counsel with their own funds. For the next two years or more an elaborate discovery procedure was followed, and trials were scheduled, but as noted above, most of the defendants ultimately entered plea agreements.

IN SEPTEMBER 2020, during the height of the COVID-19 pandemic, the trial of Rossen Iossifov—the money launderer from Sofia, Bulgaria—began in Frankfort, presided over by Judge Robert Wier. Kate, Frank Lin, and I formed the trial team. John Kevin West represented Iossifov. Boiled to its essence, the issue at trial was whether Iossifov knew he was assisting a team of scammers by providing the service of converting bitcoin to fiat currency. It was beyond dispute that Iossifov ran what is known as a money services business, which provides to the public currency-related services such as international currency conversion, check cashing, and loans. It was also clear that the scammers in Alexandria had used his services to convert large amounts of bitcoin into cash. However, the defense argued that Iossifov had been tricked by the scammers and didn't realize the bitcoin came from fraudulent activity.

The trial had at least two unusual features: the anti-COVID-19 transmission efforts we employed, and the use of a Bulgarian interpreter. The wearing of masks in the courtroom was required by all, with one exception. When a lawyer questioned a witness or made an argument to the court—i.e., engaged in a speaking exercise—he could remove the mask, but he had to stand at a specifically positioned podium behind a plexiglass shield. When finished speaking he had to disinfect the podium and surrounding area with spray and tissues before returning to counsel table. Instead of having sidebar conferences with the judge we used a closed microphone system wherein counsel and the judge could hear each other but the jury could not hear the conversation.

A Bulgarian interpreter sat beside Iossifov and translated the proceedings quietly by speaking into another closed transmission system that only the defendant and interpreter could hear. Using interpreters at trial always frustrates, as it interrupts and changes the normal flow of the proceedings. The lawyers must pause after asking very clear questions and allow the interpreter time to make the translation before proceeding to the next question. Care must be taken to avoid idioms and local slang that doesn't translate well into the other language.

Kate had divided up the various trial functions between the three prosecutors. Kate would give the opening statement, Frank Lin was assigned the first closing argument, and I the rebuttal closing. The direct examinations of government witnesses were divided among us based on who would have the most knowledge and background regarding the subject of the witness's testimony. Kate and Frank handled most of the very technical witnesses, such as those that explained how bitcoin works, or how the criminal enterprise operated. I handled all the victims of the fraud scheme because this was a compartmentalized portion of the case that lent itself to "Okay, what happened next" type of questioning.

Kate's opening reflected extensive preparation and organization. When she finished and set down at our table, I showed her an index card on which I gave her a grade—I wrote *A+*.

The victims did a wonderful job, despite some trepidation and fear we had about a couple of them before the trial. We selected around ten who had compelling stories of loss and despair. At least one of them balked at the prospect of taking off work, flying to Kentucky and testifying. He wanted to get on with his life. But we insisted that he honor our subpoena. That's always a very delicate process because our ultimate recourse, if he refused, was to have him arrested for contempt and hauled into court. How willing would he be to testify under those circumstances? Ultimately, after a lot of reassurance and coaxing from Nate Moore, a KSP and Secret Service task force officer, he got on the plane and came to Frankfort.

The transformation in attitude of this reluctant witness was remarkable. Under the glare of the courtroom lights, and with the jury's collective attention fixated on him, he exuded anger and righteous indignation. His story was very compelling, and the jurors were eating it up. I'll never forget that glare he gave Iossifov as he exited the witness stand.

The witnesses walked the jury step-by-step through the process of being defrauded, showing them the ads that they responded to, complete with realistic eBay or Amazon logos, and bank records showing the debit from the bank account and the meager balance that was left. They showed the emailed instructions from the scammers containing false reassurances, claims and promises. They described the fear and frustration they felt when day after day went by, and the car or truck never arrived as promised. They told how the scammers went silent, and they could no longer communicate with them. Then they described that sinking feeling in the pit of their stomach when they realized they had been duped. Several testified that the lost money essentially was all they had. Dreams were shattered. Self-confidence and trust of others was lost, and bouts of clinical depression ensued in some. It was very moving. Judge Wier highlighted this testimony at sentencing.

Of course, the plight of the victims was terrible, but was it attributable to Rossen Iossifov? How could we place Rossen in the RICO conspiracy? Iossifov had cashed out the scammer's bitcoin, which we argued was the final step in the overall conspiracy. Our cooperating witnesses had testified about how the defendant had turned a blind eye to what was obvious—that the bitcoin was the proceeds of fraud. We introduced emails between some of the scammers and Iossifov, or one of his associates, wherein they had explicit discussions about avoiding the police. We proved that the scammers drove far out of their way from Romania to Bulgaria to visit Iossifov. Several cooperating scammers testified that this was because Iossifov asked no questions about the source of their funds, and he gave them a better exchange rate. An analyst for the Secret Service, Richard Yancey, introduced a summary of financial records from Rossen's business that showed that the identified scammers who used that business were far and away the lion's share of his operation. Would this be enough to convince a jury that Iossifov joined the conspiracy?

Frank Lin gave a compelling closing argument. Like Kate's opening statement it reflected hours of preparation and organization. I had heard about Frank's practice session at another colleague's house the night before where he gave the argument in front of other prosecutors from the office. He digested their comments and went back to work up into the wee hours of the morning. I graded him out at A+.

Defense counsel Kevin West made some persuasive points in his closing argument. His main argument was that Iossifov's business methods were wholly inconsistent with what one would expect from the operation of an illicit money-laundering business. He set out all the facts pointing to the legitimate nature of this money services business. Iossifov operated out of a brick-and-mortar location using his real name, not an alias, with business cards and his name on the door. He sought government licenses and permits. He purported to follow money-laundering detection protocols. He had several demonstrably legal and valid customers in his money services business. In short, this was no back alley, clandestine operation.

Sitting at counsel table listening to West's facially valid points about the legitimacy of Iossifov's business, I knew, in my rebuttal closing, I had to counter with some way of showing that this was not, for the jury, a binary choice of either a totally illegal or totally legal business. Two things can be true at once. A legal, legitimate business can have a dark side. It can present itself to the public one way and to a criminal enterprise in another. A metaphor came to mind. This business is like a mullet haircut—business in the front, and party in the back.

I told the jury about an otherwise legitimate business that had a gambling side hustle. Big Red liquor store in Mount Sterling, Kentucky, sold liquor up front but made book in the back room I used the metaphor for Iossifov's operation, calling it a *mullet business,* a legitimate business on the surface, but money laundering behind the scenes. The joke stuck with our trial team and became a running gag. At my retirement, Kate and Frank gave me a mullet wig as a nod to the moment.

WE ALL FELT good about our case when the jury retired to deliberate early on a Friday afternoon. But after several hours of deliberation the jury sent a message to the judge that indicated that one juror was refusing to even consider the jury instruction regarding *deliberate ignorance.* That was not a good sign for us, as that instruction was at the heart of our theory of the case. Judge Wier instructed the jury to resume deliberations. Next came a message to the judge stating that one juror was asking to be dismissed from the jury because he didn't believe he was knowledgeable enough or smart enough to participate. Again, the judge instructed the jury to continue. Finally came a bizarre question that I ponder the meaning of to this day. "Is Rossen Iossifov a conspirator or an alleged conspirator?"

The attorneys gathered in the courtroom to discuss with Judge Wier that last question. I'll never forget that look on his face—half amused and half quizzical. He said bluntly with a smirk, "That is the question, isn't it?" He instructed the jury to consider each count under his prior instructions.

Around 5:30 p.m. the jury announced it wanted to recess for the day. The trial team gathered in our little office. Kate was stressed. We all knew that we had a bad egg on the jury, and it was the wiry little guy with a beard in the back corner. The jury's body language in the courtroom told us the other jurors had had it with him. Undoubtedly, he was behind all the jury questions, and he was probably going to hang the jury. "He's a true believer," Kate said, a reference to a person who is an anti-government contrarian. Now we had to spend the long weekend contemplating a retrial of the case.

Trial, or jury deliberations to be exact, began again the next

Tuesday. To our great surprise the jury returned a guilty verdict after about one hour. I wondered what happened to that holdout juror over the weekend. What brought him around? Regardless, there was great joy in our little office at that point. Kate arrived late to court that day because she awoke to COVID-19 symptoms and went for a test, which fortunately was negative. When she joined us, we opened and shared a fifth of Eagle Rare bourbon that someone (I'll not rat him out) had purchased while the jury was deliberating. It really went down smoothly.

For months before and after this trial, Kate handled dozens of sentencings for the various Romanian and American defendants in this case. Iossifov received around ten years. There was great variation in the sentencings of other defendants, based on their respective levels of culpability. Kate's hard work on this monumental case was rewarded in 2023 when she received a Director's Award for Superior Performance from the Department of Justice. Coincidentally, at the same ceremony in Washington, DC, I was awarded the Lifetime Exceptional Service Award. Kate and I coordinated our trip to Washington, where we connected with Frank Lin and Neeraj Gupta, my former colleague in the Lexington office who then worked for DOJ in Washington, and we took in various touristy venues and nice restaurants. It was a nice postscript to our work on the Romanian case.

Mike Crawford

Unit One

In July 2020, while on my annual timeshare vacation in French Lick, Indiana, I received a call from US Attorney Rob Duncan, my boss. He had just gotten off the phone with Fayette County attorney Larry Roberts who asked whether our office could pursue a federal case against a couple of individuals involved in an open state case. Larry had been appointed as a special prosecutor in a Scott County case due to a conflict of interest by the prosecutor in that circuit. The case had become mired in a morass of procedural motions and appeals, and he wanted to see if we could carve out a federal case and get things moving toward a resolution. I called Larry to discuss the matter and he had my head spinning.

Larry explained that John Goble was a well-known and respected coroner in Scott County. He was a former Marine, security chief for Georgetown College, city councilman, and a retired state trooper. He had served several terms as the elected coroner.

Goble was a rotund man with an outsized personality to match. He loved taking fellow first responders to lunch at his favorite dives all over Central Kentucky. He was known for his war stories and his frighteningly fast driving. He said if he had a wreck, he wanted to ensure that he didn't walk away. He had recently gone through a bitter divorce and now lived in a small apartment over the coroner's office. He was loving his new simple life. His coroner's office was the frequent site for drop-in conversations with law enforcement officers and first responders. But most people were not seeing the side of Goble that two of his deputy coroners were seeing.

Goble had several deputy coroners. Two of them had become concerned about procedures and conduct by Goble they had witnessed while working in his office. Goble was stealing narcotic drugs from the bodies, cars, and homes of deceased individuals and taking them himself. The deputies had seen pill bottles bearing the name of the deceased in Goble's vehicle, and the pills disappeared over time. He was leaving corpses in his vehicle overnight—a violation of regulation. He had amassed large quantities of what appeared to be state police ammunition and stored it in the basement of the coroner's office. His reckless driving was disturbing, and his deputies had witnessed him using his county vehicle for private errands and trips as well as picking up and delivering bootlegged moonshine.

Two deputies took their concerns to the Scott County attorney and the county judge executive. The county judge, in turn, contacted the KSP due to the ammunition allegation. Detective Sergeant Gerald Wilson was assigned to investigate. Wilson was provided photos taken by the deputies of the ammunition in the basement and he took it to the KSP armory to see if the personnel there could verify that this was indeed KSP property. But the photos were not conclusive. The armorer would have to see the actual boxes with serial numbers to determine whether they had once been in the KSP inventory.

Wilson traveled to Goble's apartment to interview him. Goble admitted that he had acquired ammunition, had temporarily stored it in his office basement. He said he had been storing it as a favor to a KSP armorer Mitch Harris. Goble said he assumed Harris was accumulating a stash of ammo for retirement that Harris had paid for. He said he had recently moved the ammo to the garage of a friend and former deputy coroner Nathan Morris. Goble denied that he had moved it because of the investigation. Goble said Harris was calling all times of the day and night drunk and Goble had decided he didn't want to store the ammo any longer, so he moved it to Morris's place. None of this made much sense. Wilson was convinced that someone, either in the county courthouse or within the KSP, had alerted Goble to the investigation, prompting him to move the ammunition so it would go undetected.

Immediately, Wilson and his crew made their way to Morris's house in Georgetown, Kentucky, and recovered 187 cases of various calibers of ammunition, worth approximately $40,000. The ammo was taken to a KSP storage facility and dusted for finger and palm prints. Several latent palm prints were obtained. They then went to interview the armorer, Harris, whom they requested to meet at the Frankfort KSP post. The meeting lasted into the wee hours of the morning.

Harris eventually would become a critical witness for our prosecution, but he withheld information in his first interview. He initially claimed he gave the ammunition over several years to his superior, Colonel Mike Crawford. In later interviews he admitted giving directly to Goble, at Crawfords direction, but was reluctant to say so because Goble wasn't his superior. He feared greater consequences for that admission. Harris also revealed illegal surplus gun sales involving Crawford and Goble, violating KSP property regulations.

The mechanics of the firearm sales basically involved a violation of KSP regulations governing the disposal of outdated or surplused firearms. A trooper is allowed to purchase a weapon issued to him, but any outside third party is prohibited from buying them. Any firearm not purchased by the trooper who formerly carried it, is supposed to be sold to outside gun dealers who had a contract with the state to provide this service. But a practice had arisen within the KSP where false inventory records were created to falsely show that weapons were purchased by troopers who had used them, when in fact the gun was going to an outside, unauthorized purchaser.

FAYETTE COUNTY ATTORNEY Roberts had indicted Goble, Crawford, and Harris on various state offenses some months earlier. I didn't know at the time, but the case had been taken to the FBI at the beginning of the investigation and that agency had declined it as not meeting their theft amount guidelines. Essentially, Larry was angling for a fresh look at the case from a federal perspective.

I was not overly enthusiastic about taking the case to federal court. It just seemed to be more of a state administrative matter, but Larry and I go way back, and I found it hard to say no to him. So, I decided to give it a good look. But what was the federal crime? I scoured the federal gun laws, but nothing seemed to fit the facts. I called a contact I had over at the ATF for his input. He indicated they had looked at the case on behalf of the FBI at the time of their declination and could not find a gun sales violation of federal law.

Then it occurred to me. This was ultimately a public corruption case centered on Crawford, Harris, and Goble's misappropriation of state-owned property. Under federal law, it is a crime for an employee of a state agency receiving over $10,000 in federal funds annually to steal or misuse more than $5,000 of state property. That would form the basis of our charge.

My colleague Kate Smith seemed like the logical person to enlist as a second chair in this prosecution. When she came to the office several years prior, she joined me on several corruption cases in Eastern Kentucky, and we had tried at least one case together. I admired her insight and instincts, and she was a pleasure to work with. She had recently mentioned we needed to do another case together. So I stuck my head in her office one day and said I had just the case for us. She quickly agreed. FBI Agent Chelsea Holliday was assigned to the case based on a new legal theory. With the team in place, the investigation began.

OUR FIRST MEETING with Roberts at his office left us feeling overwhelmed. Tons of transcripts of state grand jury proceedings and Gerald Wilson interviews of dozens of witnesses. We saw the mess of state pleadings and various accusations that had been made toward the prosecution in state court, including issues about misconduct in the state grand jury. Larry had a massive case file with reams of his handwritten notes, analyzing phone cell tower records, and dissecting grand jury testimony. He had an outline of a closing argument. It was obvious he had spent hours on the case and was essentially ready to try it. Of course, none of those state proceedings and problems affected our case directly, but it just gave the case a certain odor.

A key challenge in the case was that much of the evidence relied on the credibility of the now-cooperating codefendant Mitch Harris. He was the only witness who could tell the full story, but his credibility was compromised by a history of disciplinary issues, including a televised news account of overtime fraud. His punishment had been reassignment from road trooper to the armory as an armorer—a person in charge of maintaining the inventory of firearms. The official who sent him there was Colonel Crawford.

Harris had been suspended earlier in his career for some type of misconduct involving a woman he met in a bar. Topping it off was the fact that, as noted above, Harris had lied when first interviewed. But despite his baggage, Harris, in person, was very convincing when he said he felt indebted to Colonel Crawford for giving him a tolerable punishment by assignment to the armory. He came to believe that Crawford put him in that position to obtain the ammunition.

We indicted Crawford and Goble in March of 2021 on conspiracy charges related to the federal misappropriation statute—one conspiracy count related to the firearms and another related to the ammunition. We gave Harris a pass on federal charges because of his steadfast cooperation, believing as we did that a state conviction was sufficient justice for his wrongdoing. He had been fired from the state police and was now living in Florida, working for a swimming pool installation company. Thus began a year and a half of pretrial proceedings that were fraught with issues.

ONE SATURDAY MORNING shortly after the indictment of Goble and Crawford, but before they were arraigned in open court, my fiancée, Rebecca Feland, and I decided to stop at one of our favorite breakfast spots, Callie's diner in Versailles. We were seated facing the front door when two men entered. One was helping the other walk. The face of the struggling man looked so familiar, but I could not place it. Where had I seen that face? Suddenly, I thought, that looks like the picture I saw in Larry Robert's case file of the defendant John Goble. I had never met the man, but Larry had mentioned that Goble was in bad health and could barely walk. The man I saw was large like Goble, and his age would be consistent as well. And though Goble was from Georgetown, not Versailles, Goble was notorious for visiting quaint restaurants all over Central Kentucky. Callie's would have been right up his alley.

I glanced outside and saw a black Chevy Suburban like the one I knew he drove. One of the state charges involved using a state-owned black Suburban for personal trips. I told Becca quietly that I thought the man was someone I had just indicted. As we left the diner, I casually strolled past the rear of the Suburban and saw the official Kentucky license plate. I was then sure the man was Goble.

A few days later, I was in court when Goble entered the courtroom for his arraignment. Characteristically, Goble was friendly and affable. He stuck out his hand and introduced himself. I couldn't resist telling him that we had breakfast together last Saturday. He looked puzzled and I said, "Callies, Versailles." A big grin crossed his face, and he shook his head in agreement. We had a nice conversation as if we were old friends. I couldn't help but like John Goble, even if it was my duty to prosecute him.

OUR LEGAL THEORY, based largely on Harris's testimony, was that Colonel Mike Crawford began directing Harris to give him cases of ammunition, which Crawford then stored at John Goble's home. Harris stated that he never delivered the ammo to Goble's house, only that he met him at arranged locations.

At the time, Crawford led the division overseeing all state troopers, holding the influential *unit one* position, just below the commissioner. Though not in Harris's direct chain of command, Crawford had significant influence over trooper careers.

Crawford's defense was complete denial. He had never handled the ammunition and had not told Mitch to take it from the armory.

Goble claimed he simply stored it as a favor to Harris. He said Crawford was not involved with the ammunition. Therefore, cell tower records and palm prints taken from ammo boxes were big issues. Would the cell records show that Harris did not visit Georgetown? Would Crawford's finger or palm prints be on the ammo boxes?

The process of *discovery,*—sharing the evidence with defense counsel—was frustrating. Nearly every week we uncovered new information that should have been disclosed and required further action. While I don't recall all the details, there were complications involving cell tower records, the form they were in, and the inferences that could be drawn from them. A significant issue also arose around determining the value of the ammunition. Kate took the lead on these technical matters, working with the KSP administrators to establish pricing and coordinating with the firearms expert to assess the value of the misappropriated guns.

There was a big issue with the fingerprint and palm print analysis. Crawford was refusing to cooperate with us to obtain his palm prints for comparison to prints that were lifted off ammunition boxes. I had mistakenly informed the court that the prints already had been compared to Harris's and Goble's, when they had not.

When all was said and done, the palm prints from the boxes remained unknown—not Harris's, not Goble's and not Crawford's.

At some point it came to our attention that one of the deputies had related to Gerald Wilson during an interview that Crawford had, in the deputy's presence, made a very incriminating statement, implicating him in knowing about the ammunition. It was to the effect that if anything happened to Goble someone needed to get the keys off his body that opened the basement to the coroner's office because what's down there would put a lot of people in prison. This disclosure had never been provided to the defense. Of course, they protested loudly when we provided the new information.

AS TRIAL APPROACHED, Goble's attorney, Fred Peters, filed a motion to have Goble examined for competency to stand trial. He argued Goble had recent memory issues, but a clinical exam confirmed he was competent to stand trial.

Shortly after that finding, Goble decided to work a plea deal. Through his lawyer, he offered a preview of what he would say if he testified. This was done in his effort to get a lighter sentence in return for helping the prosecution. The information was a bombshell. Goble now claimed that the ammunition in the basement was the result of a very specific conspiracy headed up by KSP Colonel Crawford. The ammo belonged to Crawford, but he still insisted that Harris had delivered most of it. While this placed Crawford directly in the conspiracy, it also contradicted Harris, who continued to insist that he never went to the coroner's office.

We had a dilemma. Do we use Goble at trial to incriminate Crawford, even if he contradicts our star witness on a critical issue? Do we drop Harris as a witness and go with Goble? Kate, Chelsea, and I struggled to make this call. If we put both on the stand, which one do we argue is telling the truth, and why are we putting on someone we don't believe? Ultimately, we decided that Harris' story came across more credible than Goble's.

Crawford's attorney, Bernie Pafunda, believing that Goble was going to testify, sought to obtain all the evidence behind the motion to have him examined for competency. The claim was that if he had memory issues, he could not be trusted to testify truthfully. That issue was mooted by our decision not to call Goble at trial.

This was classic *Giglio* material—evidence that can be used to impeach a witness. We had a duty to tell Crawford about Goble's intended testimony, despite not calling him to the stand. That put the defense on the horns of a dilemma. They could call Crawford to contradict Harris as to who transported the ammunition to the coroner's office, but that would come with the testimony that Crawford was the grand master of the plot. Goble did not testify. The Crawford trial was held in the summer of 2022. It was my last federal trial—number 108. When Harris testified, I was afraid we had made the wrong decision to put him on the stand. The setting brought out a side of Harris we had not seen in trial preparation. Instead of calmly laying out the facts, he appeared to be trying too hard to convince the jury that he was telling the truth. He would begin his answers by turning and facing the jury with a serious look and say, "Ladies and gentlemen . . . " It was as though he was delivering a closing argument. To this day, I don't know what the jury thought about Harris' credibility. The verdict seemed to indicate they had some doubt about his testimony as it related to the ammunition conspiracy.

Despite having focused most of our attention on the ammunition part of the case, the firearms violations proved more readily provable. The paperwork behind the gun sales showed clear violations of the KSP regulations dealing with the manner of disposing of surplus guns. Crawford had admitted that he had been involved in the gun purchases, but that he didn't think he had done anything illegal. The verdict was guilty on the firearm purchase conspiracy, but the jury deadlocked on the ammunition conspiracy.

I RETIRED IN September, 2022, so I had no substantive involvement in Crawford's sentencing which occurred in early 2023. Kate Smith took over those duties, and her experience there merits some mention. From my subsequent conversations with Kate and a brief review of some sentencing documents, I learned that Kate was very exasperated by the letters written to the court in support of Colonel Crawford. A KSP sergeant who had worked in the investigation of Crawford, and in fact was the sole investigator who interviewed Crawford, wrote a letter recommending that Crawford be probated. Other troopers wrote in support of Crawford. A former colleague of hers, a former assistant US attorney, had also written a letter in support of Crawford. To Kate this was all outrageous. She felt that Crawford had betrayed the trust placed in him by the KSP and that what was going on was an attempt by the KSP "old boys club" as she called it, to circle the wagons around one of their own.

In her sentencing memorandum, Kate mentioned the letter-writing campaign and argued that it demonstrated that Crawford should be sentenced to the top of the sentencing guideline range set out in the presentence report—twenty to twenty-seven months—in order to serve as a deterrent to those who would be tempted to pilfer government property. She said that probation would unduly minimize the seriousness of the crime. Judge Van Tatenhome was tasked with determining whether probation or a substantial prison sentence was appropriate. It was a tough call, to be sure. Here before him was a high-ranking member of the KSP who had provided praise-worthy service to that agency. Crawford deserved some credit for that. But Kate's arguments against probation were strong. The judge split the baby so to speak and sentenced Crawford to eight months imprisonment. For some observers, that doesn't sound like a lot of time, but it was a long fall for this man—from unit one to federal inmate. It was a loud statement.

www.ingramcontent.com/pod-product-compliance
Lightning Source LLC
LaVergne TN
LVHW100258210926
848480LV00003B/959